Starving for Salvation

The Spiritual Dimensions
of Eating Problems
among American Girls
and Women

Michelle Mary Lelwica

New York   Oxford

Oxford University Press

1999

Oxford University Press

Oxford   New York

Athens   Auckland   Bangkok   Bogotá   Buenos Aires   Calcutta
Cape Town   Chennai   Dar es Salaam   Delhi   Florence   Hong Kong   Istanbul
Karachi   Kuala Lumpur   Madrid   Melbourne   Mexico City   Mumbai
Nairobi   Paris   São Paulo   Singapore   Taipei   Tokyo   Toronto   Warsaw

and associated companies in
Berlin   Ibadan

Published by Oxford University Press, Inc.
198 Madison Avenue, New York, New York 10016

Oxford is a registered trademark of Oxford University Press, Inc.

Library of Congress Cataloging-in-Publication Data
Lelwica, Michelle Mary.
Starving for salvation : the spiritual dimensions of
eating problems among American girls and women / Michelle Mary Lelwica.
p. cm.
Includes bibliographical references.
ISBN 0-19-512743-9
1. Eating disorders—Patients—Religious life.
2. Women—Health and hygiene—Religious aspects.
I. Title.
RC552.E18L44   1999
616.85'26'0082—dc21   98-50120

1 3 5 7 9 8 6 4 2

Printed in the United States of America
on acid-free paper

Starving
for
Salvation

PREFACE

When people ask me about my work as a scholar in the field of religion, most of them are surprised to learn of my interest in eating disorders. Over the years, I have come to appreciate the raised eyebrows and vexed smiles, for at the heart of this confusion resides the challenge of my study: to articulate connections that are not obvious, processes that are hard to see. This articulation is appropriate, I assure those who remain interested in my work, insofar as religion has long been in the business of calling attention to that which ordinary vision cannot clearly see.

In the course of writing this book, I have come to believe that the difficulty in seeing the spiritual dimensions of girls' and women's struggles with anorexia, bulimia, and related problems has much to do with the way many of us have been taught to look, with what we are encouraged to want and assume, and what we have learned to do without. There is much talk about pleasure, but rarely joy; much striving, but little freedom; many words, but not a lot of understanding.

In reality, most people today are very busy. In this land of maldistributed abundance, some work day and night just in order to make ends meet; others strive around the clock in a wishful effort to "succeed." Amid this hustle and hurry, however, widespread social phenomena—from the popularity of consumer culture, to the breakup of communal ties and cultural traditions, to the wave of religious fundamentalism, to the spread of eating disorders—suggest that many people are also hoping and searching for something more. It seems there is a sense that something precious is seriously endangered, or perhaps it is already missing, from the language and habits that make up the fabric of life on the evening of the twentieth century.

To explore the spiritual dimensions of girls' and women's troubled relationships to food and their bodies is to take up this question of what is threatened or missing from this culture at this historical juncture. While my study suggests an alternative to conventional approaches to "eating disorders," it does so by raising a series of larger questions that I believe these problems present: questions about where to turn and what to do in the face of cruelty and injustice; questions about how to make sense out of suffering and uncertainty. These queries are central to my analysis because in many ways women's eating problems epitomize the reality that in these revolutionary times, so little seems to have changed. In particular, remnants of the religious legacies that have historically effaced the diversity and complexity of women's spiritual yearnings and struggles are alive and well in a host of "secular" practices, pictures, and promises. Until these legacies are recognized, contested, and changed, many girls and women will continue to turn to the symbolic and ritual resources most readily available to them—food and their bodies—in a passionate but precarious quest for freedom and fulfillment.

ACKNOWLEDGMENTS

To study the world of eating disorders is to encounter a universe of pain. Navigating this sad and troubled turf would have been impossible without the tremendous support and keen vision I received from my teachers, students, family, and friends.

I thank first of all my friends at Harvard Divinity School, where this project was first conceived. My fellow students in the Religion, Gender, and Culture doctoral program—Irene Munroe, Julie Miller, Nancy Nienhuis, Lynn Miller, and Emily Neill—encouraged me and gave helpful feedback on early versions of this project. Jess Gugino and Elizabeth Lemons coached me through the academic vicissitudes and emotional conundrums that make up the rhythm of graduate school. Others who helped sustain my mind, body, and spirit during my years of doctoral study include Jane Shaw, Jennifer Manlowe, Nancy Goldstien, Susan Trabucchi, and Adam Chase. I am also extremely grateful to the professors who mentored me at Harvard, especially Gordon Kaufman, Elisabeth Schüssler Fiorenza, and Margaret Miles, whose creative geniuses and critical spirits nourished this book into being.

Friends, colleagues, and students at Saint Mary's College of California picked up where my grad school support-system left off, cheering me to the finish line of this book, while helping me learn the ropes of being a new professor. I want to especially thank the members of the Religious Studies Department and the Women's Studies Program.

Another community that has indirectly supported my work are the members of Berkeley Aikikai. I want to especially thank I. Shibata Shihan and all my sempai for teaching me the art of balance and blending and for exposing me to a different kind of knowledge. I also give thanks to the late Sylvain Sensei and his amazing daughter Chloe, who continue to inspire my struggle for harmony and fullness.

I have my own parents to thank for teaching me that religion is central, that music is sacred, and that rivers and trees are healing. The vitality of their own quest for spiritual meaning, as well as their capacity to continue to grow, have enriched my life and made it possible for me to flourish. The rest of my family—my sister Sue Lorette and my brothers Mark, Jim, and John Lelwica (along with their spouses and children)—have all shown un-shakable faith in my process as a "professional student."

Finally, on days when finishing this project seemed both imperative and impossible, a few close friends insisted that I not lose hope. I want to es-pecially thank Theresa Traynor, Julia Freedgood, Bobby Angotti, and Anne McGeary, whose abiding friendship and faith in me brought this book to fruition.

CONTENTS

FIVE

A DIFFERENT KIND OF SALVATION
Cultivating Alternative Senses, Practices, and Visions, 125

Starving

for

Salvation

INTRODUCTION

There is an empty space in many of us that gnaws at our ribs and cannot be filled by any amount of food. There is a hunger for something, and we never know quite what it is, only that it is a hunger, so we eat. One cannot deny the bodily responses to starvation, and that is part of the reason, some nights, I sat in the basement of the dorm; locked in a bathroom, catching myself in the mirror as I stuffed candy bars, chips, vending machine anything into my mouth, and then threw it up. There is also a larger, more ominous hunger, and I was and am not alone in sensing it. It squirms under the sternum, clawing at the throat. At school we were hungry and lost and scared and young and we needed religion, salvation, something to fill the anxious hollow in our chests. Many of us sought it in food and thinness.

—Marya Hornbacher, *Wasted: A Memoir of Anorexia and Bulimia*

In the closing decades of this century, a majority of girls and women in the United States have spent an incalculable amount of time, money, and energy worrying about their weight and its appearance on their bodies. Nearly two-thirds of adult women surveyed report that one of their greatest anxieties is becoming fat. Roughly the same percentage of high school girls monitor what and how much they eat; and in some urban areas, up to 80 percent of fourth-grade girls have dieted. While the average woman in the United States is 5' 4" and weighs 144 pounds, the average female model in this society is 5' 10" and weighs 111 pounds. Not surprisingly, diet books outsell any other books on the market—except the Bible. Indeed, Americans today spend some $50 billion a year trying to shed their "excess" flesh. Meanwhile, nearly 5 percent of adolescent girls and young women suffer from anorexia, and up to 20 percent of college women suffer from bulimia. Still, it is not uncommon to see TV ads like the one for "Nutri Systems," in which a slender, young white woman announces that "changing your body is as easy as changing your mind."[1]

What are so many girls and women trying to change through their pursuit of a slender body? What cultural values and social conditions make this transformation seem possible, if not necessary? Most psychologists explain girls' and women's problems with food and their bodies as pathological responses to developmental issues that should be treated therapeutically. Most sociologists see these problems as reflecting a societal preference for slender female bodies, a preference that needs to be challenged through public education. Many medical doctors contend that aberrant eating behavior results from biochemical imbalances that can be treated pharmaceutically. Finally, many feminists interpret these problems in terms of an eclipse of women's true identity and nature, which must be resisted through organized protest against a misogynist culture.

Popular lore on women's eating problems echoes and embellishes the more official views. Many people subscribe to at least one of the following beliefs: that these problems reflect individual pathologies, including a host of personal deficits and unresolved issues; that they are self-inflicted bad habits that could easily be abandoned with the proper amount of will; that they reflect an unreasonable desire for slimness caused by the unrealistic images of the fashion world; that they are rare, affecting only young women who are white, middle- or upper-class, and heterosexual; that they are transitory, reflecting the innocuous preoccupation with appearance that is characteristic of "normal" adolescent girls; and, last, that they are essentially secular phenomena, mirroring the prominent features of the social landscape in which they have become a regular feature.[2]

One would hope that all the popular and professional energy devoted to these problems would somehow help to reduce their prevalence. Indeed, a mixture of formal discourse and popular myths has made "eating disorders" a subject of national attention. Too often, however, this attention reflects the very mentality that these problems embody: a way of thinking that seeks to reduce ambiguity and control the unknown. This way of thinking also makes it difficult to notice certain aspects of these problems, aspects I refer to as spiritual.

The human body has been a crucial subject of religious discourse and imagination. Until quite recently in Euro-American history, religious symbols, beliefs, and rituals, especially Christian ones, provided shared idioms for people to articulate what is most important in their lives and to reconcile experiences of longing and pain. Christian attitudes and ideas are deeply woven into our culture's moral fabric. Prior to the twentieth century, Christian symbols and beliefs also played a central role in mediating girls' and women's relationships to their bodies, to others, and to the uncertainties and vicissitudes of their daily lives. Particularly in times of conflict or pain, girls and women turned to the ideals and practices of their religious traditions to help them make sense of their lives, creating and discovering a sense of purpose in relation to the whole of life.

Today, the declining and contested authority of traditional religion has made it possible for many girls and women to envision and embody new ways of being female. However, the need for meaningful symbols, beliefs, stories, and rituals has not disappeared amid the plurality of truths this shift has engendered. For many girls and women, including those who believe and participate in organized religion, a media-saturated, consumer-oriented culture provides the primary images, beliefs, and practices through which the truths of their lives are sought and defined. In both public and private spheres, "secular" ideals and rituals coexist alongside Christian beliefs and disciplines, whose assumptions and forms they frequently resemble.

In particular, consumer-media culture's prevailing ideals of womanhood, along with the self-correcting disciplines that these ideals inspire (e.g., dieting and exercise), are the icons and rituals by means of which a vast number of girls and women organize and manage their daily hopes and fears. For many of them, a network of symbols, beliefs, and rituals centering on bodily appetites and appearances constitutes an ultimate frame of reference—a "secular" salvation myth[3]—despite its seeming banality. This frame helps define the margins of the current sociopolitical order. This frame becomes a prison in the lives of those whose energies become trapped inside its narrow lines.

Anorexia, the most notorious though least common type of eating disorder, involves self-starvation and excessive weight loss, along with a dread of gaining weight. The related and often overlapping problem of bulimia, which is considerably more common but less conspicuous than anorexia, revolves around cycles of bingeing and purging. Bulimics consume large quantities of food, purging themselves by various means, the most common of which is self-induced vomiting. Laxatives, self-starvation, and/or strenuous exercise may also be used to rid the body of unwanted material. Besides anorexia and bulimia, a number of other related eating problems also damage the lives of contemporary girls and women. On the same continuum as bulimia and anorexia, these problems include compulsive eating, chronic dieting, and preoccupation and discontent with body shape and size.

Both popular and professional discourses on "eating disorders" tend to concentrate their attention on the more visibly extreme and less common types of troubled eating, especially anorexia. This focus creates a kind of depoliticizing voyeurism, obscuring the greater incidence of related problems (bulimia, compulsive eating, chronic dieting, body-hatred) and erasing the continuities between the "pathological" extremes and the eating practices that cultural authorities recommend to girls and women as "healthy." Girls' and women's own accounts suggest that their eating problems develop out of these socially endorsed, normalizing disciplines. Moreover, the hyperattention to the problem of anorexia encourages an exclusive focus on the struggles of those who are believed to be most vulnerable to developing eating problems, namely, females who are young, white, middle- to upper-class, presumably heterosexual, and "high achieving."

This narrow focus reflects and reinforces an interface between professional paradigms and popular ideologies of womanhood. The stereotyped anorexic[4] is one whose social privilege keeps her in the purview of health professionals, media culture, and intrigued academics. She is also presumed to be most affected by the pervasive cultural imperative for female slenderness because of its associations with racial, sexual, and economic privilege and with youth. These stereotypes not only overlook the multiple and often insidious ways that dominant cultural ideals, such as slenderness, infiltrate the subjectivities of those in marginalized groups; they also imply that the desire to lose weight is at the core of eating problems. Most popular and professional conceptions of these problems thus not only reproduce (however unwittingly) stereotypical visions of race, class, age, size, sexuality, and gender; in so doing they also divert attention away from the broader and deeper issues that these problems intimate.[5]

In this book, I probe what I believe to be the broader and deeper issues by looking at the full range of eating problems as they afflict diverse girls and women. I aim to better understand such problems by situating them within American society at the end of the twentieth century, a context in which we are seeing a culmination of the historical shift from a predominantly religiously oriented culture toward one that has been described as "disenchanted" or "secular": a media-saturated and profit-driven culture in which religious questions about the meaning of life are often relegated to the universe of the individual self, or treated with absolute assurances in the public sphere, or commodified in the interests of consumer capitalism. It is both in spite of and because of this seemingly "secular" context that I am asking how spiritual issues are present in girls' and women's troubled relationships to food and their bodies.

Interestingly, several authors who address the topic of eating problems from a self-consciously nonreligious perspective have noted the quasi-religious character of women's preoccupations with their bodies and food. Historian Roberta Seid calls our pursuit of slenderness a "new religion," with moral codes that are "worthy of the strictest Calvinist"; sociologist Richard Gordon says that the fanaticism with which girls and women pursue the perfect body points to "an underlying religious ideal" masking itself as "the epitome of secular rationalism"; feminist sociologist Sharlene Hesse-Biber draws a parallel between religious cults and the popular "cult of thinness"; feminist philosopher Sandra Bartky argues that feminine images of beauty have replaced the religious symbols of the past; and best-selling author Naomi Wolf spends an entire chapter in *The Beauty Myth* comparing contemporary women's obsessions with achieving a perfect body with the medieval "superstition[s]" of traditional religions.[6]

Although none of these authors say exactly what they mean by "religion," their common insight into the religious function that preoccupations with weight and eating serve is significant. In this book, I analyze the quasi-religious quality and function of girls' and women's struggles with food and their bodies. On close examination, this quality and function are not hard to see: the obsessive, imaginary, sacrificial, ritualizing, ascetic, penitential, dogmatic, and devotional aspects of anorexia and bulimia all resemble certain features of traditional Christianity. Using the categories of religion, gender, and culture, I examine girls' and women's accounts of their eating problems, and I situate these problems in relation to dominant cultural icons and rituals of womanhood and the historical legacies embedded in them. My analysis suggests that eating problems are not simply oriented toward the obvious goal of getting thin. Instead, I argue, eating problems point to spiritual hungers—desires for a sense of meaning and wholeness—and such hungers are inextricably intertwined with the politics of these problems.

When I characterize these hungers as "spiritual," I do not mean that they are beyond or untouched by material reality. On the contrary, the phrase "spiritual hungers" calls attention to the *embodied* character of girls' and women's desires for a life that is meaningful. These desires are shaped by cultural norms and social institutions that are historically specific. Thus, the spiritual hungers that eating problems suggest are neither "existential" nor "metaphysical" insofar as these terms are supposed to refer to a transcendent realm of experience. Instead, they can be seen as the embodied effects of living in a society whose "order" continues in this "postmodern" age to be organized through a logic of dualism and domination: spirit over body, men over women, thought over feeling, white over colored, individual over community, rich over poor, and so forth.

My study suggests that living in this "order" leaves many girls and women feeling profoundly empty. On some level, many of them experience the rules and values of the dominant culture as void of truth, and they carry this void in their bodies, feeding it, starving it, vomiting it up. I characterize the hungers that this emptiness breeds as *spiritual* because I believe they signal a desire for meaning and wholeness in the face of injustice, suffering, and uncertainty. To understand girls' and women's struggles with food and their bodies, we must see how these struggles function as precarious solutions to a crisis of meaning: as symbolic-ritualizing attempts to fill a void, to construct some hope. "Of course we went on a diet," a woman who spent half of her young life purging, bingeing, and starving explained. "We were scared and hollowing out; we needed a religion."[7]

Implicitly, the self-negating beliefs and health-destroying rituals that girls and women with eating problems turn to in their quest for a sense of purpose underscore the impoverishment of this culture's prominent myths, symbols, and rituals. More specifically, the sufferings of anorexic and bulimic girls and women point to a tragic failure on the part of traditional religion, especially the dominant tradition in this culture: Christianity. Part of what makes consumer culture's salvation myth of female slenderness so powerful is that it gels so well with the anti-body, misogynist attitudes that became dominant in this tradition. Sin itself, the ancient story goes, entered into the world through the disobedient appetite of a woman.

Throughout Christian history, this legacy fostered an association between women, sin, and bodily cravings, even as it promised women salvation through the mastery of their flesh and through their subordination to men. Tacitly, such a legacy lives on in the contemporary promise of female slenderness: control your appetite, be thin, and you will be beautiful/loved/successful/saved. In both scenarios (the biblical legacy and the popular cultural myth), women are condemned to the very flesh they must transcend in order to be saved.

The history of female oppression and marginalization within biblical religion has left many women feeling spiritually rootless and disconnected, harboring a kind of inner void. Perhaps not surprisingly, some believe that organized religion is either irredeemable or irrelevant when it comes to their most pressing concerns. On the other hand, women who continue to place their faith in traditional religious institutions may find that the only avenues available to them for cultivating a sense of spiritual power require obedience and submission to a "higher" (read: male) authority.

But if traditional religion is part of the problem, it is also, in its less dominant and more subversive forms, potentially part of the solution. The body-transcending, female-subordinating attitudes that became dominant in Christianity overshadowed, but never completely eliminated, the more egalitarian and incarnational elements of this tradition. Nevertheless, insofar as contemporary religious leaders and people of faith fail to recognize, challenge, and transform the misogynist, anti-body legacies of their traditions, women will continue to turn elsewhere in an effort to feed their spiritual hungers.

Notions that religious faith is inherently otherworldly, reactionary, or just plain antiquated have made many feminists and cultural critics suspicious of organized religion, theology, and even spirituality more generally defined. Often such notions reflect and reinforce both the growing privatization of religious beliefs and the concomitant absolutization of certain groups' religious values within the public sphere. Whatever their bases, these notions stifle prophetic critique of dominant cultural norms and institutions whose values, though commonly taken for granted, may serve to undermine social and personal well-being.

My analysis of the spiritual hungers that eating problems intimate presumes that critical religious thinkers can and should be engaged in the social and political challenges of their time and that questions of spiritual significance need not be restricted to the sphere of organized religion. The works of feminist and liberation theologians demonstrate the interdependence of spirituality and social change. In the words of Jewish feminist theologian Judith Plaskow, "For spirituality to matter, it must be poured out into the world in which we live, just as enduring social change must be rooted in some intuition of a richer and more humane future." Ecofeminist theologian Sallie McFague makes this point from a Christian perspective: "Social justice and spirituality are not opposite tracks; rather, staying the course on any justice issue appears possible only by being grounded in a power and love beyond oneself." And feminist thealogian Carol Christ says that such views articulate a vision of political and spiritual commitments as "two dimensions of a single struggle."[8]

In this book, I draw on the insights of those who recognize the connections between social and spiritual revolutions, between changing values and changing cultural conditions. Among religious feminists, such insights are often informed by, but not confined to, commitments to particular religious heritages. Today, a growing body of feminist-oriented theo(a)logy[9] and spirituality includes voices of women from Jewish, Goddess, Mujerista, Buddhist, Womanist, Catholic, Asian, Wiccan, Native American, Protestant, and other spiritual heritages.

My own spiritual tradition is Roman Catholicism. Undoubtedly, this heritage shapes my perspective both in ways that are obvious and in ways that are hidden (even to myself). However, the concerns and commitments that ground my work as a theologian and cultural critic are rooted in the struggles and insights of feminist and other liberation communities, especially those whose spiritual practice and vision is shaped by critical consciousness.[10] Ultimately, a radically mindful spiritual perspective provides an alternative frame of meaning within which girls' and women's struggles with food and their bodies can be compassionately and critically understood.

Critical and compassionate assessment of these struggles, rather than dispassionate or pathologizing analysis, is necessary in the current cultural climate of denial and blame. In our society, female bodies are trained through a network of symbols, beliefs, disciplines, and institutions that privilege the material interests of elite men. In order to transform the myriad pains and anxieties which eating problems create and to which they respond, a change in consciousness is required. Such transformation becomes possible in the space of communities committed to social justice and spiritual well-being, communities whose stories, beliefs, and practices challenge the dualistic logic and controlling ethos through which eating problems develop. With the support and inspiration of such communities, girls and women can learn to redirect the energies they devote to changing their bodies into struggles to transform the dominant ways of thinking and being that, in varying degrees and ways, jeopardize the well-being of every body.

As these preliminary remarks indicate, neither my theoretical lens, nor my interpretive method, nor my overall argument in this book is value-neutral. I assume that all scholarship is "interested" and that clarity about one's own concerns and loyalties constitutes a step toward greater objectivity. I assume that girls' and women's struggles with their appetites and bodies are problems. Compulsive eating, chronic dieting, and body-hatred slowly drain girls and women of their creative energies, making their lives feel like a living hell. Bulimia and anorexia are life-threatening illnesses. In this light, the large-scale political and spiritual revolution I call for is a long-range response to eating problems. It is meant to supplement rather than undercut the efforts of those in the fields of mental and physical health. Although I believe my interpretation will broaden and deepen our understanding of and response to these problems, it is limited in its capacity to address the very urgent needs of some women and girls, particularly those who are dying.

Acknowledgment of this limitation points to another assumption that underlies the way I situate my work in relation to others in the field of eating disorders. I believe the spiritual hungers that bulimia, anorexia, and related problems suggest must be seen as *one* of their several facets. I do not claim to be talking about the *real* or *ultimate* truth of (or solution to) these problems. I understand their spiritual aspect to be a tremendously important piece of the puzzle, rather than a picture of (or answer to) the puzzle in its entirety. My aim is to highlight this previously neglected piece, especially as it connects with the politics of these problems. In so doing, I hope to show how the spiritual dimensions of eating problems relate to their other aspects (biological, sociological, psychological) and thus how a more integrative perspective may help both those who struggle with, and those who treat, these problems.

The spiritual and political interests of this book dictate a method of interpretation that is *critical, contextual*, and *imaginative*. This method draws on three distinct yet often overlapping areas of study: feminist studies, cultural studies, and religious studies. This interdisciplinary approach allows me to attend to the complexity of girls' and women's eating problems. Although a survey of the literature on eating disorders reveals numerous acknowledgments of their "multidimensional" character, few analyses actually reflect this multiplicity. Common assumptions about the secular nature of troubled eating behavior and beliefs inhibit most experts in the field from exploring their spiritual dimensions, even though women themselves frequently use the terms and conventions of traditional religion (e.g., "soul," "purity," "sin," "salvation") to describe and interpret their troubled eating patterns.

In my view, this language points to the quasi-religious function that the symbolic worlds of anorexia and bulimia implicitly serve: that of constructing an ultimate frame of meaning that provides what seems to be a transcendent source of values, power, comfort, and order. This language, and the logic it presumes, reveal the multiple levels of struggle that eating problems entail: the links between a woman's efforts to redefine the margins of her own body, her desire for a self-determining voice and presence in society, and her need for a sense of meaning and fulfillment amid the conflicts and disappointments surrounding her life as a whole.

It is essential to recognize these multiple levels because the yearnings for meaning and fulfillment that eating problems suggest are multifaceted and diverse. Girls' and women's accounts of their troubled relationships to food are full of tensions and contradictions: the desire for a sense of connection *and* independence, the longing for a sense of order *and* creativity. Such tensions point to the depths and complexities of girls' and women's subjectivities today, intensified and diversified as they are by the social changes brought on by liberation movements in the past few decades.

Attention to the diversity, the complexity, and the agency of girls' and women's subjectivities is central to the feminist angle of this project. My analysis takes seriously the diverse experiences and discourses—the "subjugated knowledges"[11]—of girls and women who have grappled (or are grappling) with bulimia, anorexia, and related problems, and it interprets these "knowledges" from a critical perspective. By "critical perspective," I mean a way of seeing that recognizes the interrelatedness of all forms of life and that is therefore suspicious of hierarchical divisions that foster unequal relationships of power. Throughout this book, this way of seeing provides an alternative lens for analyzing the experiences of those with eating problems and the culture that feeds them.

This book tries to bring these experiences to life by drawing on the writings of and published interviews with girls and women who have struggled with food and their bodies. This allows girls and women to describe their eating problems in words that are neither solicited by nor formulated in response to my specific questions. At the same time, the previous publication of these words suggests varying degrees of filtering. Women who are economically and/or racially privileged have more access to public/published voice. Moreover, although my sources represent a variety of voices (in terms of racial, religious, sexual, class, and generational diversity), many girls and women do not locate themselves socially. After wrestling with the question of whether this "invisibility" marks one as a member of some dominant social group, I have opted to let the unmarked stand, rather than attempt to identify a girl or woman's unstated social background. This issue underscores the need for more research on the meanings and functions of eating problems among diverse girls and women. Unfortunately, published materials also offer relatively few younger female voices, whose chances of being recorded for public hearing are limited at best. I believe it is crucial that girls become more central to both feminist agenda and religious studies, and I highlight their voices whenever possible, even when their statements are less articulate than those of their adult counterparts. I also value older women's reflections on their own girlhood struggles with food and their bodies.

The value of this book rests not in its discovery of new data but in its reinterpretation of already existing materials both in relation to other sources and through a different theoretical lens. I bring the voices of diverse girls and women into conversation with some of this culture's historical shifts (for example, secularization; changing beliefs about gender, race, class, sexuality), its pervasive trends (for example, the war on fat), and its popular artifacts (for example, women's magazines, TV ads, celebrity personalities). These present-day phenomena constitute another source of data for my study, since they shape the popular cultural landscape wherein girls must navigate the question of what it means to be a woman. Moreover, while I situate eating problems in relation to popular icons and rituals of womanhood, I analyze the contested meanings of these icons and rituals in relation to prevailing social arrangements and ideologies, as well as the institutions by means of which they are produced, circulated, and consumed.[12]

This method of historically contextualizing women's efforts to control their appetites belongs to the cultural studies angle of my interpretive scheme. It highlights the ways that girls' and women's experiences are variously shaped by their environments. More specifically, this method illustrates how eating problems emerge from and respond to this culture's prevailing social values and conditions. Situated amid the symbolic systems and social structures of America today, girls' and women's preoccupations with their bodies and appetites are extremely, though tragically, meaningful.

The argument of this book also integrates another interpretive angle, namely, the theological. To recognize the spiritual dimensions of girls' and women's struggles with their bodies and food is to view these struggles in relation to questions about the ultimate meaning and value of human life. Since this is the feature that most distinguishes my interpretation of eating problems from other approaches, it is important to clarify its assumptions.

I assume that all theological references (i.e., ways of referring to the ultimate power, reality, or meaning of life—traditionally "God") are *imaginative*.[13] People may experience divinity in their lives, but awareness and expression of such experiences are unavoidably interpretive, depending on cultural symbols and stories whose meanings are metaphorical, rather than literal or descriptive. Because theological images are products of *human* imagination, they are also invariably shaped by historical and political interests and must therefore be open to critique and revision.

When I interpret girls' and women's accounts of their eating problems to bespeak a hunger for something more, my characterizations of this "something more" are self-consciously imaginative (rather than literal). These characterizations are also meant to be iconoclastic and liberating. Thus, the theological angle of my work is both (de)constructivist and critical. Perhaps most important, it is interpretive. I am neither a medical nor a social scientist. Readers who expect to find positivist "proof" that there are spiritual dimensions to girls' and women's eating problems will be disappointed. At least in part, this argument entails a leap of the imagination: a willingness to listen to the inaudible, to envision the invisible, to consider the unknowable.

This leap constitutes a worthy risk at this time, when so many attempts to understand and address eating disorders are at an impasse. The efforts of those working in the social and natural sciences have been largely unsuccessful in slowing the spread of these problems. Most of these efforts confine their analyses to issues pertaining to women's social, psychological, or biological experiences. The imaginative addition of a wider context of interpretation—one that underlines the mysteries and sufferings of human life in relation to which girls and women search for a sense of meaning and fulfillment—may shed new light on the issues.

My use of girls' and women's own descriptions of their struggles with food and their bodies does not exempt me from the dangers of academic imperialism. While I try to let girls and women speak for themselves, I do not pretend to be a neutral observer or interpreter. The political and spiritual commitments that inform my study are shaped by my own experiences growing up in a white, middle-class family in rural Minnesota, where traditional gender and religious prescriptions were inseparable, and where the possibility of thinking differently—of thinking *critically*—seemed as far removed as the clouds on the receding midwestern horizon. At school I was a straight-A student, a homecoming queen candidate, a cheerleader. At home I consumed a steady diet of Roman Catholicism and *Seventeen* magazine. Overall, there was little question about the way my life was to unfold: I would go to college, find a man (preferably a rich one) and get married, have kids, maybe work part-time to avert boredom, and of course stay thin and pretty through it all.

I did everything I possibly could to accommodate the "truths" of this feminine indoctrination, but the dream was slowly suffocating my spirit. Thinking back now, I see how my despair was laced with a longing for a freedom I could not even imagine. Like so many young women, I turned to the one area in my life over which I seemed to have some say. After a year of eating virtually nothing but a small dinner each night to appease my parents, I became bulimic. For the next few years, hardly anyone noticed my bottomless appetite for food any more than they had noticed my insatiable craving for more in life.

I cite these experiences at the onset of my exploration neither as a confession nor as a norm but as a resource, and a very partial one at that. In many ways, my own experiences match the conventional descriptions of who gets eating problems and why. Yet my research has led me to believe that, taken alone, such descriptions obscure more than they clarify. Girls and women develop eating disorders for reasons that are infinitely varied. Only by attending to the multiple meanings of these problems among girls and women with different physical, social, and cultural histories can we begin to detect some of the "common senses" that they produce and the shared functions they precariously serve.

The specificity of my own struggles reminds me that the danger of speaking for others is especially acute where I attempt to speak about realities with which I have little or no direct experience.[14] However painful some of its effects, my socialization as a white, middle-class girl/woman growing up Catholic in rural Minnesota shielded me from many of the cruelties that girls and women with less social privilege experience on a regular basis. In fact, much of what I was taught and believed about what it means to be a woman implicitly and unwittingly perpetuated these cruelties. Such teachings and beliefs were usually very elitist, though of course they seemed "normal" to me at the time. While I cannot change this aspect of my social/personal history, I cannot ignore it, either. My memories and awareness of it inform the spiritual search and political loyalties that inspire my desire to understand. In retrospect, I have come to see the intolerable emptiness I experienced in relation to the "truths" of my specific gender indoctrination as both different from and connected to the pain and struggles of girls, women, and men in less privileged social positions, many of whom experience exploitation in the name of such "truths."

In their diversity and their ubiquity, the struggles recounted in the body of this book demonstrate the potentially lethal shallowness of the dominant cultural ideals, beliefs, and practices that are used to feed girls' and women's creative spirits. At the same time, these struggles point to the need for alternative images and rituals with which girls and women might more adequately nourish their spiritual hungers: symbols and practices that shatter rather than reinforce the legacies of silence and disempowerment that obstruct their searches for meaning and fulfillment; visions and rituals that increase our awareness of something more, while fostering our ability to be present to what is.

One

BODIES OF EVIDENCE,
BODIES OF KNOWLEDGE

Contemporary Approaches, Historical
Perspectives, New Directions

Religious thinkers have often been notorious for intellectual parochialism. The seemingly archaic language and methods of traditional theology, next to the skepticism and jargon of modern and postmodern thought, make cross-disciplinary exchange nothing short of a miracle. But what falls through the cracks between apparently disparate bodies of knowledge may be precisely what is needed in order for us to see more clearly. This chapter endeavors to explore some of this between-the-cracks material.

The explicit purpose of this chapter is to provide an overview of contemporary approaches, historical perspectives, and new directions in the study of eating disorders. The implicit aim, however, is to get us to think about the relationship between what we study and how we think: between the starving bodies of girls and women and the ideas through which we interpret these bodies—between "bodies of evidence" and "bodies of knowledge."

Contemporary Discourse on "Eating Disorders"

During the past two decades, a flood of literature on eating disorders has raised questions about the nature of these problems, as well as the numbers and kinds of persons they affect. There is confusion regarding the terminology of anorexia and bulimia, and there are debates over classification and diagnostic criteria. Demographic (who?) and epidemiological (how many?)

questions accompany these definitional issues, and a related sphere of controversy centers on the etiology (causes) and treatment of eating disorders.

Definitional Issues

The terms used to describe girls' and women's problems with their appetites and bodies tend to confuse as much as they clarify. Generally speaking, "eating disorders" refers to anorexia nervosa and bulimia nervosa.[1] However, experts today agree that "anorexia" (literally, "loss of hunger") is a misnomer, since anorexics' refusal to eat actually leaves them intensely hungry and preoccupied with food. The term "bulimia" (literally, "ox hunger") is also misleading because it fails to suggest the purging behavior that typically follows a bulimic binge. In addition, neither "anorexia" nor "bulimia" etymologically conveys the intense body-dissatisfaction that accompanies women's eating problems.[2] Finally, the term "nervosa," which is commonly appended to "anorexia" and "bulimia" to indicate the *psychic* origins of these problems,[3] is misleading to the extent that it obscures the societal, physical, and spiritual influences on psychic processes.

All of these terms originated in psychiatric discourse (see below). This discourse views these problems through a medical or disease model, which sees them as individual "pathologies," ignoring the cultural values and social conditions that encourage and reward women's obsession with their bodies. Their associations with this pathologizing framework make terms like "anorexia" and "bulimia" troublesome. At the same time, they have become part of this culture's vocabulary during the past decade. I use them because I want to communicate—not because I accept their traditional meanings, which can be stigmatizing. I often use the phrase "eating problems" as a corrective to the more pathologizing term "eating disorders," though I agree with Becky Thompson that this is only partially corrective insofar as these "problems" begin as *solutions* to a host of difficult and oppressive experiences.[4]

The question of how to talk about eating disorders is important because language does not merely reflect but to some extent also creates the realities it seeks to name. This insight pertains not only to the terminology of eating disorders but also to their diagnosis. Standard criteria for identifying anorexia and bulimia appear in the *Diagnostic and Statistical Manual of Mental Disorders* (*DSM*), published in several editions by the American Psychiatric Association.[5] Used by clinicians and researchers alike, this text's norms and definitions illustrate the links between power and knowledge: the connection between the creation of ideas and the maintenance of a political order, between the classification of reality and the mechanics of social control.[6]

Feminists have questioned the validity of the "normal/pathological" paradigm that the *DSM* employs.[7] The objectifying language used to designate an "eating disorder" masks the ambiguities surrounding a diagnosis,[8] obscuring the continuities between "disordered" and "normal" eating among women today. For example, according to the *DSM-IV*, "essential features" of anorexia nervosa are that

> the individual refuses to maintain a minimally normal body weight
> [below 85 percent of what is deemed "normal"], is intensely afraid of
> gaining weight, and exhibits a significant disturbance in the perception
> of the shape or size of his or her body. In addition, postmenarchal
> females with this disorder are amenorrheic.[9]

But the clarity of these diagnostic "essences" is blurred when one considers that, to varying degrees, *most* females in the United States are afraid of gaining weight, that many of them (including those who are underweight) overestimate their body size, and that "normal body weight" varies among girls and women, depending on their social circumstances and physical histories.

Official *DSM-IV* criteria for diagnosing bulimia have similar problems. According to the manual, "essential features" of this disorder include:

> binge eating and inappropriate compensatory methods to prevent
> weight gain. In addition, the self-evaluation of individuals with Bulimia
> Nervosa is excessively influenced by body shape and weight. To qualify
> for the diagnosis, the binge eating and the inappropriate compensatory
> behaviors must occur, on average, at least twice a week for 3 months.[10]

Again, the clarity of such criteria becomes fuzzy when one recognizes that many "normal" girls and women in the United States measure their self-worth on the bathroom scale, that a number of them regularly "compensate" for overeating through restrictive dieting and excessive exercise, and that what the *DSM-IV* considers "inappropriate compensatory methods" for preventing weight gain (such as strenuous exercise and fasting) have been deemed "healthy" by mainstream fitness and diet industries.[11]

The relationship between anorexia and bulimia is a further source of diagnostic confusion. Whether these problems are qualitatively distinct or variants of the same pathology is not entirely clear. In part, the confusion stems from the physical overlap between anorexia and bulimia. About 50 percent of anorexics become bulimic in the course of their illness, and the same percentage of bulimics have a history of starving themselves, but not to the point of becoming anorexic.[12] Amid this confusion, some have suggested that differences in body weight may be the most reliable way to distinguish anorexia and bulimia. Whereas anorexics lose about 20 percent of their original body weight, bulimics tend to remain slightly below or above or even at a weight that is deemed "desirable" for their height and age.[13] But this is not always the case.

What is troubling about standard diagnostic categories is not that they are ambiguous but that their ambiguity is generally reduced and denied. In the tradition of modern science, these standards are meant to function as objective norms rather than value-laden interpretations that are historically conditioned. Moreover, in the name of scientific "objectivity," the voices of those who suffer from these problems are excluded from the knowledge-making process of categorization.[14] As a result, standard diagnostic criteria for eating problems are exceedingly narrow. Even the newest category, eating disorders "Not Otherwise Specified," fails to illumine the range of problems that diverse girls and women have with their bodies and food.[15]

This failure is evident from some women's accounts of these problems. "Everyone's alarmed at what amounts to a nation-wide eating phobia in young women," a fifty-three-year-old grandmother observes,

> but what about the older woman trying to resist the way her body naturally thickens at the waist, the way her skin loosens and flaps below her upper arms, the way fat collects upon her stomach? . . . Every day that battle gets more difficult. It takes time and energy, and worst of all it takes space in my mind, filling my head with calorie counts and broken resolutions. . . . I know how crazy-making it is to live in a society that expects an older woman's body to be as slim as a young body, but still I fussed and fumed buttoning my slacks.

The stories of those whose troubled eating patterns do not fit into the pre-existing categories known as "eating disorders" point up the inadequacy of current definitions. The same woman concludes: "It's bizarre to spend so much time thinking about food. And I don't binge; I don't vomit. According to the literature, I don't even have a problem. If this obsessive preoccupation is normal, what is it like to have an eating disorder? I can't bear to think about it."[16]

The narrow rigidity of standard criteria rules out the pathologization of the majority of the female population. However, it also creates an either/or approach to eating problems: either she has an eating disorder or she doesn't. This erases the variations in the degrees, forms, and functions of food and body obsessions among girls and women from different generational, economic, religious, sexual, and ethnic backgrounds. At the same time, it downplays the role of common sociocultural influences, especially the mandate for female thinness, in the development of these problems. Thus, feminist therapist Catrina Brown advises,

> We cannot stigmatize anorexia and bulimia as individual pathologies or diseases, at the same time that we approve, even praise, the behavior of those women who exercise and diet to attain the culturally prescribed body ideal. The tendency to separate the social obsession with thinness from anorexia and bulimia allows the latter to be treated as individual problems and isolated diseases, disconnected from popular culture and patriarchal society.[17]

An alternative perspective locates the pathology of which these problems are symptoms in the ideals and structures of this society, rather than in the minds of those who assimilate its norms. This view recognizes a *continuum* of eating problems, from the more extreme incidences of anorexia and bulimia to the more common but related problems of compulsive eating, chronic dieting, and body-discontent.[18] The aim is not to collapse the differences between anorexia and dieting, for example, but rather to see these differences as a matter of *degree* rather than *kind*. This illuminates the continuities between "disordered" eating and the "normal" food patterns of many girls and women today (those based on some degree of restriction, dissatisfaction, obsession, and/or loss of control).

It is important to underscore that while "obesity" may in some cases accompany eating problems, it does not belong on the continuum I am developing here. Not only do medical experts disagree on the origins of obesity; a growing number of them also question whether being overweight is automatically unhealthy and thus whether it should be treated at all.[19] Proponents of the "set point" theory, the notion that each person has a set weight that their body "defends," are especially articulate in this regard.[20] Although obesity can be a physically and mentally debilitating condition, it is not *necessarily* so. Given that most people who are fat have an extremely difficult time getting thin, it seems likely that much of the physical and mental stress they experience is an effect of *cultural*, rather than *natural*, pressures to be thin. That people who are fat do not necessarily eat more than those who are thin suggests that obesity itself is unreliable as a sign of underlying eating patterns.[21] Finally, studies suggest that many fat persons who begin dieting to "normalize" their bodies not only decrease their ability to discern whether they are hungry but also lower their metabolic rate and as a result end up gaining more weight. Some doctors believe that such "weight cycling" presents a more serious health hazard than obesity.[22]

Epidemiological and Demographic Issues

Positing a continuum complicates an already confusing set of questions regarding the demography (who?) and epidemiology (how many?) of eating problems. Most experts agree that the incidence of eating disorders has increased during the past few decades, that females represent the majority (90–95 percent) of those with anorexia and bulimia, and that bulimia is the more common of the two problems.[23] Outside of these points of agreement, however, the map becomes a lot less clear.

Reports on the number of girls and women who struggle with eating disorders vary, depending on how these problems are defined, which tests are used, and which population is represented. Conservative estimates (based on *DSM-IV* criteria) suggest that between .5 percent and 1 percent of females in late adolescence and early adulthood have symptoms that meet the full criteria for anorexia, while between 1 percent and 3 percent of this population could be diagnosed as bulimic. Confusingly, however, these low percentages conflict with the findings of other studies based on similar criteria, which show up to 20 percent of college women suffering from anorexia and/or bulimia.[24]

When less rigid criteria are applied, these percentages rapidly escalate. Using more flexible measures, one study found 40 percent of a group of college women showing "anorexic-like" behavior. Nearly half of these women reported bingeing and vomiting, and all of them knew women with similar practices.[25] Surveys of female college populations reveal up to 67 percent of self-reported binge eating in "normal" (i.e., nonclinical) student samples.[26] Problems with chronic dieting, compulsive exercising, and body-dissatisfaction are at least as widespread. A 1987 Harris poll showed that nearly 75 percent of women surveyed wanted to lose weight. Another survey found that 95 percent of young women who exercise do so primarily to control their weight.[27] These numbers suggest that many women and girls who have problems with their appetites and bodies are not diagnosed. Standard discourse on "eating disorders" renders their struggles invisible.

It is commonly assumed that eating disorders are unique to Western industrialized countries. This appears to be generally true, although girls and women from some non-Western industrialized nations, such as Japan, have also shown signs of troubled eating.[28] In addition, some cross-cultural studies cite evidence of disturbed eating among females from nonindustrialized societies that are heavily influenced by Western norms and institutions.[29] In any case, however, the United States continues to be a context in which such problems flourish.

Conventional portraits of females with eating disorders—as young, white, and economically privileged—are to some degree accurate, but they are also misleading. While many anorexics and bulimics do come from families that are socially privileged,[30] many do not. Clinical evidence seems to suggest that anorexic girls and women are more likely to come from a smaller, affluent slice of society, whereas bulimics tend to be more socially diverse.[31] This discrepancy may reflect the influence of popular cultural associations between social privilege and self-control on clinical research, rather than "the facts." In any case, the frequent overlap between anorexic and bulimic behavior suggests that theories about who gets what kind of eating problem are tentative at best.

In the past decade, however, the prevalence of debilitating eating problems among girls and women who are not socially privileged has become indisputable. For example, one study revealed that 74 percent of Native American girls and women surveyed were trying to lose weight and that 75 percent of this number were using potentially dangerous methods to do so, including bulimic techniques.[32] In another study, Asian schoolgirls showed a disproportionately higher percentage of bulimia and bulimic symptoms than their Caucasian peers.[33] Other research indicates that eating disorders have become more common among African American females and that these problems are affecting the lives of both younger girls and older women.[34] Some studies show that girls and women from lower socioeconomic classes are increasingly vulnerable to bulimia in particular.[35] And there is evidence suggesting that lesbian and bisexual women are no less likely to develop problems with food than their heterosexual counterparts.[36]

The social geography of eating problems is even more diverse further along the continuum. As the title of one study states, "minorities join the majority" when it comes to problems related to anorexia and bulimia. This study found a greater degree of body-discontent and disturbed eating among Native American and Hispanic girls than among their white counterparts.[37] These quantitative findings are supported by Becky Thompson's qualitative study of troubled eating among women who are racially, sexually, religiously, generationally, and economically diverse. Her interviews attest to the pervasiveness and variety of eating problems among women in diverse social locations. By showing how women with different cultural and physical histories developed eating problems as "survival strategies . . . in response to myriad injustices, including racism, sexism, homophobia, poverty, the stress of acculturation, and emotional, physical, and sexual abuse," Thompson's work challenges popular and professional myths about who develops eating problems and why.[38]

The common clinical presumption that minority females are "protected" from eating problems by their exposure to subcultural values overlooks the various and insidious ways that prevailing cultural ideals can colonize the experiences of nonprivileged girls and women, who are often rewarded for assimilating dominant (white, middle-class, Protestant, heterosexual) cultural values and norms.[39] Several studies besides Thompson's document a relationship between eating problems among minority women and acculturative pressures.[40] In sum, a growing body of evidence—both quantitative and qualitative—suggests that the underrepresentation of minority females in conventional discourse on eating disorders reflects not the absence of eating problems among these groups but, rather, stereotypical expectations about who these problems affect, narrow professional definitions, biases built into standard criteria for measuring and defining eating disturbances, and minority girls' and women's unequal access to traditional medical and/or psychiatric services.

Current Approaches to the Etiology and Treatment of Eating Disorders

Any overview of conventional approaches to eating disorders[41]—psychological, biomedical, and sociocultural—must begin with two caveats. First, with some important exceptions, these discourses tend to focus on anorexia and bulimia, ignoring the less extreme forms of troubled eating and weight preoccupation. Second, there is overlap among these approaches. Rhetorically at least, many experts acknowledge the "multidimensional" nature of eating problems. Even so, a high level of specialization among professionals makes dialogue across disciplinary boundaries difficult at best. And where dialogue is difficult, assumptions can easily go unquestioned. The following overview aims both to familiarize the nonspecialist with current models of interpretation and to highlight and assess some of their unstated assumptions.

Psychological Models

Some of the most popular approaches to eating disorders share a common view of anorexia and bulimia as manifesting disturbances in psychological development and functioning. Most of these approaches fall under one of three interpretive models: psychoanalytic, family systems, or cognitive behavior.

The psychoanalytic model generally views anorexia and bulimia as pathological responses to developmental conflicts, especially those related to childhood and adolescence. This model builds on the work of Hilde Bruch, who was the first to move beyond Freud's belief that troubled eating expressed underlying sexual disturbances. Like Freud, Bruch saw the typical age of onset (adolescence) as key to understanding these problems: the anorexic's desire to keep her body childlike signifies her fear of the demands of adult female sexuality. Unlike Freud, however, Bruch insisted that sexuality is only one aspect of an anorexic's refusal to eat and that such refusal also represents a desire for control—a desire that conflicts with the anorexic's need to comply with the perceived demands of others. Such conflicts inhibit the development of the internal cues that enable a person to recognize hunger.[42] In addition, Bruch noted the ineffectiveness and fear of ordinariness that anorexics typically feel, despite their above-average intelligence and achievement-orientation. In her classic work, *The Golden Cage*, she concludes that "inner doubts" and "underlying self-deceptions" are at the heart of eating disorders:

> The main thing I've learned is that worry about dieting, the worry about being skinny or fat, is just a smokescreen. . . . The real illness has to do with the way you feel about yourself. . . . This illness is the supreme effort to establish for oneself the conviction that I can do what I want to do.[43]

If "self-devaluation is the essence of the illness," acceptance of one's "genuine self" is the key to getting better. For Bruch, such acceptance is best cultivated in the context of a therapeutic relationship. Thus, in the spirit of Freud, she upheld the "talking cure" as the optimal method of treatment.

The psychoanalytic emphases on adolescent development and identity formation are incorporated into a second psychological model: the family systems approach. This model sees eating disorders as family pathologies that are rooted in familial dynamics that impede a young woman's growth as an individual.[44] Frequently, mothers are implicated in this failure; they are depicted as frustrated, depressed, perfectionistic, passive. Fathers are often conspicuously absent from the clinical picture.[45] In any case, family therapy is the centerpiece of treatment in this model.[46]

Cognitive-behavioral therapy represents a third psychological model. This approach focuses on an anorexic or bulimic woman's present beliefs and behaviors (rather than childhood development or family interactions), with the aim of "restructuring" her "grossly abnormal" attitudes and patterns relating to food through positive and negative reinforcements.[47] Some cognitive-behavioral therapists think that this restructuring process is enhanced by a patient's exposure to psychoeducational materials, whose correct information can help them modify faulty eating patterns.[48]

The attention that psychological models devote to personal history, family dynamics, and present habits and thoughts about food is crucial for understanding and treating eating problems. Exploring the anorexic or bulimic's psychological development may help us to learn why some girls and women are more vulnerable to developing unwanted eating patterns. Moreover, the effort to change self-destructive attitudes and behaviors must be an integral part of recovery from such problems. At the same time, these models' common focus on individual (or family) pathology obscures the factors that make girls and women see anorexia and bulimia as viable responses to psychic turmoil, namely, the social conditions and cultural values that promote and reward women's self-negating eating practices. Consequently, psychological models cannot explain the prevalence and diversity of eating problems among girls and women at this historic moment. Many such models also ignore the physiological influences on the development of these problems.

Biomedical Models

Biomedical perspectives see eating disorders as rooted in physical, rather than mental, disturbances. In this view, anorexia and bulimia are involuntary illnesses, not (un)consciously chosen. Medical researchers point out that many of the psychic disturbances anorexics and bulimics experience (irritability, lack of concentration, preoccupation with food, compulsiveness, etc.), can be explained as the result of inadequate nutrition.[49] Psychotherapy is thus futile without some stabilization of a patient's physical health.[50]

The physical complications accompanying anorexia and bulimia make the biological aspects of these problems hard to ignore. They include electrolyte disturbances, cardiac irregularities, endocrinological imbalances, kidney dysfunction, neurological abnormalities, swollen salivary glands, edema and dehydration, gastrointestinal disturbances, dental deterioration, and menstrual irregularities, to name some of the more prominent.[51] Some medical studies set the mortality rate for anorexia and bulimia at 18 percent.[52]

Proponents of a biomedical model see physiological imbalances as central to these illnesses, but there is disagreement as to whether these aberrations are primary or corollary. Broadly speaking, medical experts fall into two groups: those who posit an organic *basis* of eating disorders and those who emphasize the centrality of the biological *components* of such problems.

The difference between these two groups is illustrated by their views on the role of the hypothalamus in the development of eating disorders. Researchers generally agree that this part of the brain, which is headquarters for the regulation of hunger, satiety, metabolism, and other homeostatic processes, plays a decisive role in the development of anorexia. Some insist that the chemical imbalances associated with anorexia originate in the hypothalamus. Others, however, point out that its heavy interaction with the higher part of the brain opens the hypothalamus to external (cultural) influences; thus, its role may be central in the development of anorexia but is not necessarily causal.[53]

Bulimia has also been linked to hypothalamus-related dysfunctions. Unusually low levels of serotonin, a neurotransmitter that contributes to the regulation of satiety, are believed to trigger binge eating.[54] Again, some doctors think that this imbalance begins in the brain. Others, however, argue that it is more likely a result of—or a response to—externally imposed changes (i.e., dieting).[55] On this view, depriving oneself of food leads to involuntary overeating. The urge to binge is thus rooted in physiological needs that are culturally induced.

Some biomedical treatments of eating disorders focus on the chemical similarities between persons with eating disorders and those who suffer from affective disorders. These similarities have given rise to the "affective variant hypothesis," which holds that anorexia and bulimia have the same physiological basis as other mental disorders, particularly depression. In this theory, eating disorders are symptoms of depression rather than diseases in their own right. The tendency among bulimic and anorexic patients to respond positively to antidepressant drugs is cited as strong evidence for this view.[56]

The debate over whether biochemical imbalances are a cause or a component of severe eating problems has not slowed the advance of pharmaceutical solutions, including the widespread prescription of antidepressants. Such methods of treatment are part of a long line of medical efforts—from the administration of thyroid extract, to shock therapy, to prefrontal lobotomy—aimed at altering the physical chemistry of those who starve, gorge, and/or purge themselves.[57] While many doctors support the use of drugs as an adjunct form of treatment, those who posit a primary biochemical basis for eating problems are especially enthusiastic about "pharmacotherapy," despite the lack of clarity regarding its long-term efficacy and safety.[58]

By highlighting the physical aspects of anorexia and bulimia, biomedical perspectives illumine a component of these problems that others tend to overlook. Many of the mental and emotional difficulties that anorexics and bulimics suffer are inextricably tied to inadequate nutrition. The body attempts to compensate for this deficiency by lowering its metabolic rate while increasing its cravings. Biomedical models become implausible, however, to the extent that they view physical aberrations as causes rather than components of eating problems. Causal interpretations ignore the myriad ways that physical processes are influenced both by social conditions and by (un)conscious thoughts and feelings. Largely decontextualized, biomedical theories typically ignore the diversity and range of female eating disturbances. Like psychological models, they cannot account for the uneven distribution and increase of these problems during the latter part of this century. Seen in this light, pharmacological solutions are particularly disturbing. By failing to challenge the cultural norms that encourage women to eat in ways that upset their body's chemistry (whether by starving, gorging, or purging), pharmaceutical solutions indirectly perpetuate the very problems they medicate.

Sociocultural/Feminist Models

The most recently developed model for understanding eating disorders—the sociocultural model—attends to much of what is missing in other approaches. Its basic premise is that eating disorders are "culture-bound syndromes," rooted in shifting social norms and expectations, rather than individual pathology or biochemical imbalances.[59] In contrast to other models, which tend to focus on anorexia or bulimia, this model highlights a range of problems with food and body, insisting that such problems are "*learned habit[s]*."[60] Its proponents tend to be critical of popular and professional discourses that reward women for slenderizing their bodies while stigmatizing those who go too far.

By emphasizing the sociocultural context, this approach underscores the political aspects of eating problems, particularly those relating to female gender socialization and oppression within a patriarchal culture. Feminists have called attention to the double standards inherent in traditional gender norms: men are encouraged to develop their minds, women are rewarded for refining their bodies; men are supposed to be sexually attracted (to women), women are supposed to be sexually attractive (to men); men are encouraged to satisfy their physical appetites, women are taught to deny their own needs for the sake of others; men's concerns are institutionalized, women's tend to be trivialized. The continued prevalence of these double standards helps explain what many psychological and biological theories cannot, namely, why the vast majority of those with eating problems are female.

A sociocultural/feminist perspective also sheds light on the growing incidence of these problems during the past few decades. Many feminists attribute this growth to society's increasingly narrow body ideals for women, along with its changing beliefs about gender. According to feminist therapist Kim Chernin, these two trends are related. The ideal of the thin, childlike female body reflects this culture's fear of women of mature body and mind, a fear that has intensified in the wake of the women's movement. When internalized by girls and women, this fear conflicts with the new options open to women (Chernin does not specify *which* women), resulting in an identity crisis for those who transgress conventional gender norms.[61] Some authors contend that this ambivalence over gender identity contributes to the development of anorexia and bulimia, especially among "achievement-oriented" women.[62]

Many feminist interpreters of eating problems suggest that the struggle with gender identity symptomized by women's obsessions with thinness reflects an attempt to navigate the competing demands of womanhood today: the traditional requirement that women be selfless, nurturing, and caring for others (especially their families), alongside new pressures on women to be independent, self-reliant, and successful in the public sphere. Whether the anorexic or bulimic woman's attempt to forge an identity out of such competing expectations represents an act of heroic resistance or tragic compliance is not clear. Some feminists compare the struggles of anorexic women to those of early-twentieth-century hunger strikers, who refused food to protest their social inferiority.[63] Others see the bulimic's struggle as reflecting acceptance of, rather than resistance to, stereotypical femininity.[64] Recently, some feminists have argued that eating problems involve *both* acceptance *and* resistance. Like the hysterics of the nineteenth century, anorexic and bulimic women today express through their bodies the contradiction inherent in the coexistence of new freedoms alongside continued oppression.[65] Several feminist studies indicate that a disturbing number of present-day anorexics and bulimics also share the hysterics' history of sexual abuse, the trauma of which may contribute to the development of eating problems.[66]

Believing that eating problems are culturally determined, those working out of a sociocultural framework advocate social methods of treatment: from women's support groups, to public education, to organized speak-outs.[67] These efforts challenge what they take to be the real sources of such problems, namely, the oppressive conditions of a patriarchal society.

Sociocultural approaches are most capable of addressing the questions "Why women?" and "Why now?" At the same time, they downplay the bodily aspects of these problems, particularly the loss of control that anorexics and bulimics typically experience. This points to the limits of a view of eating problems as political protest. Some feminists also weaken their own insights by appealing to a "natural" female body (as if the body existed outside of culture) and by presuming an authentic feminine identity or nature (as if there were an essence of womanhood unmediated by social values and norms). Such rhetoric reveals a lack of understanding of the ways that race, class, sexuality, and other social variables influence the course of gender socialization. In sum, those working out of a sociocultural model often fail to pursue their most important insight: the *historical* character of women's struggles with their bodies and appetites, and the shifting meanings of these struggles in different cultural circumstances.

Historical Perspectives on Female Fasting Practices

Joan Jacobs Brumberg notes the historical shortsightedness of present-day discussions of eating disorders.[68] Conventional models of interpretation overlook both the historical precedents of these practices and their various meanings in different epochs. Long before slenderness was the hallmark of the ideal female body, fasting was a means for women to define themselves and manipulate their environment. Moreover, the historical record shows that prior to the modern era, women's refusal to eat or digest their food held a decidedly religious significance.

The refusal or inability to eat, and sometimes the need to vomit, played a central role in late medieval women's piety. From about 1200 to 1500 C.E., these practices were a means for cultivating the religious ideal of suffering with Christ for the sake of others. In cases where abstinence was prolonged, fasting was deemed miraculous. Later historical authors referred to it as *anorexia mirabilis*: the miraculous loss of appetite. One of the most famous medieval holy women, Catherine of Siena (d. 1380), reportedly lived on the Eucharist alone and stuck twigs down her throat to induce vomiting. The notoriety she gained as a result of these practices enabled her to intervene in the political and religious crises of her time, until she died of starvation.[69]

Ascetic fasting was not the sole prerogative of exceptionally holy women like Catherine. For many of her female contemporaries, food (rather than money, property, or institutional power) was the most accessible social and symbolic resource for defining one's relationship to God and others. Medieval Christian holy men also practiced asceticism, but fasting for them was merely one of several forms of renunciation (alongside poverty, chastity, and mortification of the flesh). For medieval women, hunger, food, fasting, and feeding were *the* central means and metaphors for becoming one with Christ's sufferings, for achieving holiness, and for saving souls.[70]

Two important studies on medieval women's ascetic food practices, Rudolph Bell's *Holy Anorexia* (1985) and Caroline Walker Bynum's *Holy Feast and Holy Fast* (1987), interpret this behavior differently. In *Holy Anorexia*, Bell uses a modern psychological framework to analyze the fasting practices of Italian women from circa 1200 to the present. For Bell, the modifier is key to interpreting the relationship between medieval women's religious fasting and the practices of modern anorexics: "whether anorexia is holy [*mirabilis*] or nervous [*nervosa*] depends on the culture in which a young woman strives to gain control of her life." Despite this acknowledgment of contextual difference, however, Bell sees anorexia as a "timeless" struggle: the modern quest for thinness and the medieval pursuit of holiness reflect a singular desire for female autonomy in the face of patriarchal control.[71] This argument is ultimately ahistorical because it implies that medieval women's ostensibly religious motives were really psychological.

In contrast to Bell, Bynum argues that these women's fasting practices cannot be understood through modern psychiatric categories. They must be seen in the context of medieval Christianity, with its emphasis on Eucharistic devotion, world-renunciation, *imitatio Christi*, and ecclesial moderation, along with its traditional associations between women, food, and body. For centuries Christian authors had depicted women as representing the "physical" aspect of human life, in contrast to men, who were seen to represent the "spiritual" part. Women were thus deemed responsible for taking care of the body's needs. They prepared meals, fed their families, and distributed food to the sick and poor. Moreover, women's bodies, by virtue of their capacity to give birth and to lactate, were seen as analogous to both ordinary food and to the body of Christ. By refusing to eat and directing their hunger toward the nourishment of Christ (literally and symbolically ingested in the Eucharist), medieval holy women became "the suffering and feeding humanity of the body on the cross."[72]

Seen in context, Bynum argues, medieval women's fasting represents neither internalized misogyny nor hatred of the flesh. Rather, it signifies women's creative efforts to use the resources and roles most available to them—food, feeding, and their bodies—to shape their worlds and to achieve sanctity.[73] This interpretation stresses the *religious* import of food-refusal for medieval women, especially the *redemptive* quality of their sacrifice and suffering. For Bynum, this meaning does not transfer to the behavior of modern anorexics. She believes women today starve themselves for reasons that are far more narrow and negative, such as the pursuit of thinness or the desire for control. In her view, modern interpretations of contemporary women's starving practices are similarly flat.[74]

By affirming the ingenuity of medieval women's asceticism, Bynum wants to prevent us from seeing these women as fanatical or helpless victims. In my view, however, the notion that women's salvation requires their self-annihilation needs to be challenged rather than praised. The belief that female sacrifice and selflessness are salvific has functioned throughout Christian history to sanctify female suffering and oppression. Moreover, as Kathleen Biddick argues, the model of female holiness that Bynum's analysis appreciates pivots on the damnation of "other" women: those outside the scope of proper Christian womanhood (i.e., pagans, heretics, prostitutes, and Jews).[75]

Bynum's aim is to highlight the social power and symbolic richness that female asceticism generated in medieval Christianity. She is not claiming this model of female sacrifice as a universal ideal. Nevertheless, her appreciation of it downplays the extent to which this construction of female holiness has supported oppressive ideologies of womanhood and the pursuit of feminine virtue into the present.

Ultimately, Bynum's reluctance to question the belief that female suffering and sacrifice are salvific contributes to her distinction between the symbolically fruitful fasting practices of medieval women and what she sees as the superficial motives of present-day anorexics. This distinction reflects both Bynum's sensitivity to the world and experiences of medieval Christian women and her lack of familiarity with the struggles of their present-day sisters. When female students in my class on women in Christianity read about the fasting practices of Catherine of Siena, they are shocked at first, but before long many of them identify with Catherine's strategy for cultivating purity, virtue, and public admiration through the sacrifice of refusing to eat. "I feel like I'm a better person when I'm hungry," one of my students told me, "like, everyone, including God, is more pleased with me if I'm really hungry and don't give in to the temptation to eat."

If we listen carefully, we will hear that contemporary girls' and women's accounts of their struggles with food and body are multifaceted, diverse, and permeated with symbolic and ritual—one might argue, *religious*—significance. The complex meanings of these present-day struggles become apparent when we survey the shifting and contested interpretations of female fasting in the modern era.

Joan Jacobs Brumberg's *Fasting Girls: The History of Anorexia Nervosa* picks up where Bynum's analysis left off, beginning with the breakdown of medieval Christendom. By the seventeenth and eighteenth centuries, the fasting practices that had previously been seen as a sign of female holiness became suspect as a form of demonic possession, or, in the eyes of science, fraud. Nevertheless, Brumberg notes, formulaic stories of miraculous "fasting girls" circulated against the tides of modernity well into the nineteenth century, testifying to the power of God in the eyes of those who rejected the disenchanting march of scientific positivism and progress.[76]

For the leaders of this march, such stories provided both a source of frustration and an opportunity to demystify. Empirical measures (round-the-clock surveillances, weighing the body, calculating food intake, measuring excrement, etc.) were used to test the authenticity of a young woman's claim that she did not need to eat. Occasionally, such methods proved fatal.[77] According to Brumberg, medical assertions that the "supernatural" loss of appetite was actually a symptom of insanity or hysteria began to prevail in the nineteenth century. By the 1870s, despite lingering popular belief in *anorexia mirabilis*,[78] science had succeeded in turning what had initially been seen as miraculous behavior into a full-blown disease.[79]

In Brumberg's account, this secularizing shift—the transition from sainthood to patienthood—was shaped by a specific intersection of gender and class. Fasting girls' appeals to otherworldly powers bespoke their lack of temporal authority. There were, Brumberg observes, no reports of "fasting boys."[80] Moreover, stories of miraculous fasting maidens typically involved rural girls with little education or wealth, most of whom fell outside the purview of the medical establishment. By contrast, the self-starving daughters of the urban, educated, and secular-minded bourgeoisie were not only more likely to be diagnosed with the new disease (i.e., anorexia *nervosa*), but their motives for refusing to eat were more likely to involve a mixture of resistance and conformity to Victorian ideals of femininity.[81]

According to Brumberg, a combination of Victorian femininity and modern bourgeois family norms made appetite problematic for middle-class females. A woman's desire to eat was seen as a moral barometer of her sexual desire. Moreover, as slenderness replaced girth as the bodily sign of prosperity, not eating provided a way for privileged women to distinguish themselves from their rural and working-class peers. Within the context of the Victorian family, refusing to eat was also a specifically gendered method of rebellion, an unintrusive but powerful expression of female discontent.[82]

By the turn of the century, fewer girls appealed to religious faith to explain why they did not eat, and by the early twentieth century the authority of medical and psychiatric views prevailed.[83] The merits of sociocultural analyses were not recognized until the 1970s, with the emergence of second-wave feminism. Brumberg's account adds a crucial background for these analyses by tracing the shifting and competing meanings of female fasting throughout Euro-American history. Her account situates contemporary females who starve themselves on "a long line of women and girls who . . . have used control of appetite, food, and body as a focus of their symbolic language." From this viewpoint, Brumberg concludes,

> it becomes evident that certain social and cultural systems, at different points in time, encourage or promote control of appetite in women, but for different reasons and purposes. . . . In the earlier era, control of appetite was linked to piety and belief; through fasting, the medieval ascetic strove for perfection in the eyes of her God. In the modern period, female control of appetite is embedded in patterns of class, gender, and family relations established in the nineteenth century; the modern anorectic strives for perfection in terms of society's ideal of physical, rather than spiritual, beauty.[84]

Brumberg's distinction between the secular and religious meanings of female appetite control among women in different historical periods echoes the closing remarks of Bynum (minus the value judgments). Brumberg's appreciation of this distinction leads her to overlook the fluidity of the categories—"secular" and "religious"—through which it is created. This very fluidity, however, is a compelling and intriguing aspect of the story that Brumberg so aptly tells.

In fact, this oversight characterizes most discussions on eating problems today: a presumably timeless distinction between religious and secular beliefs and behaviors is shared by psychological, biomedical, and sociocultural perspectives. The paucity of speculation about the religious significance of anorexia and bulimia in contemporary discourse reflects both the historically stormy relationship between science and religion and the narrow definitions of "religion" and "science" that this relationship presumes. In the field of eating disorders, the few published studies that attend to religion tend to perpetuate the very assumptions that prevent researchers from taking spiritual issues seriously. These include the beliefs that religious and secular experiences are intrinsically distinct and that spiritual issues and concerns are the exclusive property of religious institutions.

Existing research in the area of religion and eating disorders points to the need for further exploration. In general, this research reveals both a high level of traditional religious beliefs and observances among anorexic and bulimic girls and women and a significant change in these beliefs and practices as a result of eating problems. One study found that two-thirds of its subjects participated less in Eucharistic rituals for fear of the calories in the host and wine. In this study, a woman reported that she occasionally received Communion and considered it her allotted meal of the day.[85] Several of the women whose discourses I examine in this book mention similar conflicts over receiving Communion. One woman refused to eat the host, fearing that it would whet her appetite for more. Another tried to relieve her guilt over vomiting the host (she feared its caloric contents) by confessing her "sin" to her parish priest, who told her to recite "the usual number of Hail Marys."[86]

Not all girls and women with eating problems express such recognizably religious concerns. Nor are these women's experiences generalizable. Implicitly, however, they point to some of the connections we will see between "secular" rites of womanhood today (counting calories, regulating hunger, expelling "excess") and those deemed holy in traditional Christian constructions of female piety.

As a teenager, I was consumed with the desire to be thin. Never mind that I was born with the short and rounded body of my Polish and Swiss-German ancestors. Never mind that I was already thin—at least in the eyes of the doctor's chart. I wanted to be angular. I wanted to be so skinny that people would look at me and wonder what it felt like to have bones protruding through the surface of my body. I wanted people to wonder whether it hurt to be so hungry. I wanted people to wonder. I wanted to be holy.

There is much about my adolescent struggle with anorexia and bulimia that I do not remember—whether for want of adequate nutrition or other reasons, I do not know. Some days stand out in my mind more vividly than others, however. One such day was Holy Saturday when I was sixteen years old. It was a day of mourning, my mother told me: the day that Jesus lay in the tomb, after his death and before his resurrection. It was a day to recall his suffering for our sins, a day to remember the sins of the world. Having spent what seemed like an eternity in church the day before (Good Friday), I welcomed this part of the Easter scenario, as it did not signal another holy day of obligation. Even so, the image of being trapped in a dark tomb, bleeding from nail holes in hands and feet, waiting to be raised from the dead, was one with which I could somehow relate. Determining that I had to do something, I decided not to eat all day. It was by then a familiar and inconspicuous rite. Normally I used it to perfect my body. Why not use it to purify my soul?

The story of "anorexia nervosa" suggests that the seemingly obvious distinction between secular and religious ways of making meaning is both a product and tool of modern Western history. In many ways, this story also illustrates the intersection of several historical shifts that are important for my analysis. These shifts include the dispersion of religious beliefs and practices alongside the rise of scientific models and methods; the growth of a consumer- and market-based economy, along with the reorganization of class and family relations; and the "discovery" and reification of gender, sexual, and racial differences in the bodies of men and women. By illustrating the junctures of these trends, the history of anorexia points to the epistemological revolution they embodied: the mechanization of the search for truth and the disenchantment of the world.[87]

New Directions: Constructing an Alternative Frame of Interpretation

An overview of contemporary and historical interpretations of girls' and women's fasting practices demonstrates an important insight of critical thinking (by which I mean the ability to question what is typically taken for granted), namely, that what we know depends on the categories through which we seek to understand and that these categories are defined and selected in relation to specific historical and cultural conditions. In late-twentieth-century America, the terms and methods of the natural, social, and human sciences provide the authoritative frameworks for understanding anorexia, bulimia, and related problems. But these frameworks obscure important aspects of these problems, namely, the religious function they serve and the spiritual needs they intimate.

We need to examine this culture's symbolic and ritual resources—its prominent ideals, practices, and institutions—and ask how girls and women use these resources to make sense out of the uncertainties, suffering, and injustices of their lives. Until we see the spiritual dimensions of girls' and women's struggles with food and their bodies, we cannot discern the harmful forms of religiosity they employ, and we cannot envision better ways to address the needs to which they point.

There are good reasons why explicitly religious approaches have been marginalized in the field of eating disorders. These approaches have thus far included comparisons between contemporary female self-starving practices and medieval women's asceticism;[88] autobiographical accounts of salvation from unholy eating compulsions;[89] evangelical endorsements of dieting, such as the 1978 *Help Lord—The Devil Wants Me Fat!*;[90] Jungian analyses of overeating and self-starvation as flights from an archetypal Feminine Self;[91] a heuristic construction of a "theology of eating" with a reinterpretation of the "deadly sin" of gluttony;[92] and a self-help program called Overeaters Anonymous, where recovery from food addiction depends on submission to a "Higher Power."[93]

Despite their differences, these religious or spiritual approaches share some assumptions that (to varying degrees) limit their usefulness. In general, they presume a view of spirituality and religion as separable from and unshaped by cultural values and social conditions. They fail to see the ways that religion and religious experiences are always already interacting with other social and symbolic systems. An ahistorical view of religion also obscures the ways that gender and other social variables shape humans' searches for meaning and fulfillment.

A more critical perspective understands religion, culture, and gender as historical and thus fluid categories (rather than transcendent and isolatable essences). Used constructively, these categories function as lenses that help bring into focus certain aspects of girls' and women's struggles with food. Used critically, they enable us to assess the dogmatic ways of thinking and the controlling ways of being through which these problems develop.

More specifically, the category "gender" provides a lens for analyzing how differences *between* men and women and *among* women are socially produced and individually experienced. This analysis highlights the prevailing cultural ideals, images, institutions, and disciplines through which girls are taught what it means to be a woman, and it underlines the ways that diverse girls and women accommodate and/or contest these teachings. Such an analysis examines the pivotal role that popular ideals and practices of womanhood play in shaping a girl's or woman's relationship to her body and to the wider social order.

In the United States today, this "order" comprises what Patricia Hill Collins calls an "overarching matrix of domination": a hierarchical social system whose prominent institutions and values foster a variety of unjust relationships.[94] This system privileges the particular values, rules, and material interests of those who are white, male, heterosexual, adult, Protestant, able-bodied, middle- to upper-class, and educated. Ultimately, the dualistic mentality and controlling ethos that keep this system intact undermine everybody's well-being by fostering relationships characterized by domination, subordination, and alienation.

In such a "culture of domination,"[95] various forms of oppression feed off each other. Sexist attitudes and practices are inseparable from other forms of exploitation. Thus, sexism is not the only injustice contributing to women's eating problems. White females with eating problems may suffer injustices on the basis of gender while enjoying privileges on account of race and/or class. Women of color, lesbian, and/or working-class women may use weight control as a means of adjusting to the white, heterosexist, bourgeois norms of mainstream Protestant culture, while rejecting the stereotypes that such norms create.[96]

The meanings of cultural ideals and norms (such as female slenderness) are produced, circulated, and consumed by persons in different social positions.[97] To illuminate this circuit of meaning production, we need a concept of "culture" not simply as shared webs of meaning that humans create to gain a sense of direction in life but also as webs of unstable relationships among a common repertoire of stories and symbols, diverse individual and group experiences, and the existing sociopolitical order. Culture is the *contested terrain* where persons in different social positions and with unequal resources engage in multifaceted struggles over meaning.[98]

This concept of culture illuminates the struggles over meaning that are embedded in girls' and women's struggles with food and their bodies. As the term "struggle" itself suggests, issues of power are central to this understanding of culture. To analyze the politics of eating disorders is to ask how power operates in the development and persistence of these problems.

The work of French philosopher Michel Foucault is helpful here. Foucault's view of power helps explain a puzzling aspect of eating problems, namely, how the suffering and repression surrounding a woman's starving, gorging, and/or purging behavior appear to be brought on by herself. It seems as though a woman is punishing *herself* when she runs five miles and/ or downs a box of laxatives to compensate for having eaten ice cream the night before. In Foucault's view, however, this kind of self-inflicted chastening and the disciplines accompanying it (such as counting calories) represent modern forms of social control, wherein punishment for disobeying social norms (such as the requirement for women to be thin) is self-administered.[99] Foucault refers to this kind of power as "disciplinary."[100]

Foucault's view of power recognizes the multiple levels at which cultural domination is sustained. At one level, social control is exercised through a culture's formal "knowledges": the norms that circulate in scientific, moral, artistic, and popular discourses and images (such as the norm of female slenderness). These knowledges are institutionalized in the public codes of health, morality, and beauty, proffering practical rules for everyday conduct through which individuals assume their place within society.[101]

To the extent that they are not recognized as such, dominant cultural norms can be said to be *hegemonic*, their power operating in an invisible manner: through their ubiquity.[102] The term "hegemony" describes the power of institutions and beliefs that are so omnipresent and commonplace that they seem natural; their arbitrariness is hidden by their banality and repetition.[103] The belief that slenderness is the most desirable form for a woman's body is "hegemonic" insofar as this belief is so widespread that it usually goes without saying. The gripping power of this belief is rooted in the self-policing bodily practices of individual women, who are rewarded with social approval for maintaining a figure that is thin.

Women are taught to take pleasure in the self-monitoring body disciplines that perpetuate their social subordination to men.[104] The internal self-scrutiny and sense of reward at the heart of "disciplinary power" (Foucault's term) is epitomized in women's efforts to regulate their appetites. In her psychiatric work with anorexics, Hilde Bruch noted that many of them referred to an internal voice that interfered with their hunger, warning them not to eat. The girls characterized this voice in various ways: as "a dictator who dominates me," "a ghost who surrounds me," "the little man who objects when I eat." Bruch notes that when anorexics described this dictatorial part of themselves, its voice was almost always male.[105] Some of the girls also expressed a desire to "look more like a man," "to be equal to men," to prove that they had the same "endurance." Interestingly, this desire parallels a central trope of female spirituality in early Christianity, namely, the need for women of exemplary virtue to "become male."[106]

The bulimic or anorexic woman's internal longings and inquisitions illustrate the strength of disciplinary power: a girl may feel compelled to diet, even when no one forces her to do so. This compulsion is rewarded and reinforced on a number of levels. Rituals as quotidian as counting fat grams or peddling a stationary bicycle for hours not only shape a female body that conforms to dominant codes of health and beauty; in so doing, these rites create a feeling of aptitude and achievement, a sense that counteracts a girl's experience of herself as inferior, her body as inadequate, her life as insignificant.

To analyze the politics of girls' and women's eating problems is to probe the relationships between these internal desires and fears and the prominent norms and codes of the existing social order. When we see the multiple levels at which this "order" is maintained, it becomes clear that no one person or group controls the cultural production of meaning. Bulimia, anorexia, and related problems are not the result of a conspiracy, which is why the forces that fuel these problems can be so difficult to resist.

Both the prevailing sociocultural order and the power on which it feeds depend on the values they generate. Creating and assigning values is an intrinsic aspect of cultural struggles over meaning. Insofar as these struggles raise questions about the ultimate meaning and value of life, they require a third category of analysis, namely, "religion."

Religion here refers to cultural systems of meaning consisting of rituals, symbols, stories, and beliefs, whose special task is to present a picture of the whole of life in relation to which human experiences become meaningful. Religions provide idioms for articulating what is most important in life, a task that becomes especially important in times of suffering and confusion.[107] Our need for such pictures and idioms stems from our inability to know for sure the whence and aim of our existence. To refer to such needs as "spiritual" is to suggest that they touch on questions pertaining to ultimate meaning and human salvation in the face of pain, injustice, and uncertainty. To characterize these needs as *hungers* is to indicate their essential role in human survival and flourishing.

Because it deals with questions of ultimate value and meaning, religion has been a powerful force in the lives of girls and women—for better and for worse. Feminist, Womanist, Mujerista, and Asian women and transgendered scholars of religion explore the ambiguity of religion for women in their analyses of traditional Christianity. These analyses highlight the capacity of Christian faith to sanctify or to mitigate the sufferings of socially marginalized persons. In varying ways, these scholars show how religious faith has been used both for and against the empowerment of women. Religion, from the word *religio* ("to bind"), can foster a sense of connection as well as bondage, a sense of freedom as well as domination.[108] While this ambiguity suggests that religious traditions are neither inherently oppressive nor intrinsically liberating, it also implies the need for suspicion with regards to claims about "ultimate" value, especially when such claims potentially sanction unfair and abusive relations of power.

In my analysis of the spiritual dimensions of eating problems, the term "patriarchal religion" provides an interpretive tool of suspicion. This term is not synonymous with Christianity as a whole. Rather, it names a particular legacy within the Christian tradition whose influence continues today. This legacy sees the body as the site of sin, which is associated with all that is female and which is to be purified and transcended through the denial of physical cravings and needs. From this view, women are seen as spiritually inferior to men: they are objects of temptation or revulsion. Their only hope for salvation resides in self-sacrifice, suffering, and submission. In this scenario, women's subordination to men puts them in competition with each other, an antagonism that is expressed in the classic juxtaposition of Mary and Eve and whose drama has been rehearsed for centuries in portraits of "good" and "evil" women. Patriarchal ideals of female holiness (martyrs, saints, virgins, and mothers) are typically defined through the disavowal and/ or taming of female flesh and appetite. Patriarchal images of female sin (heretics, witches, heathens, and whores) tie women so closely to their bodies that "woman" herself becomes synonymous with the dangers of "carnal lust."

Although the pernicious dynamics and effects of this scheme are most obvious in the sufferings of girls and women, it is worth noting that this legacy also damages the lives of boys and men. Historically, the tendency within patriarchal religion to denigrate the bodies of most women while placing a select few up on a pedestal has contributed to the exploitation of men in nondominant positions. Moreover, even the most elite men are hurt by the quality of relationships and kinds of values that patriarchal religion calls holy. The material privilege of such men may protect them in important ways from the terrors and losses that affect the lives of persons in less fortunate social positions; such privilege cannot, however, save them from the loneliness and pain that domination insidiously masks.

The hallmark of the legacy of patriarchal religion is not misogyny per se. Rather, in its various methods and manifestations, this way of constructing ultimate truth is fueled by a dogmatic and dualistic way of thinking that makes meaning by reducing pluralities and polarizing differences, by subjugating the "other" and conquering uncertainty with the illusion of an Absolute.[109] In both traditional Christianity and its "secular" counterparts, such a logic creates and draws on an ethos of domination: an attitude and habit of control that stems from a sense of disconnection from oneself, from others, and from the transformative powers of life itself.

To underline the patriarchal elements of Christianity is not to suggest that this religion is inherently or entirely oppressive. Throughout Christian history, misogynist and anti-body messages have frequently overshadowed, but never entirely eliminated, the more egalitarian and incarnational aspects of this tradition. A variety of Christian thinkers and activists today are returning to the subversive message and ministry of Jesus—especially his empowering connections to people who were poor, vulnerable, socially outcast, and/or deemed inferior by the prevailing status quo—to inspire their work for social justice and to help them deal with their own everyday anxieties and sorrows. Some Christian theologians have reinterpreted the promise of salvation to mean not simply a blissful state that the righteous achieve when they die and go to heaven, but rather the practice of liberation and pursuit of wholeness here and now. Such a practice is symbolically portrayed in the gospel stories of Jesus sitting down to share a meal with the people his society most despised.[110]

Highlighting the ambiguity and the politics of religious faith calls into question the modern division between "religious" and "secular" reality.[111] What makes a symbol or ritual religious is not its inherent holiness but its practical function in orienting humans' myriad quests for salvation by providing shared (public) structures of meaning that designate what is most valuable and true.

Until relatively recently in U.S. history, biblical religion, especially Christianity, provided the symbolic and ritual resources with which people navigated the vicissitudes of their lives. Although surveys indicate that most people still believe in God,[112] traditional religious symbols and practices are no longer the unique or even the primary means through which they find and create a sense of meaning. In practice, such faith now competes with other systems of value and truth. For a vast number of Americans today, a variety of "secularized soteriologies" (salvation myths) provide the most comprehensive pictures for understanding life's ultimate significance.[113]

This is not to say that "secular" ideologies and practices have simply *replaced* those of traditional "religion." Rather, as the faith and teachings of the Church came increasingly under fire in the modern era, certain Christian beliefs and practices provided models for newly emerging "secular" views and institutions. While not specifically Christian, these new perspectives and organizations retained some traditional religious features that made them familiar to those whose worlds were steadily changing. Max Weber captured this dynamic when he argued that certain aspects of Christianity were incorporated and transposed into the calculating, routinized, measured modes of life that enabled the emergence of modern industrial capitalism.[114]

In many ways, the evolution and extension of this economic system into its current prominence suggests that rationalism and enchantment are not mutually exclusive. On the contrary, the present-day hegemony of consumer capitalism—an economic system owned and oriented by the commercial profit of a privileged few—thrives on its promises to alter reality, to alleviate pain, and to give "ultimate satisfaction." Like patriarchal religion, this imaginative system of material values feeds on the very dreams it functions to defer: dreams of freedom, equality, abundance. But in this technosymbolic universe of meaning, "ultimate values" are created and circulated through consumer commodities, relationships are negotiated through monetary currency, freedom is sought through perpetual consumption, and reality is apprehended through glossy surfaces.

Over a hundred years ago Karl Marx outlined the continuities between religious and economic modes of making meaning, both of which, he argued, involve processes wherein values became reified, that is, turned into *things*.[115] More recently, Raymond Williams has suggested that one of consumer capitalism's most indispensable institutions, advertising, is functionally similar to the magical systems of less developed cultures.[116] One might further note advertising's resemblance to some of the otherworldly conventions of Christianity: its quasi-religious images and ploys produce a "way of seeing" that looks beyond the banal concerns and material hardships of life in this world toward a transcendent realm of the "really real."[117]

Guided by a "dream of wholeness,"[118] the spirit of capitalism is not opposed to what have historically been called religious ways of seeing. On the contrary, some of Christianity's familiar paradigms undergird this system's ephemeral promises: to defy the laws of gravity, the rules of embodiment, the pain of finitude. Today, the otherworldly rhetoric of Christian conservatives coexists with popular cultural beliefs and images, largely thanks to their affinities. In the chapters that follow, these affinities become evident as we examine the prevailing icons and rituals of womanhood through which contemporary girls and women are encouraged to seek salvation.

If the prominence of consumer-media culture in the United States today creates the impression that "God is dead," it also attests to the vitality of the spiritual needs and religious imagination that created "Him." In exploring how such needs are embedded in the struggles of girls and women with eating problems, it is important to keep in mind the double-edged quality of religious faith in relation to contemporary social problems. Although some of Christianity's paradigms and beliefs contributed to the emergence of a culture that is largely oriented by empty promises and dehumanizing market values, other Christian beliefs and practices—those that inspire and enact the search for justice and wholeness in *this* world—clearly challenge this orientation.

The concept of religion that I use in this book emphasizes the ambiguity of religion for girls and women, while it deconstructs the division between "sacred" and "secular." In so doing, it points to the need for spiritual perspectives that challenge the cultural and political status quo. Such perspectives may retrieve or reconstruct the more subversive aspects of traditional Christianity, and/or they might draw on a variety of nontraditional religious resources. In any case, such visions must critically address the spiritual crises of these times: crises of freedom and meaning that girls' and women's eating problems embody. And they must do so not with an army of overarching explanations but by raising questions and exploring meanings, by fostering compassionate criticism along with alternative ways of seeing and being, ways that nourish the diversity and complexity of girls' and women's struggles for a life that is meaningful and whole.

Two

THE GOOD, THE TRUE, AND THE BEAUTIFUL FEMALE BODY

Popular Icons of Womanhood and the Salvation Myth of Female Slenderness

Throughout Western history, religious ways of seeing—humans' ways of searching for and imagining the utmost truths and purposes of their lives—have created a pantheon of sacred symbols: from the full-bodied statuettes of goddesses in ancient Neolithic cultures, to the images of Yahweh that fill the Hebrew Scriptures, to the Christian stories of a divine man who is sent to redeem the world. Despite their obvious variances, these symbols share the common task of pointing their users beyond the vicissitudes of ordinary life by envisioning a view of the whole and by focusing attention on that which is believed to bring fulfillment.[1] While the beliefs that sacred symbols inspire become especially important in times of acute crisis and loss, they are also a vital aspect of day-to-day living.

The imaginative use of such orienting symbols is an indelible aspect of being human. Without them, our searches for meaning would be aimless, our experiences would lack a sense of value, and we would have no way of seeing a "bigger picture." Yet the meaning-giving power of religious symbols is double-edged. Some of humanity's most horrific acts of violence are committed and sacralized in their names, their fundamentally imaginative basis being forgotten. Theologians refer to this process of turning religious values into reified norms as "idolatry."[2]

For more than a century now, feminists have criticized the idolatry of certain Christian symbols and beliefs, particularly those that sanctify the suppression and abuse of women. While this critique has dealt an irreparable blow to the authority of patriarchal religion, it has not negated girls' and women's needs for integrative symbols and stories. In this chapter, I explore how such needs are present in the beliefs of girls and women for whom popular cultural visions of womanhood have come to function religiously. More specifically, I analyze the religious and political valences of one of media culture's consumer icons: the female model who fills the pages of mainstream women's magazines. These magazines function as "sacred texts" for millions of American girls and women.

In their analyses of the sociocultural influences on eating disorders, most feminists incriminate the narrow standards for female body size that popular media images circulate. Surprisingly few, however, explore the complex processes through which the ideal of slenderness that these images circulate becomes meaningful for girls and women. As a result, they tend to imply an overly simplistic relationship between these images and eating disorders: images of skinny models are accused of causing such problems, which are subsumed under the category "anorexia," which is further presumed to affect only young women who are white, middle to upper-class, and heterosexual. These assumptions obscure the extent to which popular myths of womanhood shape the internal visions of diverse girls and women. They also misleadingly imply that the desire to be thin is at the heart of eating problems.

Icons of Womanhood: Different and Common Ways of Seeing

In rethinking the role that media images play in the development of eating problems, my decision to focus on women's magazines was initially a matter of convenience. I wanted to analyze widely accessible depictions of "ideal" female bodies, and this genre of images seemed more manageable than those of either television or film. Produced primarily (though not exclusively) by and for young, white, middle to upper-class, presumably heterosexual women, the images of mainstream women's magazines bear the imprint of this culture's ruling ideologies of race, class, sexuality, and age. The more I studied these representations, the more my choice of genre seemed fortuitous for several reasons.

Unlike female actors in both television and film, the models in these magazines are esteemed not so much for their creative talents as for their bodily appearances.[3] The model's body is her "performance," her beautiful physique a "work" of art. Another advantage of focusing on this genre of images is that the monthly circulation of the magazines I consider makes them widely available.[4] Whether or not you purchase them, you see them practically everywhere: passing by the newsstand, waiting for a doctor's appointment, standing in line at the grocery store. Their relatively affordable price and portable form makes it possible for most girls and women to view them virtually anytime, anywhere. Unlike the shifting images of women on the TV or movie screen, readers can study a magazine's photos an infinite number of times, for as long as they wish, with little effort.

Precisely the frozen form of these pictures contributes to their mirrorlike quality: they are both "models of" and "models for" what it means to be a woman.[5] Moreover, unlike written texts, such images do not appear to be interpretations. Neither moving, nor changing, nor situated within a story like the sequential images of television or film, these still-life models of womanhood evoke what Susan Sontag calls a "sense of the unattainable."[6]

The religious resonances of such representations are neither obvious nor inherent. They can, however, be inferred from the role these images play in generating and circulating symbolic ideals that help their users orient their lives. In her book *Natural Symbols*, Mary Douglas argues that "one of the most obvious forms of religious behavior . . . is the use of bodily symbols to express the notion of an organic social system." Bodily symbols function as microcosms of the larger whole: images of the human body both express and shape the order of the social body. People use such images to help them integrate various levels of their experiences: their relationships to their own bodies, to society, and to the cosmos as a whole.[7]

The pictures in women's magazines are not simply images of women. They are also bodily symbols. More specifically, they are icons of womanhood, pointing to a seemingly transcendent truth—a feminine ideal—that many girls and women recognize as Ultimate. This recognition is neither fully conscious nor unconscious: it is habitual. While the meanings of such icons are not fixed, they are also not open to any interpretation.[8] In a culture where few other models of womanhood enjoy such public visibility and influence, these icons are the visions in reference to which many girls and women learn to relate to their bodies, to others, and to their deepest anxieties and dreams. For many of their viewers, these images serve what has historically been a religious function: that of mediating the search for meaning in a world of uncertainty, injustice, longing, and pain.

Throughout the history of the Christian West, girls and women have turned to images of holy persons and saints as a means of focusing this search. For Christian women before the modern period, most of whom were illiterate, such visual images were more central than verbal language as a means for defining themselves in relation to others and powers beyond their finite control. Through their visual conventions and designs, religious images functioned as windows through which believers viewed the invisible truths and cosmic hierarchies that were seen to ground the social order.[9]

It is reasonable to speculate that for many girls and women today, visual images continue to be just as important as—perhaps even more important than—verbal texts as conduits for self-definition. Yet the iconography of traditional Christianity differs significantly from present-day images and ways of seeing. In contrast to the "realism" of most photography today, religious icons are painted in two dimensions in order to exaggerate the differences between the natural and supernatural realms. While such icons are seen to partake in the invisible realities to which they point, they are deemed idolatrous to the extent that they absorb the devotion they are supposed to mediate.[10] As Margaret Miles points out, historical Christians were keenly aware of these images' formative power. Unlike most present-day viewers, whose repetitious exposure to a plethora of visual images tends to dilute awareness of the images' influence, medieval persons *expected* to be shaped by the images they saw.[11] Such discrepancies between past and present images and ways of viewing suggest that both *what* and *how* we see are historically conditioned.[12]

Religious ways of seeing did not become obsolete when the authority of Christian images came under fire in the modern era. The search for ultimate truth and fulfillment continued in projects as seemingly distinct as modern science and consumer capitalism. In science this search was carried forth by what Michel Foucault refers to as the "normalizing gaze" of scientific reason: a way of seeing that evaluates its object according to a hierarchical norm or standard.[13] This gaze incorporated rather than abolished moral and aesthetic concerns. It compared, measured, and classified persons according to their bodily features, reifying and ranking their differences and locating them on a single scale, according to which some bodies are good, true, and beautiful, while others are deviant, degenerate, and ugly.[14]

The normalizing gaze of modern science did not simply oppose the religious search for a metaphysical anchor. Rather, it relocated its course: from the ethereal verities of the cosmos to the essences of human bodies. Thus, a scientific way of seeing did not merely supplant traditional religious concerns about the state of one's soul with new interests in the truth of the body; it conflated them. On the moral-aesthetic-scientific scale of bodies, the virtue of the invisible soul became deducible from the signs of the external physique. Bodies came to be seen as windows to the self.[15]

The modern Western understanding of the body as the tangible ground for individual identity has particular significance for persons traditionally associated with physicality. Throughout the history of the Christian West, women have been publicly identified with and (de)valued through their bodies, not as the subjects of their own experiences but as figures (both obstacles and stepping stones) in male spiritual drama. In the continued absence of a major iconographic tradition that represents female bodies as the sites/sights of spiritual struggle, many women today learn to define themselves as objects rather than subjects of meaning-making and desire.[16]

That women have rarely been depicted as subjects of their own spiritual journeys does not mean they have not constructed their own worlds of meaning. But it does suggest that the symbolic provisions available to them for orienting their search for a sense of purpose have been limited and limiting. Today, the most readily available images of what it means to be a woman keep the idealized female body (or its antithesis) at the center of female subjectivity, functioning as the symbolic ground, means, and aim in the quest for ultimate fulfillment.

During the course of this century, traditional associations between women and bodily concerns, along with the presumed correspondence between external body and internal self, have become technologically standardized and spread through the reifying magic of photography. Like the abstract categories of modern science, the camera functions as an "arm of consciousness": a seemingly rational, neutral observer, silently identifying and ranking different bodies with the "objectivity" of the scientific gaze.[17] Like the visual icons of historical Christians, magazine photos give flesh to what are believed to be intangible truths. In so doing, they fill an artistic and imaginary vacuum created by the rise of modernity.[18]

A scientific-moral-aesthetic scale of bodies permeates the pages of popular women's magazines, where idealized images of model women illustrate articles reporting the latest findings in health, happiness, and beauty. These images are uniquely suited to circulate such knowledge while cultivating a way of seeing. In the disenchanting wake of modern science, they create another world in an instant. But not just any world. For these images register in a shot and a flash what it took cultural authorities in different contexts countless theologies and theories to sacralize and explain: the hierarchical scale of bodies that grounds the social order.

Debunking the "Myth": Insights and Oversights

Despite the quasi-religious quality of popular cultural images and ways of seeing, the subject of religion rarely enters into critical discussions of media culture's forms and effects. When it does, it is often used to describe the masses' blind and gullible faith in popular culture's magic. In her best-selling book *The Beauty Myth,* Naomi Wolf devotes an entire chapter to comparing women's obsessive pursuit of a "perfect" body with the "medieval superstition[s]" of traditional religion.[19] Insightfully, Wolf sees a functional affinity between religious faith and what she calls the "beauty myth." Unfortunately, this insight is cut short by her assumptions about religion, feminism, and women's experience.[20]

Wolf argues that "we are in the midst of a violent backlash against feminism that uses images of female beauty as a political weapon against women's advancement: the beauty myth." Wolf's critique of this myth rejects the stereotypical belief that women can have a mind or a body but not both. She insists that women can have both breasts and footnotes, can be both serious and sexual.[21] While the appeal of this argument has made feminism attractive to a wider audience of women, it is based on a definition of feminism that prioritizes the interests of certain women.

A narrow definition of womanhood tacitly permeates *The Beauty Myth.* It underlies Wolf's comparison between the beauty myth and what Betty

Friedan called the "feminine mystique"—both of which are said to function as sexism-producing "religions."[22] Just as Friedan ignored the effects of the feminine mystique among a diversity of women, so Wolf overlooks how the beauty myth hurts different women in varying ways.[23] Wolf's analysis of the beauty myth ignores the racial, economic, (hetero)sexual, and generational subtexts of this "religion." It therefore leaves intact the standard hierarchy of bodies through which the myth gains its prominence.

I would not criticize Wolf's concern that "the affluent, educated, liberated women of the First World, who can enjoy freedoms unavailable to any women ever before, do not feel as free as they want to."[24] But I would argue that the beauty myth that idealized images of women constructs does more than damage the self-esteems of socially privileged, "liberated" women. Insofar as these images are seen as vehicles for sexism alone, their contributions to a wider network of injustices are obscured, and so are the sufferings of many women.

Wolf's limited notion of feminism is connected to her broad assumptions about religion. By relegating religion to an age in the past, an era prior to modernity's "rational" ways of being and knowing, Wolf uses "religion" as an idiom for describing a "legacy of female credulousness." This rhetoric turns religion into the enemy of female liberation not only because it involves a kind of "thought control" but also because it promotes denial of unjust social conditions.[25]

Most religious feminists would agree with Wolf's insight that "the antiwoman bias of the Judeo-Christian tradition" has played a defining role in instructing women that our bodies are flawed and in need of correction.[26] Wolf's undifferentiated view of religion, however, overlooks both the imaginative character of religious beliefs and symbols and the creative, albeit encumbered, agency with which women have negotiated their meanings. Ironically, this oversight leads Wolf to attribute to religion the kind of monolithic power that she rightly criticizes. Implicitly, it also leads her to trivialize a certain dimension of women's experiences, the part that uses symbols to search for meaning in the face of confusion, longing, and despair.

Wolf's sweepingly negative depiction of religion is based on views that are fairly common in white feminist discourse within and beyond the academy, including the notion that spiritual and political struggles are antithetical and the belief that a liberated woman can control all aspects of her life.[27] Such views not only presume an exceedingly flat understanding of "religion"; they also imply a narrow notion of "women's experience," one that enables Wolf to characterize feminism as "women's entry into the secular public world."[28]

Wolf's criticism of the beauty myth clouds as much as it clarifies, insofar as it fails to see the links between the body-hatred of many privileged women and the racial, economic, generational, and/or sexual inequities on which their privilege is tenuously built. To see these connections, we must analyze the ideologies of race, class, and sexuality through which popular ideals of womanhood are visually produced and consumed, and we must see how these "secular" visions of feminine salvation function to mediate girls' and women's desires for ultimate meaning and fulfillment.

Standard Models of Womanhood

Idealized visions of womanhood do not address their viewers evenly. While images of female models are the icons in reference to which *some* women measure and value themselves, they represent both the norm and the ideal in reference to which *all* women—young, old, colored, white, rich, poor, disabled, corporate executive, and housewife alike—may be measured and valued within the social hierarchy. For some, the power of these icons operates through their viewers' identification with the ideal they represent. For others, such power flows through the racial, economic, sexual, and generational stereotypes that the ideal constructs and conceals.

To understand how such images make meaning in the lives of diverse girls and women, we must see them in the context of the mass cultural "circuit" in which they are produced, circulated, and consumed.[29] Magazine images are created and circulated for capitalist purposes: cover models selling the magazines themselves and models inside selling myriad products. But the ideal of womanhood they represent is consumed by girls and women with different racial, class, sexual, religious, and family histories. Given these tensions, we must not simply ask "What model of womanhood do these images represent?" but also "What *conventions* or *cues* within these texts and in society make this ideal recognizable? How does this visual ideal address diverse girls' and women's searches for meaning?"

Standard models of womanhood today represent the apex on the dominant culture's moral-scientific-aesthetic scale of female bodies: they are typically young, white, able-bodied, and thin, available to please the very gaze they embody. Moreover, a host of visual cues, from male cohorts to designer clothes, mark them as heterosexual and wealthy. Like Christian images of female sanctity, visions of these bodies represent an ideal; like the standards of modern science, they constitute a kind of knowledge. In their uniform ubiquity, they define the virtue and truth of womanhood through the "beautiful" female body. As pictures of womanly perfection, these icons seem to partake in the invisible ideal to which they point. Describing this immanent-but-transcendent essence, a famous fashion photographer remarked: "A very small group of models project this quality. . . . There's an air that transcends mere physical beauty. It has to do with femininity."[30]

But the archetypal ideal that traditional models represent is not simply "femininity," the presumably incommensurable difference that separates women from men. It is, more specifically, young-white-wealthy-heterosexual femininity: a dominant cultural ideal whose social makeup is neither arbitrary nor accidental. In a society where most overt forms of discrimination are rhetorically proscribed, popular models of womanhood play a key (if subtle) role in maintaining oppressive attitudes and social arrangements.[31] Standard ideals of femininity sanctify these injustices by defining a model of womanhood through conventions of social privilege.

Standard models of femininity gain their meaning not only in subordinate relation to their masculine counterparts[32] but also in dominant relation to other visions of womanhood. Patricia Hill Collins specifies some of these images in her critique of stereotypified portrayals of black women: the subservient but happy mammy, whose large body conveys a sense of nurturance for white children and other privileged folks; the black matriarch, a maternal figure who dominates the homes of black families; the welfare mother, the poor black woman who threatens the state with her financial dependence; and Jezebel, the dark whore whose sexual aggressiveness unsettles the stability of society's moral order.[33] Such exploitative images stand in sharp contrast to the visual ideals with which elite white girls and women are encouraged to identify.

In *Beyond the Pale,* Vron Ware argues that the contrast between popular models of Euro-American womanhood and stereotypical images of colored women reinscribes the relationship between "white femininity" and America's history of colonialism and slavery. In this history, the white woman's image has served as a "symbol of civilization" in contrast to the savages and barbarians of "other" lands.[34] Chinese theologian Kwok Pui-lan identifies these colonizing tactics in her analysis of the role of Western ideals of womanhood—especially that of the "white lady"—in the nineteenth-century Christian missions.[35] The imperializing effects of this "white lady" ideal continue in today's media images of women.[36] To understand the politics of such present-day visions, Ware warns, we must see how "the memory of colonialism is constantly being recycled and reconstructed" through them.[37]

Images of white women's privilege circulate beyond and within the borders of the so-called civilized world. Girls and women in developing countries are prime targets of corporate ad campaigns that feature Euro-American models of womanhood.[38] These models also set the norms for women of color in the United States—though *recognition* of such norms does not necessarily imply *acceptance.* One black woman remarked: "If I hear 'beautiful woman' the image of a white woman surfaces in me sooner than that of a Black. Strange, because I generally do find Black women a lot more beautiful than white."[39] This discrepancy illustrates how the uniformity, accessibility, and ubiquity of standard (white) models of womanhood affect the imaginations of diverse girls and women.[40] No female in this culture is immune to the influence of such ideals. Even those who do not subscribe to their "truths" learn to recognize their prominence.

Among young women and girls, most of whom have neither the institutional power nor the subjective training to represent themselves, Euro-American models of womanhood do not merely signal social ascension. In their glossy, air-brushed forms, these images promise a kind of salvation.

Produced and marketed as a recognizable ideal, many young women consume this promise in the hopes that they too might be recognized, that their lives might be seen as valuable, or that they might be seen at all.

Given the invisibility that many girls feel, the desire to *be* a model, which is common among these images' younger readers, can be seen as a desire for presence: a desire to be seen and taken seriously. In the United States today, young girls are reported to know the names of more models than former presidents. "Girls have pictures of these models up on their walls," a high school girl reports. "They know all about their love lives."[41] Unlike female models in the first decades of this century, many of whom came from working-class backgrounds and were suspected of being prostitutes,[42] female models today are *model women* in the eyes of many of their viewers. Thus, an issue of *Young Miss* tells readers what model agents look for, how the top ten "supermodels" made it, what a typical day in the life of a model is like, and whether they could be "the next Cindy, Christy, or Kate."[43] A similar article in *Glamour* promises to reveal the "mystery" of these models' "real lives" by disclosing what they eat, buy, and earn, whether they dance all night, and how their sex lives are going.[44]

Whether a girl or woman directly identifies with such ideals, whether or not she expects herself to imitate them, their claim to truth is something she will likely have to negotiate in her struggle to define herself and her purpose in life. These icons are some of the most readily accessible visions of what it means to be a woman and of what we must to do achieve "salvation." They are thus some of the most widely used symbols with which girls and women navigate their most banal and ultimate anxieties and yearnings.

Competing Visions of Womanhood: The Dispersion and Accommodation of the Standard Ideal

During the past few decades, certain historical developments have brought these anxieties and yearnings closer to the surface of many girls' and women's experiences. In conjunction with the relative changes in gender expectations since the 1960s, gaps between the social classes have widened, tensions between different ethnic and racial groups have deepened, persons from different generations find themselves increasingly alienated from each other, and sexual minorities have become more visible and more vulnerable within the public sphere. Such changes in the sociopolitical landscape have diversified female subjectivities, reopening the question about what it means to be a woman and generating new tensions between standard paragons of womanhood and their socially differentiated consumers.

These tensions have been managed through a dispersion of the traditional ideal (young-white-wealthy-heterosexual femininity). Roughly since the mid-1970s, differences among girls and women have been accommodated through the proliferation of a variety of "femininities." Women's magazines now feature models whose racial, sexual, generational, and class identities appear to be diverse.

Ethnic and racial differences among these magazines' consumers are accommodated through the inclusion of models of color. Many of these dark-skinned icons of womanhood maintain their ties with the standard (Caucasian) ideal through their thin lips and nose—features associated with whiteness in this culture.[45] Other images of dark femininity rely on what bell hooks refers to as the dominant culture's "fantasy of the black female as wild sexual savage." Such fantasies are evoked by images of dark-skinned models posed in seemingly natural settings (for example, a jungle) that reinscribe the myth of colored women's closeness to nature and by images depicting them in postures that suggest their sexual availability/insatiability.[46]

Other variations of "femininity" include images of models whose positioning in relation to each other makes their sexuality ambiguous. Unlike traditional icons of womanhood, which sexualize the female body as an object of male desire through verbal or visual reference to men, these images depict female models enjoying the touch or embrace of each other. In so doing, they not only redefine "feminine beauty" as more than an object of male desire; they also create a vision of womanhood that can be read as pleasing the gaze of another woman. As Diana Fuss suggests, women's magazines provide "one of the few institutionalized spaces where women can look at other women with cultural impunity."[47] Although the sexual meaning of these images is ambiguous, some magazines have run articles on lesbians, which can facilitate subversive readings.[48] Still, the majority of popular images mediate this culture's compulsory heterosexuality: its formal and informal institutionalization of heterosexual norms.[49] An array of titles such as "What He's Really Looking For in a Woman" underscore this point.

Icons of womanhood that play with the representation of class further illustrate women's magazines' accommodation of diversity among consumers. I call these the "riches-to-rags" images, because while some of their models make more than $10,000 a day, their constructions of femininity appropriate the props of lower-or working-class culture. Whether this class association is made by a model's torn jeans or by her yard-sale-looking clothes, these images create a version of womanhood that *seems* democratically accessible to girls and women from all economic backgrounds.

The apparent democracy of these visions is also seen in a magazine ad for Revlon, whose model of femininity is aged to appeal to "older" women. Facing the reader/viewer, Lauren Hutton, who is now in her fifties, exclaims: "This is our prime time—let's make the most of it!" While this affirmation of middle-aged womanhood invites older women (at least those who are wealthy and white) to feel good about their bodies, the same ad tells (and shows) women that they need not (read: should not) look their age. Were the reader to believe that aging need not compromise her worth, she might wonder why the majority of the magazine's images define beauty through youthful, if not childlike, female bodies.

The effect of such representational revisions is to ease—not to explore— the tensions between the standard young-white-wealthy-hetero ideal and its socially diverse consumers. This effect is produced through what bell hooks refers to as the "commodification of otherness": one of patriarchal capital- ism's techniques for spicing up "the dull dish that is mainstream white culture" in order to preserve its hegemony.[50] Seemingly diverse models of womanhood acquire their meaning not only in relation to the standard ideal but also in reference to the stereotypes they incorporate. In effect, the new, "subcultural" versions of womanhood do not challenge the prevailing ideal.[51] In many ways, they make the "good," "true," and "beautiful" female body all the more recognizable, securing its position both at the feminine apex of this culture's aesthetic-moral-scientific scale and at the center of diverse girls' and women's searches for a sense of value.

An article in *Mirabella* illustrates the limits of these representational re- visions. There is "strength in diversity," the article proclaims, reporting that a "new range of models is busting the old stereotypes of beauty." The article displays close-ups of these models' "new and unusual faces,"[52] but the mod- els' uniformly thin bodies are cut out of such portraits of "difference." Sim- ilarly slender bodies appear in a *Mademoiselle* article featuring the "new girls in town." Whether these young, white models look as "nontraditional" as the article claims, their bodily forms are conformingly thin.[53]

The uniform thinness of so-called models of diversity suggests that slen- derness is an iconic convention, a visual cue, for identifying the beautiful female body today. It is the one feature that "diverse" models share. The slender form provides a constant as producers and consumers of magazine images shuffle with the content (race, class, age, sexuality) of femininity. Indeed, the narrow lines of these models' bodies are the invisible (because homogeneous) threads connecting various versions of femininity to the stan- dard ideal.

These slender lines are also a site/sight for establishing a hierarchy of differences among women. In women's magazines, the value of a model's thin body is produced in relation to other visual conventions and cues, especially the models' social privilege (signified by her youth, white skin, expensive clothes, and/or male cohorts). The intersection of these cues cre- ates an association between female slenderness and social privilege, a sym- bolic link that contributes to these images sacralizing power in a culture oriented by material values. In these images, prevailing codes for female body size cross-reference those of race, class, sexuality, and age, making slender- ness the physical sign of social distinction and of the health and happiness presumed to accompany this rank.[54] This means that body size, in conjunc- tion with other social variables (race, class, age, etc.), has come to play a definitive role in the production of female gender identity and subjectivity in the late twentieth century.

That slenderness has become a primary cue for identifying the "truth," "goodness," and "beauty" of womanhood today is apparent in the shifting iconography of popular culture. Nearly thirty years ago, the average model in the United States weighed 8 percent less than the average woman. About ten years ago, she weighed 23 percent less than the average woman, whose weight has generally increased during the same period. In 1992 the average model was 5' 10" and 111 pounds, while the average woman was 5' 4" and 144 pounds. This means that the average female model weighs some thirty pounds less than the average woman and is approximately six inches taller. A historian of this shrinking trend concludes that never before has the ideal female body been defined "so 'close to the bone.' "[55]

In the early 1990s, women's magazines themselves reported that the "glamazons" of the 1980s had been superseded by the "waifs," the ultra-thin, young, ethereal-looking models epitomized by Kate Moss (who at 5' 7" weighs less than 100 pounds).[56] This shift has not escaped the attention of those devoted to these icons. Among their adolescent fans, the shrinking contours of feminine perfection produce a host of new anxieties and aspirations. "My friends and I were looking at pictures of Kate [Moss]," a sixteen-year-old girl explains. "Gosh, we thought we had to look like Cindy Craw-ford" (whose slender body has more mass and muscle than the bodies of the waifs), "and now we have to look like this! [pointing to an image of Moss]."[57]

Despite their grip on the female imagination, popular icons of wom-anhood are as much an *effect* as a *cause* of the pervasive mandate for female slenderness. Such images are part of a larger mix of authoritative discourses that contribute to the tyranny of slenderness today. In *Never Too Thin*, Rob-erta Seid shows how scientific, economic, fashion, political, and moral au-thorities reinforced each other in designating the thin body as the twentieth-century feminine ideal. Early in this century, the medical establishment replaced its nineteenth-century association of thinness with sickness with a view of obesity as a catalyst for life-threatening diseases. By the 1950s, in-surance companies, using data drawn from the lives of those wealthy enough to buy life insurance policies, had set standards for "ideal weights." Mean-while, the fashion industry was shifting its focus from clothing and cosmetics to the shape of the female body itself; when Twiggy appeared on magazine covers in 1967, she weighed ninety-one pounds at 5' 7". Ten years later, the federal government issued a report entitled "Dietary Goals," which warned that Americans' (over)eating patterns "represent as critical a public-health concern as any before us." This concern has not been lost on entrepreneurs, who make billions of dollars every year selling ways to eradicate "excess" flesh. Neither last nor least in glorifying the thin ideal were religious au-thorities, especially evangelicals, many of whom demonized obesity and re-instated "gluttony" as one of the deadliest sins.[58]

Even a brief look at these trends suggests the historical underpinnings of the thin ideal. Slenderness has not always been a distinguishing feature of the perfect female body. During most of the nineteenth century, prevailing ideals of womanhood were defined in terms of purity, piety, passivity, and domesticity, qualities presumed to correspond to elite women's physical "differences" from men and from "other" women.[59] According to Louis Banner, these differences were expressed through a range of female bodily ideals, including the frail and ethereal-looking body of "the steel engraving lady," whose image persisted throughout the century; the voluptuous female bodies of the theater world, which became popular after the Civil War; the tall, athletic-looking "Gibson Girl" of the 1890s; and the smaller, boyish "flapper" model, who became prominent in the 1920s.[60]

In contrast to the relative variety of nineteenth-century bodily ideals, this culture's preference for female slenderness is axiomatic: most people take it for granted that the body worthy of representing womanhood must be thin. Omnipresent images of this ideal make the "beauty" of the slender body seem *natural,* in contrast to other signs of femininity, such as makeup or breast implants, which seem *artificial.* The ultraslender form passes as a timeless ideal, even when readers are told about the technologies through which it is produced. One magazine admits that its photographers some-times use a type of wide-angle lens that make a model's legs look longer, her arms and shoulders thinner, and her head smaller.[61] But in a culture where looking through the camera is a habitual way of perceiving "reality,"[62] the visual knowledge of images can be more compelling than the verbal details of their production. Writer Sallie Tisdale elaborates this point:

> Today's models, the women whose pictures I see constantly, unavoid-ably, grow more minimal by the day. When I berate myself for not looking like—whomever I think I should look like that day, I don't really care that no one looks like that. . . . I want to look—think I should look—like the photographs. I want her [the model's] little mir-acles: the makeup artists, photographers, and computer imagers who can add a mole, remove a scar, lift the breasts, widen the eyes, narrow the hips, flatten the curves. The final product is what I see, have seen my whole adult life.[63]

Indeed, it is the "final product" that viewers must negotiate. For many of them, magazines' otherworldly models of womanhood become more real than reality itself.[64]

According to Susan Bordo, the "reality" to which the models' slender bodies point is that of a well-ordered self and society. In *Unbearable Weight,* Bordo draws on the work of Mary Douglas to suggest that female slenderness has become a symbolic vehicle for expressing and maintaining social order and self-control. The narrow boundaries of the female body are a crucial site for managing the contradictory demands of consumer capitalism: indulge and refrain. Straddling the dual imperatives of self-abandonment and self-mastery, the thin body signifies a woman who can control her hungers amid the possibility—indeed, the necessity—of unrestrained consumption.[65]

The perceived correspondence between the tightly sculpted female body and self-controlled woman reflects the modern belief that human bodies are malleable: in Bordo's word, "plastic."[66] Magazine images convey this "plasticity" not only through technical tricks of photography but also through the models' contorted postures and in the flexibility that their thinness suggests. In 1993, *Harper's Bazaar* hailed supermodel Elaine Irwin as "the superbody of the '90s," announcing that "flexibility and form have both made a comeback. . . . Strength and stretch are what's admired—with considerable concern for contours backed by noticeably defined muscles." Some feminists suggest that the attraction and tyranny of this bodily ideal rests in its ability to express and reconcile competing demands of womanhood today: the model's body is both "strong" and "sensuous," defined by "firm muscles" and "accentuated by soft, supple curves."[67]

Indeed, slenderness comes in varying degrees and forms. While some models are literally bone-thin, others' slim bodies are accentuated by muscles or curves. More recently, the look of the abused, drugged-out, emaciated young woman seems to be in. Despite these variations, however, the model woman's body is indisputably slender and firm, delineating a self whose internal desires are well contained, and signifying a society where everything is under control. Given the instability of this "control" during the past few decades, the "plasticity" of the thin ideal has made it an enduring convention in the late-twentieth-century iconography of womanhood.

This "plasticity" also contributes to the textual ambiguity of female slenderness: its ability to mean something different to diverse girls and women. One might interpret the prominence of this form at this historical moment as signifying some women's increased activity in the public sphere. Not only are women no longer required to wear corsets, but as the models' flat stomachs attest, they can choose whether and when to become mothers. Yet amid the absence of alternative visions of womanhood, the slender ideal produces a more insidious kind of corset: one that is internalized.[68]

Ultimately, the slenderness of popular icons of womanhood proffers a symbolic ideal, pointing its viewers beyond the difficulties of their everyday lives. This ideal provides a point of reference for those who are confused by the changes and frustrated by the inequities of the current social order. For many girls and women, the dematerialized bodies of model women are not simply "plastic." They are "spiritual," pointing to the way to transcendence. In their ethereality, the slender lines of the model's body symbolize the possibility of something more, something better, something beyond life as it is. As such, these lines construct a salvation myth of female slenderness: a quasi-religious fantasy that promises fulfillment through a body that is thin. In their viewers' imaginations, the slender lines of this myth lead from mundane to mystical.

At least some of those who produce these icons recognize this spiritualizing effect. In a column entitled "The Lives of Supermodels," *Elle* magazine featured the "biography" of supermodel Niki Taylor: "The thirteenth child of a fisherman in a small village near Cadiz. Left school when discovered by God in a restaurant; at seventeen, donned the sacred vestments of her order; devoted life to illuminating the holy books, though open to the right movie role." Alongside the model's image, featuring her white but tanned and scarcely clad body, ribs protruding between her running bra and shorts, the column lists the model's "miracles": "Stopped traffic at 14th and Broadway. Lived on water." Taylor is also described as "patron saint" of child laborers and people injured in Jet Ski accidents. The column ends with a preview of the next month's holy figure: Kate Moss, rechristened "Our Lady of Perpetual Disaffection."[69] However amusing, this popular cultural "hagiography" (biography of saints) plays off a serious point, namely, the quasi-religious function that popular icons of womanhood serve.

Implicitly, this parody also suggests that the "spirituality" that fuels these icons has much in common with the models and values of patriarchal religion. The salvation myth that popular images of womanhood construct is based on the glorification of a chosen few, and the damnation of the rest to the realm of invisibility and cultural insignificance. In this paradigm, spiritual virtue itself is defined as flight from bodily pleasures and needs. The model's "sainthood" is achieved through her miraculous sacrifice—her superhuman ability to "live on water"—signified by a body that is thin. The reductive mentality and controlling ethos at the heart of this scheme of salvation becomes evident when we consider the ways that slenderness becomes meaningful—indeed, becomes an ultimate value—in the symbolic worlds of girls and women with eating problems.

Symbolic Ideals, Heretical Visions: The Salvation Myth of Female Slenderness

To consider this process is to examine how the salvation myth of thinness that popular icons of womanhood envision provides the language—the symbolic terms, idioms, and rules—through which eating problems develop. To understand these problems, we must decode the language through which they make sense and through which they are constituted.

A central idiom among anorexics and bulimics is the belief that they are "too fat." This belief makes sense—makes meaning—both in reference to popular icons of womanhood and in the context of a society where material privilege and self-control are supremely valued. Indeed, this *sense* is relatively *common*, even among women who are not "overweight," and even among those who are not diagnosed with "eating disorders." Some women become virtually paralyzed by a belief that they need to lose five to ten pounds and that this "extra weight" is keeping them from success and happiness.[70] "When I was younger," author Pamela Houston writes,

> I used to believe that if I were really thin I would be happy, and there is a part of me that still believes it's true. For a good part of my life I

would have quite literally given anything to be thin . . . a finger, three toes, the sight of one eye. . . . For the majority of my lifetime I would have traded being ugly, deformed and thin for being pretty, whole and fat.[71]

Former bulimic and anorexic Marya Hornbacher describes this myth as a "female version" of "the great American dream":

I, as many young women do, honest-to-god believed that once I Just Lost a Few Pounds, somehow I would suddenly be a New You, I would have Ken-doll men chasing my thin legs down with bouquets of flowers on the street, I would become rich and famous and glamorous and lose my freckles and become blond and five foot ten.

In this dream, the worldly "success" that being thin symbolizes is salvific:

Success, I firmly believed, was the key to my salvation. It would absolve me of the sins of the flesh and would lift me out of the life I hated. "Success" meant a perfect career, perfect relationships, perfect control over my life and myself—all of which depended on a perfect me, which depended in turn on me living inside a perfect body.[72]

The belief that thinness is the key to salvation keeps some women waiting for their life to begin: waiting until they lose weight.

For those who aspire to this dream, the promise that underlies this weight/wait is both meaningful and unbearable. "There isn't a day I don't wish I were thinner," a young woman remarked in a survey conducted by Drs. Susan and Orland Wooley in conjunction with *Glamour* magazine. This survey found 75 percent of its 33,000 respondents believing themselves to be "too fat." Yet only 25 percent of them weighed more than the "desired weight" listed on the insurance tables (whose figures are already below average for women in the United States). Moreover, 45 percent of those who were underweight according to these numbers felt they were "too fat." In view of the unanimously slender bodies on the pages of magazines like *Glamour*, a girl does not have to be overweight to perceive herself as fat.[73]

That the respondents in the *Glamour* survey were predominantly white is not insignificant. Symbolic associations between thinness and social privilege are central to the promise of fulfillment that such magazines circulate. This nexus is particularly strong among girls who come from families that enjoy and/or emulate material privilege. Describing the frame of reference in which her bulimia developed, one woman recalls:

My mother always wanted me to be happy. Unfortunately, her definition of happiness was skinny, pretty, married, and rich. . . . My conceptual system became based on comparison and contrast with other women. In a way, I had perfectly clear vision: The ideal of beauty, represented by a fashion model, was not the figure I saw in the mirror.[74]

The dualistic logic that shapes this compare-and-contrast "clarity" of vision *within* women fosters competitive ways of seeing *between* women. Another woman elaborates this point:

> I am walking down the street in Manhattan, Fifth Avenue in the lower sixties, women with shopping bags on all sides. I realize with some horror that for the last fifteen blocks I have been counting how many women have better and how many women have worse figures than I do. Did I say fifteen blocks? I meant fifteen years.[75]

Slenderness becomes meaningful in a society where women learn to define themselves through their bodies in relation to male desire (getting a husband), where physical differences among women are hierarchically ranked, and where fulfillment is equated with material privilege.

The links between this value system and the social relations it sustains become apparent when we consider the underside of the thin ideal. The symbolic authority of slenderness is defined in relation to what it is not: images of the "large" or "flabby" female body. The body that is said to have "let herself go," the body that is seen to be "out of control," the body that many Americans believe to be "immoral." The power of this unruly body must not be underestimated simply because it is usually marginalized in the public sphere. In the symbolic worlds of those with eating problems, the "heretical" body of the fat woman is inseparable from the "sanctity" of the slender ideal.

This does not mean, as some writers on body image suggest, that what bulimic and anorexic women see when they look in the mirror is the body of a fat woman. Such views are overly simplistic, a former anorexic woman explains:

> What I did see [in the mirror] was the potential to be fat. As if there was a line separating fat and thin, I was terrified of stepping over that line. The fashion models represented "thin." The things that made me different from them signaled danger, signified that I may belong to the other category: "fat." Among these signals were my double chin, a belly that protruded beyond my hip bones, and an increase on the scale.[76]

This woman is hardly alone in recognizing the "danger"—the "otherness"— of female fat. In a society fragmented by an infinity of social and political divisions, few issues elicit as much accord as the disdain for the bodies of women who are, or who are perceived to be, obese. The moral overtones of this disdain stem from a religious legacy that defines spiritual virtue through the denial of bodily appetites—appetites with which women are associated and to which they are seen to be highly susceptible. "Fat is perceived as an act rather than a thing," writer Sallie Tisdale reflects: "Fat is now a symbol not of the personality but of the soul—the cluttered, neurotic, immature soul."[77] Rooted in the belief that fat signifies a moral flaw, a chaos-driven lack of self-control, fear of fat is the other side of the dominant culture's adoration of female slenderness.

The extent to which men share this dread and devotion is an important question. Men are increasingly recruited to join the ranks of women who are dissatisfied with their bodies. Those who do so may feel doubly ashamed, since anxiety about weight is typically deemed a "feminine" concern. Author Richard Klein, who along with his mother and sister spent many years fretting about fat, observes: "A man. I'm not supposed to be as preoccupied about fat as women . . . A man of course doesn't feel the same pressure, but the pressure is there and it's internalized. Not only does the world mostly hate his fat, he hates it most himself."[78] In *Never Satisfied*, Hillel Schwartz also argues that America's demonization of fat has adversely affected both men and women.[79] Still, until quite recently, an (apparent) lack of concern with physical appearance has been a hallmark of ruling (white, heterosexual, bourgeois) ideals of masculinity. The authority of such masculine ideals is produced in part through images of large, muscular, seemingly invulnerable male physiques. But recent "beefcake" ad campaigns notwithstanding,[80] socially defined bodily perfection is still not a prerequisite for men who seek visibility and voice in the public sphere.

By contrast, women who seek admittance to formal realms of power must carefully monitor their appearance. Media critic John Berger explains how the Western artistic-religious trope of "woman as sexual object" is embedded in popular ways of seeing:

> Men act and women appear. Men look at women. Women watch themselves being looked at. This determines not only most relations between men and women, but also the relation of women to themselves [and, I would add, *among themselves*]. The surveyor of woman in herself is male: the surveyed female. Thus she turns herself into an object—and most particularly an object of vision: a sight.[81]

The salvation myth of female thinness depends on this vision and the legacy it extends. Accordingly, boys' and men's indoctrination into its narrow lines of worship and dread is vital to its maintenance.

Fear of fat supports America's social order in ways that are often indirect. While the "holiness" of slenderness is created through its symbolic association with self-control and social privilege, the "heresy" of fat bodies is constructed through racialized notions of social deviance. Throughout this century, the demonization of large-bodied women has carried economic and ethnic overtones. Today, contempt for fat women serves as a vehicle for oppressions that are somewhat less tolerated (such as misogyny, white supremacy, class elitism).[82] If, as the "Fat Liberation Manifesto" states, "fear of fat is a means of social control used against all women," it is a means that is used particularly against poor, older, ethnic, colored, or lesbian women.[83]

Widespread cultural assumptions (that fat people are lazy) and values (the ideal of individual self-control) prevent most people from seeing the war on fat as a form of social control. Yet symbolic links between "fatness" and "social deviancy" reference the social inequities they reinscribe. According to Beth MacInnis,

> "Obesity," as defined by the medical community, is seven times more common among working-class women than among women of other socioeconomic status; in fact, the American socioeconomic groups with the highest percentage of fat members is that of Black women below the poverty level.[84]

When such data finds its way into mainstream news reports, the injustices contributing to this situation—that nutritious food, safe places to exercise, and regular health care have become luxuries of the middle class—are rarely mentioned.[85] Nor is the popular assumption that "obesity" is automatically unhealthy questioned.

Ultimately, the glorification of the thin female body is established through the symbolic and material subjugation of "other" bodies. The widespread belief that thinner is better is both cause and consequence of the dominant culture's war on fat in general, and the oppression of fat women in particular. Given the verbal abuse, scapegoating, social stigma, job discrimination, and internalized self-hatred that many fat women face on a daily basis, it is not astonishing that some women will do absolutely anything to be thin.

The moral and political underpinnings of this culture's war on fat adds to the pressure that many minority women feel in relation to dominant models of womanhood. A survey in *Essence* magazine indicates that white cultural norms for female slenderness can be especially damaging for women of color. The mostly black female respondents in this survey showed higher levels of dangerous eating patterns (prolonged dieting, use of laxatives, excessive exercising, vomiting) than the white respondents in the *Glamour* survey. Like their white counterparts, a vast majority of these black women were preoccupied with a fear of becoming fat. Linda Villarosa, who reported this survey, points out that socioeconomic class may have influenced such findings, since *Essence* readers tend to be more educated and affluent than average African American women. Even so, it is clear that standard (white) models of womanhood figured centrally in the symbolic beliefs that lead black women to want to lose weight. "When I first started practicing bulimic behavior," a woman explained, "I was very much influenced by White beauty standards. . . . People treat you better when you lose weight and look beautiful." Another black woman echoed these sentiments: "Pressure to fit in with my White counterparts throws me again into a tailspin. The world we live in will be controlled by beautiful people and the thinnest people. Obesity will never be okay, no matter what people say."[86]

Both the fear of fat and the stigma attached to it present heavy burdens for girls and women who are already seen as "deviant" bodies. For racial and sexual minorities, the ideal of female slenderness may address both a yearning for visibility within the public sphere, which many straight white women now enjoy, and a rejection of images of otherness through which standard visions of womanhood are defined.

In her essay "Fat Is a Black Women's Issue," Retha Powers describes how white cultural norms for female slenderness informed her struggles as a young black girl growing up in a predominantly white neighborhood: "All of the girls who were considered pretty were ultrathin and white, and I was still teased for being ugly. Although now I realize that the ugliness my peers saw had more to do with the darkness of my skin, I reasoned then that I hadn't lost enough weight." Such reasoning made sense in view of her exposure to "aryan-like" fashion models while attending a mostly white high school and in view of the racist stereotypes that she encountered in this context. When Powers asked her high school counselor for help with the eating problem that her weight-loss efforts had spawned, she was told not to worry about feeling attractive because " 'black women aren't seen as sex objects, but as women' " and because " 'fat is more acceptable in the Black community.' "[87]

Popular and professional assumptions that girls and women of color are protected from Euro-American models of womanhood ignore how damaging such ideals can be to those who do not directly identify with them and who also reject the subordinate roles (mammy, Jezebel, etc.) that white culture reserves for them. A former Wall Street analyst described how the tremendous pressure-to-succeed that she felt as a black woman in a socially prestigious position translated into a pressure-to-be-thin:

> Working for an investment bank had always been a primary career goal. I was going to be the best Black female analyst those bastards on Wall Street had ever seen. In addition to doing impeccable work, I felt it was imperative that I look impeccable at all times. That meant wearing a size four.[88]

Eventually, the thin imperative led this woman to problems with bulimia, costing her both her job and her well-being. Not only are women of color not exempt from the Euro-American mandate to be thin, they are potentially even more vulnerable to such imperatives because their struggles for a sense of value and agency find so little support in mainstream society.

Although minority girls and women may not directly identify with standard models of womanhood, they are often well skilled at reading the racialized subtexts between their narrow lines. Christy Haubegger, a Mexican American woman, points out, "You only have to flip through a magazine or watch a movie to realize that beautiful for most of this country still means tall, blond and underfed." Though as an adult she has come to accept her rounded figure, Haubegger notes that narrow norms of womanhood made it impossible for her to enjoy her body when she was a teenager: "I remember being in high school and noticing that none of the magazines showed models in bathing suits with bodies like mine." In her experience, the dominant cultural worship of female slenderness overrode her own community's general appreciation of large-bodied girls and women.[89]

The tension between the prevailing mandate for female thinness and several subcultures' relative acceptance of ample-bodied women is familiar to some lesbian women who struggle with eating problems. One woman described the dissonance this tension created in her relationship to her body: "Here I am, a self-loving, woman-loving, strong and smart woman and I have spent years, hours, days of my life completely distracted from my life, concerned only with what I looked like and how fat I was, how fat I would be, what I was eating, and what I would be eating."[90] Even when lesbian women find support for their struggles to make peace with their bodies in their relationships with other women, this support is constantly threatened by ruling cultural imperatives for slenderness and heterosexuality. Another lesbian woman explained that it was "easier to emerge from the queer closet than the closet of fatness." Though she has learned to accept her body's "deviant" size and desires, this woman wonders whether her family will ever be able to see her as a whole person: "I suspect they feel that if I have to be a Lesbian the least I could do is be a thin one. Or if I feel a compulsion to be fat, couldn't I quit the queer stuff?"[91]

The salvation myth of female slenderness works by addressing but deferring women's desires to be recognized and valued in a culture whose prominent ideals and material conditions leave them feeling empty. The power of this myth feeds on this emptiness, even as it promises to fill it. After years of suffering from chronic dieting and body-hatred, black author Rosemary Bray recalls her struggle to unmask the illusions through which this salvation plan is built:

> There were days I wanted to die because I couldn't bear the idea of being fat my entire life. . . . I am angry about all those times when being fat made me absolutely invisible, especially to men. And I'm tired of the refrain that runs through my head like a billboard: "Now if only I were thin, life really would be perfect". . . . When I am by myself, feeling lonely or sad or tired, I long for the illusionary perfection of the thin life. I can still be persuaded, when I'm not in my right mind, that

thin people are happier, prettier, more focused, more balanced. At those moments I can still be persuaded that thin people have richer lives, that they're better people than I am.

As Bray points out, seeing the emptiness of such promises is especially hard for women whose lives are already circumscribed by stereotypes and prejudices and by circumstances where "having enough" is either not an option or where it comes at the cost of working in isolation and silence. The insidious power of the slender ideal resides in its elusive capacity to represent but forever postpone the wholeness that girls and women variously seek. "I'm hungry for the things all of us are really hungry for," Bray affirms, "hungry to be truly seen and known, hungry to be accepted the way I am."[92]

Skinny Models and Eating Disorders: The Popular Media Blitz

Recognizing this hunger is crucial for understanding the power of popular icons of womanhood in the symbolic worlds of those with eating problems. If most conventional approaches to these problems fail to see this hunger and the diversity of its pangs, its presence is even more obscured by the recent media blitz on the subject. In the past several years, a barrage of articles have stirred popular debate regarding the role of "skinny models" in the spread of eating disorders. Much of the controversy surrounds the prominence of "waif" models, particularly Kate Moss. One magazine reports that "not since Twiggy has anyone tried to draw a connection between a capriciously indifferent model and the eating disorders of thousands of women."[93]

An issue of *People* magazine illustrates the terms of this debate: is Moss "a fresh young face or an evil influence?"[94] Sometimes such reductionism is coupled with a tone of trivialization: "All this seems far too weighty for something as ephemeral as fashion.. . . .It's hard to believe that so much controversy has been pinned to the boney shoulders of this twenty-year-old girl."[95] In other cases, the debate elicits emphatic defenses. The editor of *Harper's Bazaar* responded to "stacks of angry letters . . . and phone calls" decrying their use of " 'anorexic-looking models' " by assuring readers that "these girls eat like horses," that "thin is their natural body type."[96]

Conflicting reports about the real-life practices of these otherworldly women exacerbate the questions they ostensibly aim to settle. Whereas waif models are quoted as saying they try to eat more but "can't help being thin,"[97] other models publicly discuss their battles to be thin and the eating disorders these battles engendered.[98] Still others make body-shaping central to their image. Some of the most famous supermodels are hired to promote fitness products. According to its own ad, Cindy Crawford's workout video ("Shape Your Body") "helped millions shape up and became the biggest-selling fitness program in history." Claudia Schiffer's video series, "Perfectly Fit," promises "perfect" abs, legs, arms, and buns, all for $14.98 (each).

Not only do these promotions establish a connection between the model woman's slenderness and an exercise regime; in so doing, they also imply that even the most ideal female bodies require routine maintenance.

Both the rhetoric defending the "naturalness" of the models' thinness and the confessions recounting the sacrifice through which it is achieved mask the larger functions of this debate. The proliferation of conflicting evidence generates as it feeds public fascination with the "reality" behind the "image." In so doing, it secures a need for more of itself, more "information" and more profit, while it depoliticizes the issues it claims to explore. The binaries through which the debate is construed—image/reality, artificial/natural, truth/fiction—frame the relationship between "skinny models" and "eating disorders" in reductive, dualistic terms. Thus, the media blitz not only reinscribes the very logic these problems embody but also erases the continuum between girls' and women's "normal" obsessions with their bodies and those deemed "pathological."

This normal/pathological polarization is illustrated by an article about an anorexic woman featured in *Mirabella*. While still battling her illness, Polly Evelegh let the magazine photograph her anorexic body. Graphic images of Evelegh's body show her ribs, pelvis, elbows, and knees protruding, a hollow expression in her eyes, a close-up of her famished face biting into a head of cabbage. According to the article, Evelegh "wanted publicity for the condition, and she wanted to vent her resentment—because if only she had known, if she had seen, what anorexia was, it might not have taken such a hold on her." Indeed, the written text that accompanies the photos emphasizes the connection between anorexia and the social pressure for women to be thin: "Why did everyone insist she [Polly] looked terrific when she first lost weight, only to tell her, the minute she was labeled anorexic, that she looked terrible? What can she say about the doctor who certified that she was fit for aerobics when she was wraith-thin and ailing?"[99] Within the iconography of the magazine as a whole, however, this connection disappears. The article following Evelegh's story features "The New Diet"—apparently what "normal" women do to get slim. Compared to the images of Evelegh's anorexic body, the ultrathin models in the rest of the magazine seem healthy, even robust.

Next to these idealized images, the story and photos of Evelegh's anorexia create a kind of a freak show. In this society, such a spectacle becomes a commodity, deriving its value in reference to public intrigue with and desire for the "extreme," the "bizarre," the "not me," a desire the monotony of mainstream media images creates. For girls and women who are already trying to lose weight, the value of Evelegh's "pathological" body is its silent reassurance that, unlike this unfortunate woman, they are in control. For those who produce and circulate this image, its value resides in the profits it generates, not the awareness it raises.

The popular media hype about the relationship between skinny models and eating disorders commodifies the very problems it claims to address.

The superficial framing of the issues fails to recognize the obvious: although most girls and women are exposed to the media culture's slender ideal, not all of them develop eating disorders. At the same time, this framing occludes the varying degrees and ways in which those who do struggle with eating problems are affected by or identify with this ideal.

That the anorexic or bulimic crusade for thinness often draws initial inspiration from magazine icons of model women is evident in the stories of girls and women with eating disorders. In her memoir of anorexia and bulimia, Marya Hornbacher recalls imitating and comparing herself to the ideal:

> I practiced the looks in the mirror, casting bedroom eyes at my reflection, thrusting my hips to the side and tossing my hair. My body was wrong—breasts poking through my shirt, butt jutting, all curvaceous and terribly wrong. . . . Legs too short, too round, thighs touch. *Seventeen* magazine advises that thighs should not touch. Mine touch. I suck.[100]

Hornbacher's experience is not isolated. One study of girls with eating disorders found that nearly half of them regularly scrutinized the images of models in magazines, wanting desperately to look like them.[101] Yet, as Hornbacher's memoir as a whole suggests, achieving supermodel slenderness is neither the first cause nor the final goal of the anorexic/bulimic struggle. For Hornbacher, the aim of looking fashion-model thin became steadily eclipsed as her eating disorder progressed and the physiological effects of starvation set in. At some point, she explains, her body and mind became addicted to the pain of hunger and to the "salvation" (her word) that this suffering seemed to promise:

> The pain is necessary, especially the pain of hunger. It reassures you that you are strong, can withstand anything, that you are not a slave to your body, you don't have to give into its whining. . . . In truth, you like the pain. You like it because you believe you deserve it. . . . Your ability to withstand pain is your claim to fame. It is ascetic, holy. It is self-control.[102]

Hornbacher's explanation illustrates how this culture's narrow icons of feminine perfection function—not as the cause of disordered eating but as symbolic vehicles of meaning, expressing and evoking the penance women must pay for the empowerment they seek.

The varying and complex ways that popular icons of womanhood shape the symbolic worlds of anorexic and bulimic women are further illustrated by a dialogue between two college women, Kim Lorton and Elena Levkin, who reflect back on the development of their eating problems. "Although I hate to admit it now," Lorton observes, "I did want to be on the cover of *Seventeen*. I had stacks of magazines and carefully cut out the pictures of the skinniest and, in my mind, most beautiful models. This, by the way, was a diet incentive trick that I learned in a book by Cheryl Tiegs. And what a trick it was."[103]

In contrast to Lorton, Levkin, who identifies herself as a Jewish Russian émigré dyke, sees her eating disorder as developing in response to familial experiences, including her mother's emulation of thinness and her father's physical violence. "In my pre-teen years," she writes,

> I felt that being fat made me a source of shame for the family. My mom told me that a friend of hers had commented on my weight, and that my weight made her ashamed in front of the friend. I was constantly told I should not be eating this or that, should go on a diet, should stop eating so much, etc. My dad would often focus on my fatness and slowness, telling me he was teaching me not to be lazy. . . . My anorexia was not an effort to conform to a feminine beauty ideal. . . . While I can't definitively say what caused it, I do know this: both when I was starving myself, and when my father hit me, I wished to be as small as possible and physically present to myself.[104]

While many women who develop eating problems share Lorton's close identification with images of model women, others, like Levkin, experience the effects of these narrow norms more indirectly. Families are frequently the primary locus where the slender lines of acceptable womanhood are transmitted—often without much subtlety: "Do you really need that?' my husband Alan asked. . . . 'When was the last time you looked in the mirror?' . . . 'You'd better lose weight,' my father said. 'Believe me, sweetheart, Alan will look elsewhere. No one wants to go to bed with a baby elephant.' "[105] Another woman recounts some scenes from her childhood and adolescence:

> I ask my mother for an extra half-sandwich, another bowl of peaches. She refuses, clearly dismayed by my request. I sulk. What is the matter with me? Why aren't I more like other children—exhilarated and rowdy, active and thin? . . . In later years, my parents offer to buy me a new wardrobe—all the most fashionable clothes—if I will just lose twenty pounds. They send me to Diet workshop. To tennis lessons. My father charts weeks in which I must lose two pounds in order to win freedoms. Every Friday evening I take off my shoes and step on the scale before his watchful eyes.[106]

These are just a few examples of how family rituals, relationships, and rules can provide the setting where the language of slenderness is taught and learned, even by those who do not deliberately intend to speak its potentially harmful meanings.

The connection that Elena Levkin makes between her eating disorder and her history of physical abuse is echoed by many of the women that Becky Thompson interviewed for her book *A Hunger So Wide and So Deep*.

For them, unwanted eating patterns emerged as methods for coping with a range of traumatic experiences, including sexual and emotional abuse, as well as racism, poverty, and homophobia. Although these women shared a desire to be thin, their different stories reveal how this desire masked their struggles to survive the pain and traumas incurred in the processes of becoming women. Thompson is justifiably critical of analyses that depict the pursuit of slenderness as the source of women's struggles with food and body. In her view, such depictions partake in a larger "politics of distraction": the diversion of attention away from the actual sources of eating problems, namely, women's myriad and often traumatic experiences of oppression.[107]

What Thompson's work implies is not that the ideal of slenderness is not central in the experiences of women with eating problems but that attention to this ideal must focus on its symbolic function rather than its causal significance: its capacity to both mask and address girls' and women's struggles for wholeness and agency in a world whose prevailing conditions and values tend to reduce, divide, and/or deny such prospects. To grasp the power of this culture's slender visions of womanhood, we must see them in relation to the crises of truth and freedom they function to address but in effect deepen. In so doing, we must see how the sense of meaning that such ideals foster is as precariously thin as the lines of womanhood through which it is constructed.

A Promised Land in a Disenchanted World

Since the beginning of the common era, the power of visual images stirred debate among religious leaders, who worried that worshipers would become too attached to the images' contents and forget the larger truths they were supposed to represent. While the iconoclastic impulses of biblical religion inform my critique in this chapter, such impulses must not become frozen into dogmatic extremes. The problem with magazine images of women is not that they exist. My discussion began with the assertion that creating and using images is a fundamental aspect of being human. Nor is the problem with media images that they are "secular" rather than "religious." Precisely such a clear distinction is what my analysis aims to confuse. Finally, the problem is not simply that media images "objectify" women or that they cause their viewers to hate their bodies. This view ignores how the "truths" or messages of such images are variously defined and experienced by their consumers.

The problem with these images is that, like the idolatrous ideals of patriarchal religion, they point both to themselves and away from the overwhelming injustices, sufferings, and challenges of life in this world. Instead of reminding us of a bigger picture, these images narrow the scope of our vision by focusing attention on a monotonous ideal. Asked whether magazines should feature "real girls" instead of glamorous-looking models, a fifteen-year-old girl replied: "I'm surrounded by reality every day, whether it's a homeless person on the street or the latest mugging on the six o'clock news. So the last thing I want to see when I pick up a magazine is more of the real world."[108] To understand the mystifying magic of popular icons of womanhood, we must see how they are some of the most readily available symbols that girls and women have for helping them imagine alternatives to real-world problems and limits. To grasp the politics of this magic, we must see how such images sacralize a culture wide denial of exploitation and pain.

The "politics of distraction" are multifaceted. They operate in girls' and women's dissatisfactions with the size of their bodies rather than the contours of their lives, in the professional and popular discourses that simplify or commodify these preoccupations, and in the opiate-like, otherworldly promises of consumer-media images. In a world of conflict, inequity, and hurt, these images promise a glimpse of the other side. In an episode of ABC's *20/20*, a reporter depicted this celestial sphere as a realm where money is plentiful, where one is guaranteed acceptance, visibility, and belonging. "Models can earn two million dollars a year," the reporter explains. By becoming a model, "you can become a member of an exclusive club, where the sun always shines, the parties are glowing. A land where there's no ugliness, no sickness, no poverty. A land where dreams come true and everyone is certified beautiful."[109] A promised land in a disenchanted world. Ironically, the same normalizing gaze that reifies and ranks different bodies, eradicating their inherent value and vulnerability, has kept the idea of heaven very much alive.

Despite its heavy reliance on the power of the visible, the salvation myth of female slenderness that this culture's popular iconography of womanhood constructs is funded by another source of meaning. In the next chapter, we will see that the transcendence that popular icons of womanhood promise gains it power from the practices that incarnate its meanings: practices that give flesh to its truths while turning its truths into flesh, which in turn must be lost in order to be saved.

Three

LOSING THEIR WAY TO
SALVATION

Popular Rituals of Womanhood and the Saving Promises of Culture Lite

D espite its lofty reputation, religious imagination has always had at least one foot in this world. Even Christianity's most otherworldly images—from Eden to Heaven, from Virgin Mother to Almighty Father—bear traces of the everyday bodily experiences and practices of those who invent and believe in them. The embodied basis of religious imagination is perhaps so obvious that it has a history of being ignored.[1] Traditional Christian theology focused on what were believed to be purely metaphysical questions. More recently, however, critically minded theologians contend that the symbolic activity of religious imagination is enmeshed with concrete, practical concerns.[2] Whether explicit or implicit, questions about ultimate meaning and value are questions about *what to do* and *how to live* amid the complex possibilities and constraints of everyday life in this world.

This insight suggests that making and finding meaning in life is not an exclusive property of the brain. Not only are our symbolic quests for truth and fulfillment anchored in those aspects of existence generally referred to as "bodily," but the *sense* of meaning that most of us seek is not merely cognitive: it is embodied. Just as our searches for fulfillment would be rudderless without orienting symbols, so these symbols would mean nothing without the rituals through which their truths are discerned and embodied.

Yet the meaning-giving power of religious practices, like that of sacred symbols, is highly ambiguous. Christian history illustrates how easily practices aimed to create a sense of freedom become patterns that reduce the scope of alternatives: how easily exercises become compulsions, rituals rit-ualistic, disciplines disciplinary. How easily the values that these practices engender come to be experienced as timeless and inevitable truths. Ironically, the reifying tendencies of traditional Christian disciplines contribute to their declining authority in an age of pluralism. Perhaps not surprisingly, many girls and women today, even those with traditional religious commitments, no longer find these practices to be relevant to their most pressing concerns. Instead, the practices of consumer-media culture—especially its rituals of womanhood—provide primary strategies and shared beliefs through which their anxieties and hopes are mediated.

The previous chapter explored how these fears and yearnings are ne-gotiated in relation to the dominant culture's narrow images of what it means to be a woman. In this chapter, we will see how the salvation myth of female slenderness that these images construct derives its meaning both in relation to the practices of its adherents and in connection with the consumer in-dustries and products that promise fulfillment through a thin body. This analysis fleshes out the language through which eating problems develop by highlighting the cultural context and the ritualizing functions of female weight control.

Rituals of Womanhood: Different and Common Ways of Acting

Such an analysis presumes that the distinction between "secular" and "re-ligious" meanings is less obvious than has been conventionally assumed. In his classic essay "Religion as a Cultural System," Clifford Geertz cites the difference between ascetic fasting and dieting to illustrate the distinction between "religious" and "secular" behavior. This distinction, Geertz argues, is based in these practices' diverging ends and the varying frames of meaning and dispositions they foster. Whereas weight reduction aims to achieve a finite or "conditioned" goal, religious fasting seeks to attain an "uncondi-tioned end." Whereas dieting is tied to worldly values (presumably health and beauty), ascetic fasting takes its meaning and motivation in reference to a cosmic scheme, a picture of "a general order of existence," of "the way things in sheer actuality are."[3]

At first glance, Geertz's distinction makes a lot of sense. One need only watch TV for an evening, page through a popular women's magazine, join a diet club, or listen to a schoolgirl insisting she is "too fat" or to a doctor telling you to "watch what you eat" to witness the this-worldly quality of America's pursuit thinness. Yet a closer reading of popular, professional, and experiential discourses on weight control suggests that something more, something of vast importance, is being summoned, weighed, and reckoned in this pursuit, especially among its female participants. The more one probes this "something," the more the distinction between "secular" and "reli-gious" behavior fades and the more one begins to see that for many girls and women, creating a slender body is a matter of all-pervading significance, an end whose achievement feels tantamount to ultimate salvation.

Over thirty years ago, anthropologist Mary Douglas recognized the fluidity of the distinction between sacred and secular practices. In her book *Purity and Danger*, Douglas argued that "rituals of purity and impurity" such as dietary restrictions and avoidances are central to religious behavior. At the same time, she noted, "very little of our ritual behaviour is enacted in the context of religion." Instead, ordinary practices of purification (such as refusing to eat certain foods) are the activities through which we regularly create a larger sense of meaning and value. Secular explanations of these practices (such as medical hygiene and aesthetics) reduce their symbolic meanings and functions by ignoring their multiple layers of significance: their capacity to suggest a picture of the ideal social and cosmic order and to unify experience within that grand scheme.[4]

If Douglas's insights blur the distinction between sacred and secular behavior, Catherine Bell's work shows how power operates in the creation of this distinction. In *Ritual Theory, Ritual Practice*, Bell uses the concept of "ritualization" to highlight how meanings are produced in ritual activity.[5] The significance of ritual practices rests not in their inherent difference from other ways of acting but in their capacity to constitute themselves as distinct from—and *holier than*—more mundane ways of acting. Such practices are rooted in the "ritualized body": a body that has been socialized to look, feel, and act in culturally mandated ways. Ritual meaning is thus strategically created in relation to prevailing social norms and in reference to "realities thought to transcend the powers of human actors."[6]

Bell's work offers a way of thinking about female dieting as a popular cultural rite of womanhood: a ritualizing practice through which a woman's body is distinguished and sacralized, her fears and dreams generated and regulated, and the prevailing social order negotiated and reproduced. As part of a broader system of cultural beliefs and symbols, weight-loss rituals do not simply create an ideal female body; they generate a worldview, an embodied sense of self-definition, and a precarious method for coping with the problems and possibilities of life in the late twentieth century. "After a time," Sallie Tisdale reflects back on her years of compulsive dieting,

> the number on the scale became my totem, more important than my experience—it was layered, metaphorical, *metaphysical*, and it had bewitching power. I thought if I could change that number I could change my life. . . . I would weigh myself with foreboding, and my weight would determine how went the rest of my day, my week, my life.[7]

Historical Precedents, Shifts, and Meanings

I will never forget the day my friend Atema, who is from Kenya, told me that she had never weighed herself before she came to the United States. "I didn't even know what a scale was, much less a calorie," she said. To her, the idea that people made value judgments about themselves and each other based on body size or weight seemed silly. The practice called "dieting" seemed equally bizarre: "In my country, people eat what is available when they are hungry, and they stop eating when they are full. This is the best way to ensure that there will be enough food to go around for everyone."[8]

I do not want to romanticize the eating practices of persons in the Two-Thirds World, where food shortages are directly and indirectly shaped by the mundane habits and social policies of consumer-oriented societies like the United States. My aim is simply to underscore the contrast. In America, land of maldistributed abundance, most girls know the language of dieting—often from first-hand experience—by the time they are ten years old. Rituals of avoiding some foods while measuring others are not only common among females in this culture: they are habitual. So are the ritual encounters on the bathroom scale, and so are the losses of control that frequently follow restricted eating.

The range of dieting varies considerably. Some diets involve specific food plans; others focus on technique. Some are formally prescribed by doctors; others are commercially bought and sold. Still others are informally devised and implemented, broken and resumed.[9] Despite these variations, however, dieting involves the routinization, calculation, and regulation of eating in an attempt to control the body's appetite and reduce its size. For many girls and women today, this disciplined mode of nourishment is not only habit-ual; it is, true to its name, "a way of life."[10]

Yet the desire to minimize the female body's appetites and size is neither natural nor universal. In many cultures, especially those where food supplies are unstable, large female bodies are not only tolerated, they are desired.[11] The same was true in this country prior to this century, when female plump-ness was seen as a sign of health, beauty, and prosperity, and when restrict-ing or calculating one's food intake entailed an interruption of ordinary ways of eating.[12]

A network of historical shifts and cultural conditions have made slen-derness a prevailing ideal and weight loss a seemingly viable strategy for making meaning and seeking wholeness among girls and women today. The axiomatic belief that women can and should monitor what they eat stems from a confluence of modern developments, including the belief that "the self" is an autonomous individual; the reconception of the body as a ma-chine; and the rise of new scientific, technological, and economic institu-tions, in conjunction with long-standing and still powerful symbolic associ-ations between spirituality/transcendence and women/bodily concerns.

These developments and beliefs are evident in the history of dieting in the West. This story begins with a new mode of restricted eating that emerged with the rise of modern science.[13] This method combined the quest for spiritual truth with the pursuit of improved health; it focused on regu-lating one's food intake, and its rules and guidelines were initially encoded in the texts of religiously motivated men.[14] Such texts began to circulate in the early modern period. Frequently their authors had drastically changed their eating patterns in midlife due to a combination of physical and spiritual malaise.

For example, Luigi Cornaro's problems with gout led him, at the age of forty in mid-sixteenth-century Italy, to develop a regime that limited his consumption to twelve ounces of food and fourteen ounces of drink each day. This program not only cured him of his painful disease but also inspired his formula for overall health: "Every Man [sic] . . . might become his own Physician if only he would keep a strict watch over his appetite, which indeed ought to be every one's Chief Business and Concern."[15] By advocating that individuals should take responsibility for their own physical and spiritual health, Cornaro's regimen represented wider trends across the sociocultural landscape of early modern Europe, including a new emphasis on individual spiritual authority, the development of more "civilized" codes of conduct, and the emergence of a mechanistic picture of human life in the world.[16]

In *The Death of Nature,* Caroline Merchant traces the rise in the sixteenth and seventeenth centuries of a new paradigm for understanding human beings, society, and the cosmos, namely, as ordered systems made up of mechanical parts, governed by immutable laws and knowable through deductive reason. Such a worldview reconceptualized the body, an extension of the earth, as passive, manipulable, subject to and in need of rational mastery and control. The image of an autonomous self housed in a machinelike body reflected as it responded to the historical changes amid which it emerged: the post-Reformation anarchy of truths, the incipient rise of commercial capitalism, and the initial discoveries of modern scientific reason. But the belief that the body requires mastery and supervision legitimated the already timeworn notion that women, who were closely associated with the body, need to be controlled.[17]

According to Bryan Turner, the emergence of a mechanistic worldview in the modern period involved a "secularization of the body," whereby the body as the site of sin and salvation became the object of scientific scrutiny.[18] Religious concerns about the body did not simply disappear with the expanding authority of science. By the eighteenth century, new medical regimes had much in common with the spiritual disciplines they implicitly took as their models. Scientific treatises of the time advocated regulated exercise and eating. The aim of these programs was not slenderness per se but the improvement of health and prolonging of life. According to Turner, the growing emphasis on monitoring one's appetite and overall health was part of a wider historical trend in which the physical body became an outward tool for cultivating the virtue of the inner self.[19]

This trend was evident among the first diet-conscious individuals in this country: the disciples of Sylvester Graham (1794–1851). Graham was the first American to formulate a systematic response to new anxieties about the human body and society that emerged with the shift from a household to a marketplace economy. Drawing on his experiences in both the evangelical ministry and the temperance movement and on his selective readings in medical theory, Graham's "Science of Human Life" proffered techniques through which ordinary persons could protect themselves from the health threats posed by their rapidly changing world. To achieve spiritual, physical, and social improvement, Graham insisted, persons must bring their unexamined bodily routines to a level of conscious scrutiny and control, thus turning the habits of daily life into a "regimen."[20]

The primary goal of such regimes was not trimming the body but purifying the appetite. With evangelical zeal that reflected the perfectionism of the age, nineteenth-century health advocates and reformers insisted that hygiene and holiness were inseparable. Inspired by the belief that the immutable laws (physical and spiritual) of an all-knowing creator supported rather than contradicted each other, they held proper diet to be a moral obligation whose fulfillment would bring social purity and religious righteousness.[21] In effect, their programs made health and disease an individual duty rather than a passive result of God's will. This modern confidence in the autonomy of the individual will and the malleability of the flesh set the stage for William Banting's "Letter on Corpulence" (1864), the first widely circulated diet aimed at the reduction of *both* appetite *and* body size.[22]

Around the turn of the century, Americans' growing preoccupation with weight control became increasingly systematized under the increased prominence of science, whose authority had begun to erode religious reasons for appetite surveillance. Between 1870 and 1930, the ideas that people should not necessarily eat what they want, that the vital components of food are hidden (calories, fats, vitamins), and that science had a set of rules and measures that could prevent illness and increase longevity became widely dispersed.[23]

Initially, these new ideas were designed to improve and to "Americanize" the eating habits of poor, immigrant, and working-class groups (especially Italian and Jewish women), who had come to be associated with fatness.[24] Eventually, however, with the help of government channels, the rise of giant food corporations, the spread of mass advertising, and the new female science of home economics, such strictures made their way to the tables of most middle-class families.[25] These new codes of conduct allowed for and demanded greater precision in supervising the body. They not only implied that individuals can and should take charge of their health; they made monitoring the body's appetites and size the centerpiece of this task.

In the early twentieth century, questions about what and how much to eat became increasingly important for those caught up in new signs of American "progress" and "abundance." Scientific views on the properties of food and the mechanics of the body meshed with economic, technological, and kinesthetic developments that placed great value on *efficiency*. This emphasis fostered new symbolic relationships between thinness and control, obesity and lethargy. By the 1920s, old associations between girth, health, and prosperity were giving way to a preference for bodies that looked and felt dexterous and lean. Summarizing the effects of these shifts, historian Hillel Schwartz identifies a new model of bodily motion and size that resonated with other cultural paradigms in its focus on managing excess:

> With the advent of the powered flight, modern dance, scientific management and home economics, a new kinesthetic ideal appeared, insisting on the dynamically balanced, centrally controlled body. . . . Americans sought to master the spiral and flow of things—in the body, the home, the factory, and the national economy itself, for which there was also a new model concerned rather with abundance than with scarcity. . . . Slimming became an acceptable strategy for dealing with the problems posed by abundance, gluttony (or "overnutrition") and the "dead weight" of fat.[26]

By midcentury, the mechanical model of the sleek, malleable, and efficient body lent authority to medical and psychiatric discourses, whose postwar theories demonized obesity, turning it into a full-fledged disease. In the rational codes of modern science, variation came to mean deviation—for which there was scant excuse given the presumed autonomy of the self: if 3,500 calories equals one pound, then losing weight should be a matter of simple arithmetic.[27]

For all its scientific underpinnings, the expanding pursuit of the narrow physique hinged on a symbolic system whose patterns resembled the moral codes and ritualizing techniques of traditional Christianity. In her historical account of this society's obsession with weight control, Roberta Seid suggests that the fervor with which contemporary Americans pursue thinness borders on the religious:

> If sloth and gluttony have always been condemned as sins, we have taken those sins as the cornerstone of a new faith. We believe in physical perfectibility and see its pursuit as a moral obligation. The wayward are punished with ugliness, illness, and early death. The good get their just rewards: Beauty and a blessedly long, happy and fulfilling life. The virtue that presumably will put us on this road is our ability to control one of our most fundamental instincts—eating.

This "new religion" has become so pervasive, and so persuasive, in the latter half of this century because it blends so well with some of America's most cherished beliefs, including a faith in the objectivity of science and a belief in the ideal of individual self-control.[28] During the past few decades, these beliefs have come to support a network of commercial products and programs that promise fulfillment through a fat-free physique. I refer to this system as "Culture Lite."

Less Fat, More Filling: Introducing Culture Lite

Mainstream manifestations of Culture Lite are evident in the explosion of various slenderizing industries during the second half of the twentieth century. In the 1950s, sales of weight-loss aids, from bathroom scales, to diet books, to low-calorie foods, to amphetamines, began to soar.[29] In the 1970s and 1980s, the profits of commercial diet centers grew exponentially, despite statistics indicating that up to 95 percent of those enrolled in these programs regain their weight (and more) within a few years. During this period, over-the-counter drugs for weight control became popular—and profitable, with sales climbing 20 percent each year. Meanwhile, sales of diet food and soda were increasing three times as fast as those of regular foods and beverages. Some 90 percent of Americans today regularly consume low-fat, sugar-free, and/or low-calorie foods and drinks. In 1997, losing weight was estimated to be a $50 billion business, and by this century's turn, Americans are predicted to spend $77 billion trying to shed their "excess" flesh.[30]

The mechanisms of Culture Lite have not simply accelerated during the past few decades; they have also changed, making the pursuit of the fat-free body more dispersed, more mandatory, and more deeply entrenched in profit-seeking ventures. This trend is illustrated in the rise of the "fitness ethic," a prominent but distinct current within Culture Lite that emerged in the late 1960s.[31] What distinguishes the fitness ethic's practices from its "mainstream" counterparts is that both its marketers and its consumers claim that its primary goal is not slenderness per se but overall "health," signified by a body that is light and lean.

The fitness ethic began as a "countercultural" challenge to mainstream eating and dieting practices. It promoted nutritious food and moderate exercise as means of mental, spiritual, and social renewal. By the late 1970s, however, this alternative was taken over by the very powers it meant to criticize: the giant food and weight-loss industries. While this co-optation produced the current markets for "natural" foods, it reinterpreted the fitness ethic beyond recognition. Concerns about eating healthy and "living lightly," by which the counterculture meant watching the earth's resources, came to mean counting calories and fat grams, whereby mostly middle-class white women were encouraged to watch their waistlines.[32]

The difference between the "mainstream" weight-loss practices and those comprising the "fitness ethic" is far from clear. In the wider context of Culture Lite, the call to "overall health and fitness" is not easily distinguishable from the mandate to lose weight. Given this culture's axiomatic preference for female slenderness, fitness-oriented rhetoric usually implies the need for women to reduce. Surveys indicate that most women who exercise do so primarily to lose weight.[33] Commercial exhortations to "Get Healthy! Feel Fit! Lose Weight!" (to quote an ad for Joan Lunden's "Workout America" video) conflate aesthetic, moral, and health concerns. This conflation contributes to the apparent "naturalness" of the slim ideal, an aura that makes the call to thinness all the more difficult to resist.

The commercial takeover of the fitness ethic by various weight-loss industries illustrates the mechanics of modern domination: prevailing cultural hegemonies operate by accommodating and profiting from new developments within the social order, even when these developments are critical of its systems. The profit-seeking ethos of consumer capitalism seems both omnipresent and omniscient, supplanting an omnipotent creator as the invisible source of transcendent power. Given its quasi-religious function, it is not surprising that some of this system's rhetorical maneuvers selectively employ certain terms and conventions of traditional religion.

Traditional religious motifs are relatively common in the symbolic galaxy of consumer-media culture. Conventions like choir music and personal confession are regular features of TV ads; terms like "ultimate," "pure," "total," and "perfection" are invoked to sell an assortment of products, from new cars to breakfast cereals. Given that the average American is exposed to 1,500 ads each day and is likely to spend one and a half years of her or his life watching television commercials, it is reasonable to suggest that advertisements are a crucial conduit for communicating religious values, in spite of and because of their "secular" content.[34]

The commercial use of traditional religious idioms and terms plays a particularly prominent role in circulating the promises of Culture Lite. Within this system, producing a body that is lite and lean has become a middle-class mode of "enlitenment." That such enlitenment depends on consumption is not a problem within the logic of late capitalism. A magazine ad for a fat-burning candy bar, featuring a trim, athletic-looking woman, tells us that by eating this product we can "burn it off." The ethic of control that underwrites this trope of forgiveness is seen in another ad for a fat-burning product, which summons its readers to "show those pesky fat cells no mercy." More subtle tactics of domination-enlitenment are sold in products like the "Cellulite Solution," the "Chews to Lose" weight-loss gum, the "Totally Fit" workout video (available in Spanish), or the "Think Like a Thin Person" tape series (at the Sharper Image for just $69.95!).

Precisely because weight-reducing rituals engage their users' hungers for a sense of meaning, many of their terms and promises resemble those of traditional religion. The penitential aspects of losing weight are implicit in the New Year's cover stories of *People* magazine: "Diet Wars: Who's Winning, Who's Sinning" (1992) and "Diet Winners and Sinners of the Year" (1994).[35]

The continuities between the language and promises of Culture Lite and certain terms and values of biblical religion are especially lucid in evangelical Christian circles, as the title of one diet book—*More of Jesus, Less of Me*— makes clear. In the past few decades, evangelical diet and fitness programs have made the quest for thinness, conservative Christian piety, and big business something of a trinity. Best-selling books like Marie Chapian and Neva

Coyle's *Free to Be Thin* spawn church-based weight-loss workshops where believers are encouraged to see connections between their "slavery to food" and the Hebrews' bondage in Egypt, between their desire to be thin and the broader Christian story of sacrifice and redemption. "Sweating and working out don't seem as bad when you're praising the Lord at the same time," a student of Body and Soul Aerobics gives witness. Such sweat may now be deemed all the more necessary, given a recent study which found that Christians who are most active in practicing their faith are more likely to be overweight.[36]

According to R. Marie Griffith, weight control and thinness are central concerns for the members of Women Aglow, the largest women's evangelical organization in the world. This group's teachings on food, appetite, and body size tend to reinforce the dominant cultural worship of female slenderness, despite its efforts to define the goal of dieting as pleasing God rather than society. For women in Aglow, Griffith explains, "Overeating is both sin and sickness, construed as gluttony and as rebellion against authority."[37] A thin body is therefore seen as proof that a woman is obeying God's Word. Aglow literature on overeating stresses that Jesus conquered the power of carnal appetite, to which women are most susceptible. In *Slim for Him*, Patricia Kreml relates the dangers of overeating to the disobedient appetite of Eve. Through the rhetoric of self-control and surrender, Christian women are instructed to give up their own efforts to conquer their desire to eat and to leave their sinful cravings in the hands of God. In the end, Griffith observes, such acquiescence to God is not easily distinguishable from obedience to wider cultural norms, especially those that glorify the fat-free female form.[38]

The mix of religious devotion and cultural norms for weight control is illustrated by one of the most popular evangelists of Christian dieting: Gwen Shamblin, whose "Weigh Down Workshop" appears in more than 10,000 churches in the United States today. Shamblin's approach to Christian dieting differs from the blatantly shame-based programs of earlier decades, such as Rev. Charles Shedd's *Pray Your Weight Away* (1957), which told believers that being fat was offensive to God. For Shamblin, the problem with fat is not simply that it displeases God but that it indicates an underlying spiritual problem: an inability to give oneself to God. "When you give your heart to God," Shamblin assures, "the body will follow," and soon the pounds will disappear.[39] Shamblin compares the success of her Christian-based approach to the failures of her "secular" competitors, whose programs cannot work because they place their hopes in worldly ends. Only when one turns from the "idol" of food to the grace of God will one's efforts to reduce succeed.[40]

That the evangelical approach of Christian dieting fails to seriously interrogate the "idolatry" of female thinness suggests its own lingering ties to "worldly" concerns and its underlying compatibility with the saving promises of Culture Lite. This compatibility is implicit in the morality of food that permeates Americans' eating patterns. Eight out of ten Americans believe that foods are inherently "good" or "bad," regardless of how or why they are eaten.[41] Just as the explicitly Christian call to lose weight incorporates prevailing cultural norms of health and beauty, so these prevailing cultural norms incorporate certain values of Christianity, especially those that define spiritual virtue as transcendence of the flesh and that see women as inordinately lured by the body's cravings. Ultimately, these two different plans of salvation—one explicitly "religious" and the other apparently "secular"—are not just compatible: they often overlap.

This overlap is evident in weight-loss programs that are not explicitly tied to traditional religion. A diet club called "Happy Losers" motivated its members with the following saying:

> The diet is within me I shall not cheat
> It leadeth me to choose the legal food whenever I have the urge to eat
> Yea though I may wish to eat sweets or cake
> I shall eat them never
> For the diet is with me
> And I shall reach my goal
> And remain slim forever. Amen.[42]

Other quasi-religious approaches to weight control assume the tone of New Age or "alternative" spirituality. Dean Ornish's best-selling *Eat More, Weigh Less* claims that followers of his "Life Choice" diet "feel more open, aware, and connected."[43] Perhaps the most vivid example of this "spiritual" approach to diet and fitness is Ray Kybartas's *Fitness Is Religion*. Personal trainer to Madonna, Kybartas contends that "the pursuit of fitness is the pursuit of wholeness, a religious regimen that can empower each of us to cope with the overwhelming pressures of our day-to-day existence."[44] While Kybartas's emphasis on "balance" distinguishes his regimen from the quick-fix, health-destroying weight-loss tactics of many of his competitors, his belief that health is inseparable from beauty assumes that being fit means being thin. This assumption is evident in the book's photos depicting bodies that are unequivocally toned and trim and in its numerous charts for measuring body fat, weight, and calories.

Sometimes Culture Lite's gospel of diet and fitness is construed through conversion idioms of before-and-after. Inspirational stories of miraculous transformation are at the heart of Richard Simmons's *Never Give Up* (1993). One of Simmons's faithful followers lost 112 pounds and saved her marriage; another achieved her life dream of becoming an aerobics instructor; another whose daughter was run over by a car and who ate as a way to cope with her grief lost weight on Simmons's Deal-a-Meal and was able to adopt a new baby.[45] Precisely this possibility of being "born again" makes losing weight a compelling ritual for women who want their lives to be different.

Several diet franchises were founded by ordinary women who confessed and capitalized on this desire by turning their "personal" weight-loss sagas into businesses devoted to helping (and profiting from) other women.[46] The evangelical tone of these commercial enterprises echoes in the words of fitness diva Susan Powter: "Stop the Insanity! Discover the Truth!" her infomercial screams. Posing as a lonely voice in the wilderness, Powter's "truth" begins with repentance: "Four years ago . . . I was an unfit person—a very, very, very unfit person," referring to the days when she allegedly weighed 260 pounds. Now weighing in at 115 pounds, with shaved and bleached white hair, she quips: "I'm a housewife who figured it out."[47]

Confessed and converted, Powter presents a female rendition of the "American Dream." Unlike the famous fitness gurus of previous decades (Jack Lalane, Richard Simmons), Powter displays a female body that many women can envision themselves developing. In contrast to her female counterpart, Jane Fonda, Powter appeals to women without unusual social privilege: women like herself, she claims, reminding disciples of her unhappy fat days in the Dallas suburbs, where her husband abandoned her and her two children for a woman who was thin. In the spirit of the fitness ethic, Powter criticizes "mainstream" weight-loss programs such as Jenny Craig. Her "alternative" includes a "wellness kit" with five motivational audiocassettes, an exercise video, a booklet with recipes and fat guides, and a caliper to measure body fat, in addition to her best-selling book *Stop the Insanity*, a quarterly audio newsletter, and a paid infomercial that reached nearly 50 million viewers every three days when it first aired. Needless to say, Powter is a millionaire. But that, she insists, is not the point. Her goal is to empower women like herself, which can only happen when they slim down and shape up so the world will take them seriously.[48]

Powter's blend of evangelical tone and democratic rhetoric is a recurrent theme in Culture Lite, where distinctions of worth are made by transforming the ordinary practices of daily life into opportunities for self-improvement: "Park a few blocks away from work and walk; or better yet, ride your bike. And take the stairs instead of the elevator. Stand rather than sit. Walk rather than stand. Walk briskly rather than slowly. This way you can nudge up the caloric expenditure."[49] On an obvious level, such advice makes burning calories the ultimate goal of fitness-oriented activities. More subtly, however, the banal focus of this rhetoric masks the ritualizing function that weight-loss strategies implicitly serve. Walking fast, taking the stairs . . . such practices create much more than a body that is trim and lean. They also produce a renewed sense of purpose, an embodied sense that links an individual's experience not merely to a social order but also to a cosmic scheme, a conception of a "general order of existence" (Geertz).

The ritualizing function of Culture Lite, its capacity to transform life's mundane materials into ultimate meaning, is further illustrated in popular food products whose labels bear the saving words "low-cal" or "fat-free."[50] An ad for Diet Coke, featuring the standard figure of a slender young woman, entices consumers by reference to ecstatic religious experience. "To the Novice," the copy reads:

Many of our loyal drinkers equate the indescribable taste of a Diet Coke with that of something in the spiritual realm. However, if this is your first time, we do advise that after drinking one, you resist the urge to run out into the street, toss your beret in the air and exclaim to a slightly bewildered crowd "I'm gonna make it after all!!" While we are not disputing these emotions of exuberance, a display of this kind could be confusing to the non–Diet Coke drinker, thus resulting in ostracism from the community, perhaps to a strange land that does not serve Diet Coke.

Such is the longed-for rapture that the monotonous fare of Culture Lite can engender. Though the details of its products and programs vary, the "truths" around which the pursuit of thinness spins its often vicious circles seem as indisputable as the numerical values (both scientific and monetary) through which they are created. In the words of a smiling woman who in an ad for Weight Watchers testifies that she lost over eight pounds in fourteen days, "The scales don't lie."

Yet the saving promises of Culture Lite are fueled by a culture of self-deception. The search for a sense of meaning that America's battle with the bulge both conceals and reveals represents a large-scale attempt not merely to manage this society's abundance but, more important, to divert attention away from the damaging effects of its grossly uneven distribution. According to the ethos and logic of Culture Lite, it is good to have excess in your billfold but not on your body, and it is right to want to change your thighs but dangerous, indeed *crazy*, to want to change the world.

Organized around the pursuit of slenderness, especially the quest for the flab-free female body, Culture Lite is a central nerve in this society's politics of distraction: the wide-scale diversion of attention away from the prevailing values and actual conditions that undermine individual and social well-being. On one level, the prominence of Culture Lite stems from its ability to synthesize a number of authoritative discourses and beliefs, thus offering diverse Americans what traditional religion no longer does: a common, public frame of meaning that appeals and applies across multiple and competing party lines. On another level, this prominence stems from its resonance with certain paradigms and values of Christianity, especially those that support and sustain oppressive relations of power.

The illusory promises of Culture Lite are not simply patriarchal; they are also feminized. For the modern beliefs that fuel the quest for the lean and well-managed body, particularly the notion that individuals can and should control their own destiny, have special meaning for those whose destinies have historically been tied to their anatomies. Long-standing religious views of women as carnal vessels of devotion or temptation, together with women's historical exclusion from formal realms of power and their modern duties as domestic servants, ornaments of beauty, household scientists, and consumers, has cast them in a leading role in the quest for the fat-free body.

In this drama, modern beliefs in the autonomy of the individual self, the manipulability of the flesh, the authority of science, and the promises of consumer capitalism merge with traditional visions of womanhood, revising without upsetting women's age-old identification with their bodies by demanding increasingly strict mastery over them. In a society whose prevailing symbols, rituals, and social arrangements continue to conflate female anatomy and destiny, it is not surprising that girls and women learn to seek salvation both from and with their bodies. In a culture where female anatomy is evaluated largely according to its size and contours, it makes sense that rituals aimed to regulate the body's weight and appetites figure prominently in this quest.

The Rewards of Punishment and the Saving Promise of Being Thin

The quasi-religious quality and function of the rituals and rhetoric of Culture Lite point to the spiritual hungers of those who consume its empty promises. To understand the role of such hungers in the eating problems of American girls and women today, we must see them in relation to the historical legacies and current cultural conditions that make losing weight seem like a viable strategy for creating a sense of purpose. This is important because problems with anorexia and bulimia do not appear out of nowhere. They are part of a broader network of popular symbols and practices that tell us what it means to be a woman. Girls' and women's own accounts of their struggles with food and body suggest that eating problems develop out of the very rituals and beliefs that mainstream cultural authorities recommend to them as *normal* and *healthy*, namely, those aimed at reducing their bodies and appetites.

These recommendations are part of a context, not a conspiracy. In most cases, no one forces a girl or woman to diet. Yet losing weight is an extremely compelling, if often debilitating, practice for so many of them. What makes the pursuit of thinness so powerful is the rewards it promises and, at least temporarily, delivers. These rewards are sought and achieved on several levels: through social norms and physical sensations, through moral codes and cultural identities, and through the promise of self-determination. The reductive mentality and controlling ethos that tie these levels of meaning together become clear when we take a closer look at girls' and women's own descriptions of their ritual pursuit of the slender ideal.

The Socially Approved Body

Rituals aimed to slenderize the female body create their own rewards, including a sense of social approval, a feeling of "measuring up" and "fitting in." In a society where values are frequently defined by numbers, the reductive measures of science are not only the goal but also the means through which weight-loss practices become meaningful: "I used to weigh myself every morning," a woman recalls, "and I do mean before I drank any liquids, or even put on my perfume."[51] "Simple arithmetic," another woman sarcastically muses:

> After all, 3,500 calories equal one pound of fat—so the books and articles by the thousands say. I would calculate how long it would take to achieve the magic number on the scale, to succeed, to win. All past failures were suppressed. If 3,500 calories equal one pound, all I needed to do was cut 3,500 calories out of my intake every week.[52]

Whether weighing the body or counting calories, the values of such empirical measures reduce the internal dissonance that many women experience in relation to prevailing models of womanhood. Most women do not "measure up" to such ideals. But by slimming her body, a woman stands a better chance at gaining some of the admiration that these models monopolize in the public sphere. Social approval is thus an enticing factor in women's battles to be thin: "The more clothes hung, the more the compliments grew. 'What kind of diet are you on; you haven't looked this good in ages; why, you look like you've lost ten years.' " Another woman explains: "I've gotten a lot more attention from men as I've grown close to the conventional idea of beauty. The skinny me, apparently, has a 'great personality' that the fat me somehow lacked."[53]

The female body that loses weight is a socially approved body. Such approval is generated in reference to dominant cultural models of womanhood (traditionally white, young, bourgeois, and thin). Its power, however, reaches the subjectivities of those in less privileged social positions. A young black woman who temporarily lost forty pounds following "The Model's Ten Day Diet" recalls:

> Afterward, no one dared to call me Fat Alberta, and my relatives extolled me for my weight loss and referred to me as a "real teenager," as though prior to the weight loss I was insignificant. One aunt sent me a letter in which she wrote, "Inside every fat girl there is a thin girl dying to get out!" and drew a picture illustrating a "fat" me surrounding a "thin" me. The fat me was frowning, the thin me was—of course—smiling.[54]

For females who are multiply devalued by Euro-American standards of health, morality, and beauty, the reductive distinctions that rituals of dieting create (before/after, insignificant/real, frowning/smiling, fat/thin) are particularly insidious. Though the social applause that accompanies weight loss may temporarily ease the pain of living in an unjust society, it does so by reinstating the narrowly defined standards of womanhood that keep women starved for a broader, more integrative experience of meaning.

The Morally Upright Body

Scientific and aesthetic norms are embedded in women's reasons for wanting to reduce. The power of weight-loss rituals, however, resides not simply in their ability to produce a body that is "healthy" and "beautiful." Part of what makes these rites so compelling is their ability to create a sense of value, particularly a sense of living "right." This sense is evident in the moralizing tones that permeate girls' and women's accounts of their efforts to reduce.

For a girl or woman who wants to lose weight, the decision of whether or what to eat presents a kind of ethical dilemma. In their interviews with adolescent girls, Deborah Tolman and Elizabeth Debold asked a seventh grader to describe a moral conflict she had recently experienced. The slender blond girl responded by recounting the "conflict of whether I wanted the calories of two [pastries], or should I only have one." Basically, the choice boiled down to "whether or not I wanted the calories or to be good." When her interviewers asked what she meant by "good," the girl explained: " 'Good' means not to have too many calories, or you'll be fat like I am."[55]

The continuities between this girl's ethical universe, the popular ethos of Culture Lite, and classic Christian views on good and evil become apparent if we consider the dualistic logic they share. In some women's accounts, affinities between "Christian" and "secular" systems of value are very thinly veiled. The belief that hunger is good and eating is evil is an ongoing theme in the stories of the women Jennifer Manlowe interviewed in her study of incest survivors with eating problems. "When I was hungry, I felt like I was living right," one of Manlowe's subjects explains:

> I even felt better when I would eat only fruits and vegetables, even when hungry. Pretty soon I was able to convince my mind and my body that such feelings of purity were much better than any fattening food. I was on my way to becoming the invulnerable perfection that I really craved. . . . I believed that the kind of food that went into my body had the power to absolve or disgrace me, and I would feel these feelings deeply depending on what I had ingested.[56]

Such discourse reveals not so much an authentic religious experience as a specific cultural logic, according to which values (pure and impure) are distilled and divided, unevenly assigned and mutually opposed. This dogmatic way of thinking links this woman's seemingly private moral universe and personal disciplines not only to a network of popular cultural norms but also to a vision of female holiness constructed through the division of spirit and flesh.

This spirit/flesh dichotomy underwrites another idiom of Culture Lite that many women internalize: the separation of virtue and pleasure. "Only my senses tell me the crisp is good," a woman explains, describing this inner conflict: "The voice of civilization, speaking from inside my head, says it will bring me fat and misery . . . although I enjoy each bite, I know I am doing wrong. Moral wrong. And I'm no Puritan—I don't feel this way about other pleasures. . . . I can't help feeling it is immoral to be fat."[57] By denying herself the pleasure of eating, a woman who diets constructs a moral universe in which her hungry body is not simply morally upright: it is morally superior. "I have in my mind that if I'm thinner, I'm better," a young woman elaborates:

> Last night when everyone was going out for ice cream, I kind of wanted ice cream and I kind of didn't want it. After they were gone, I thought, now why didn't I go? I really think it had to do with, it would look good if I just said "No, thank you, I don't care for any." You know, like I'm above that kind of thing.[58]

The superiority complex that shapes this value system is rooted in a dualistic logic. In classic Christian theology, this dualism is expressed in the beliefs that good and evil are never mixed and that what is of utmost value is inaccessible, invulnerable, and indisputable.

Such beliefs not only feed the notion that "thinner is better;" they also fuel the sense of shame that the separation of virtue and pleasure creates. This sense pervades the morality of dieting, wherein the quest for self-correction and improvement is predicated on a lack of self-acceptance:

> My entire life was ruled by fat with but one desire—to be thin. . . . Unfortunately, my shame gave birth to guilt. Guilt is impalpable. It does not have form; you cannot touch it. But it pervades the mind like pain does a tooth. . . . the seeds of shame and guilt are insidious. They grow like weeds in an untended garden.

These seeds of shame are rooted in another garden as well: the biblical story of this garden depicts a cosmic battle between good and evil as pivoting on the dangers of female desire. Implicitly, the drama of this story continues to unfold in the weight-loss battles of women today:

> Now a war waged in my head. Fat vs. Thin. I visualized myself as a Vulture—the Fat Me, and as a Snake—the Thin Me. The only resolution I could see was the Snake slaying the Vulture. But the Vulture refused to die, she kept picking away at me as though I was a carrion on the road. My not-eating was in danger. Everything became black or white. Don't eat or else binge. Life became one big scale.[59]

In addition to its echoes of Eden, the apocalyptic tone of this imagery recalls a conservative Christian emphasis on otherworldly salvation: the belief that wholeness is ever beyond the present moment, the mundane moment, the embodied moment here and now. According to the saving promise of Culture Lite, fulfillment is just a few pounds (lost) away, in the form of a fat-free body: a body that seems to transcend the earthly laws of finitude and change. If the vitality of this woman's symbolic universe bespeaks the intensity of her desire, the futility of the war through which it is waged points to the shallowness of the ideals on which it draws and to the impoverishment of the moral legacies it implicitly contests and unwittingly extends.

The Ritualized Body

The "truths" that weight-loss rituals generate—whether moral, aesthetic, or scientific—are not abstract. Part of what makes losing weight so compelling is that these truths are known-felt-experienced in and through the body: through the physical knowledge of sensation. To attend to this level of meaning-production is to see how the values that weight-loss rituals create are experienced from the inside out, even as they are learned from the outside in. The meanings that such rites produce take hold beneath the skin.

Conventional discourse on eating problems focuses on women's poor "body image." However, this concept fails to convey the interplay between physical and imaginative processes. As an alternative, the term "body sense" more adequately conveys how the beliefs surrounding the desire to be thin become embedded in the biochemical processes of the dieter's body.[60] The double meaning of the term "sense" (as thought and feeling or as physical sensation) suggests that meanings are incarnated and experienced throughout the body, rather than anchored solely in the brain. The tenacity of a thin girl's belief that she is "too fat" stems in part from its embeddedness in her bodily sensations. She does not just *think* she is "too fat"; she also *feels* "too fat." Which is not to say this perception is "natural" or necessarily accurate. Body sense is both taught and learned.

Girls' and women's common sense that they are "too fat" is the product of a shared but diversely embodied knowledge, a knowledge built from the bodily rituals of self-surveillance and correction (counting fat grams, checking in mirrors, stepping on scales, doing leg lifts) that a cluster of cultural authorities recommends. Through these daily disciplines and the pain and pleasure that such rites engender, a woman's body ingests and memorizes the publicly sanctioned codes of female slenderness, storing them "beyond the grasp of consciousness" so that their truths become second nature. The dieting body is thus a "ritualized body": a body that has been trained to feel, act, and appear a certain way within a particular social milieu.[61]

A woman's desire to lose weight does not simply stem from her "poor body image." This desire is part of a specifically trained *body sense*: a sense that has been rewarded and punished through internalized social norms. Since this sense is acquired through the ritualizing activities of the body, it *feels* natural rather than learned, individual rather than social. This feeling makes it difficult for many women, even those who do not consciously worship narrow icons of womanhood, to simply "accept" their bodies. Self-help manuals often miss this point when they admonish women with poor body images to change their "mind's eye" or when they advise chronic dieters to trust their bodies' "true hungers."[62] Such advice presumes a mind-over-body distinction which, in practical experience, is often not so clear.

Despite their dualistic logic, weight-loss techniques rely on the very mind/body nexus they seem to splinter. The power of such rites works not simply by repressing the body's appetites but also by intensifying them. Invariably, women who try to lose weight become more, not less, preoccupied with food and eating, which suggests that the mind/body division is more an illusive product of language than an essential quality of experience.

Moreover, many dieters train themselves to experience intense hunger as pleasurable. In one woman's words, "Appetite is more appealing than what happens after. Appetite . . . is expectation, anticipation, fantasy and promise . . . Looking forward to the feast is always more pleasurable for me than actually consuming it." Feeling hungry is not only a strategy for achieving a morally and aesthetically superior body; it is also a technique for cultivating pleasure and concentrating desire. The intensity of a hunger deferred can serve multiple purposes among those whose longings are socially prohibited. The above woman, for example, notes the overlap between her forbidden cravings for food, for language, and for other women: "Lust keeps me hungry. Being hungry keeps me thin. Lust is the unanswered echo. . . . Lust keeps me thin. Lust for language. Lust for bodies. Women's bodies. Fantasy feeds off the homeless energy that inhabits a body fueled by hunger and denial."[63] Despite its rewards, the power of this denial feeds on the very legacy it means to contest and compensate: a legacy that fails to see the plurality and complexity of girls' and women's longings; a legacy where female pleasure is permitted only to the extent that it is attached to pain.

Within this legacy, women have been seen to represent the carnal aspects of existence, aspects that need to be tamed and transcended if salvation is to be achieved. But the dual notion that females are invariably tied to the flesh and that salvation is achieved by rising above the body creates an impossible dilemma for women. In classic Christian theology, this conflict has been resolved through the classification of "good" and "evil" women. "Good women" (nuns, martyrs, virgins, and saints) transcend their natural inferiority as females by eschewing bodily pleasures. When "evil women," by contrast, give in to those pleasures, they are merely doing what is "natural" for them, given their supposedly inferior nature as women.

Traditionally, this "good woman"/"evil woman" dichotomy has been defined in relation to women's sexual practice: "good women" are virgins or submissive wives; "evil women" are temptresses or whores. Nowadays, however, this opposition is also represented through women's relationships to food. "Good women" do not have big appetites. "Bad women" like to eat a lot. They shamelessly enjoy the sensuality of food, and they undoubtedly will be punished for their pleasure—because such pleasure (it is assumed) will make them *fat*.

And like the scarlet letter A, they will be forced to wear their girth as a sign of their iniquity for all the world to see. But those who look close will notice that the letter A denotes not "appetite" but "alienation." For ultimately it is not the body's unruly cravings that the diet rituals aim to cure, but the sense of separation: the body sense of deep division. As embodied knowledge, this ritualized sense of disconnection bears the tragic trace of a legacy that condemns women to the very flesh they must transcend in order to be saved.

The Socially Situated Body

Despite the common sense of alienation that leads many girls and women to diet, losing weight generates different meanings among diverse girls and women. Weight-loss rituals can serve as a means of shaping one's cultural identity with regards to age, race, sexuality, and class. The dieting female body is thus a socially situated body.

Among adolescent girls, the belief that one is "too fat" can serve as an idiom for navigating both the bodily changes that occur during puberty and the potential dangers that these changes can signify. Recalling the initial stages of her life-long struggle with food, Marya Hornbacher writes: "At age 10, it seemed I woke up to a body that filled the room. The hips, the rear, the chest—all of it fat. I hated it. Men were staring at me, and the sixth-grade boys snapped the one bra in the class."[64] Another teenage girl connects her sense of being "too fat" with her feeling of not fitting in: "[As a child] I wasn't obese but maybe 15 pounds overweight. Basically, I've been on and off diets since I was 11 years old. I was conscious of having to lose weight. Everyday I would go to school feeling fat and like I didn't belong. None of the boys liked me."[65] Given the relative paucity of public attention to the complex changes, anxieties, and longings that shape the lives of adolescent girls, it is not surprising that many young women feel, as one girl put it, "lost in the shuffle, like the odd one out."[66] Given the prevailing icons and rituals through which girls learn what it means to be a woman, it is not surprising that many of them experience and express this sense of disconnection in the belief that they are "too fat."

This same belief can express a sense of failure among older women who judge themselves to be physically inadequate. Seventy-year-old author Doris Grumbach writes:

> In my younger years I remember that I enjoyed feeling the firmness of my arms and legs, neck and fingers, chin and breasts. . . . [Now] I see the pull of gravity on the soft tissues of my breasts and buttocks. . . . There is nothing lovely about the sight of me. I have been taught that firm and unlined is beautiful. Shall I try to learn to love what I am left with? I wonder. It would be easier to resolve never again to look into a full-length mirror.[67]

Another older woman looks back on her years of dieting as an attempt to arrest the aging process that sealed her mother's fate as "fat and old," qualities she associated with "weakness" and "powerlessness":

> I set my body on a course to move through all the expected rituals. I vacated my premises. I learned to smile, to be "nice," learned to be an Amerikan [sic] woman. I ran away from a body that was flesh, soft, vulnerable, fat and female, threatening pain and oppression, promising certain death. I diminished myself.[68]

In the virtual absence of rites of passage with which to celebrate the changes and cycles of female bodies, many girls and women turn to the behavior and beliefs most readily available to them: those that sacralize the female body through rituals devoted to getting thin.

If cultural associations between female worth, slenderness, and youth contribute to older women's discontent with their bodies, ruling codes of heterosexual privilege weigh heavily among lesbian women who feel physically inadequate. For some of these women, reducing the body to a socially "acceptable" size aims to compensate for the socially "unacceptable" quality of their homosexual desires. "It took years to realize what was going on. Years of keeping a running total of each day's caloric intake in my head. Years of eating cottage cheese, carrot curls and radish rosebuds before I heard a word that named the nagging fear chewing away at me. Queer. Lezzie."[69] Another woman interprets her body's inability to tolerate certain foods as a symbolic rejection of the compulsory heterosexuality she was served via her parent's expectations:

> "This is the life we want you to live," they told me in a thousand different ways, offering me marriage, and my very own family; offering me boys, dresses, homemaker skills; offering me a highly socialized role that my gut knew was dead wrong for me. . . . I suspect my food allergies are not more than a systematic, automatic response my body developed to those foods which most obviously represented to me family life and the golden platter of heterosexuality. I gagged on it.[70]

Fear of fat and homophobia are connected by a dogmatic logic that defines "truth" by suppressing whatever deviates from the norm or ideal. This logic links a range of meanings that cling to female body-hatred, a multiplicity that is determined by women's and girls' varied relationships to prevailing ideals of womanhood.

The ambiguous power of weight-loss rituals is further sketched in the discourses of girls and women of color. These accounts illustrate how girls' and women's relationships to their bodies are influenced by the values, norms, and histories of the culture(s) with which they identify. A Mexican

American woman explains how her culture's traditional acceptance of ample-bodied women makes it possible for some Latina women to value their girth and to see it as a sign of value:

> Latinas in this country [the United States] live in two worlds. People who don't know us may think we're fat. At home, we're called *bien cuidadas* (well cared for). . . . Whether we're Cuban-American, Mexican-American, Puerto Rican or Dominican, food is a central part of Hispanic culture. . . . You feed people you care for, and so if you're well cared for, *bien cuidadas*, you have been fed well.[71]

Despite the alternative values available to them through their families and cultures, most girls and women of color learn that some degree of assimilation is needed for survival in America. Black feminist therapist Julia Boyd suggests that for black women, "learning to comply publicly with white standards has not been as much a choice as a dictate necessary for survival."[72] Moreover, access to multicultural values does not necessarily shield female minorities from internalizing dominant cultural norms. One black woman describes how such norms colonized her self-consciousness as a girl:

> I soon realized that I was different—not white, rich or beautiful. . . . By my eleventh birthday, I had gained a substantial amount of weight. . . . Truth is, I was more perplexed than disturbed by my increasing girth. But that changed forever after one of my classmates referred to me as "tub". . . . I laughed with everyone, but the humiliation I experienced was indescribable. All my life I had strived to fit in or fade in and now here I stood, exposed to the derision of my friends.[73]

Female slenderness may serve as an elusive and precarious passport for entry into mainstream social life. As we saw in chapter 1, a number of quantitative studies suggest a correlation between troubled eating among minority females and assimilation to white, bourgeois values and norms.[74] Qualitative work in this area confirms this pattern. Several of the Latina and black women that Becky Thompson interviewed for her multicultural study connected the pressures they felt to lose weight with their parent's hopes of becoming middle-class. In this study, dieting also served as a means for gaining acceptance among women who belonged to religious/ethnic minorities. An Italian Catholic woman who had attended a predominantly Protestant school recalled how her " 'loud, aggressive and emotional ways' " made her an outsider among her classmates, a status that becoming thin was supposed to counteract. Several Jewish women in Thompson's study said that losing weight served as a means for reducing their sense of alienation among their Protestant peers, who perceived them as talking, dressing, and looking "different."[75]

Weight-loss rituals may also serve as a strategy for focusing attention away from the anxieties of financial instability. "I wouldn't eat," a woman recalls, "because I was worried about money, about paying the rent." But refusing to eat was also this woman's way to achieve her goal: "To be thin. Slight. Slender. Sleek. Weightless."[76] Among women who are poor, pressures to conform to the slender, middle-class ideal, and the costs of trying to do so, are extremely high, leaving many of them feeling even more bankrupt of the dignity that losing weight was supposed to establish. Discussing her life-long eating problem, one woman remembered her struggle as a large-bodied black girl whose family was poor, trying to fit in at a predominantly white school where most of the students came from money: "I felt like I was being forced into a tube that was too small."[77]

By highlighting a variety of meanings that weight-loss beliefs and practices generate among diverse girls and women, I am not suggesting a formula for understanding the relationship between cultural diversity and weight reduction. Differences both among and within girls and women in any cultural group preclude any such typology. Nevertheless, examining how variances in social location determine the meaning of girls' and women's weight-loss efforts reveals what these struggles have in common, namely, the symbolic-ritual language through which they speak and the reductive logic and controlling ethos through which they are construed.

This logic and ethos permeate the beliefs and rituals that make the promise of slenderness meaningful. This promise accommodates the longings of diverse girls and women by reducing them. The rituals of womanhood that keep this promise alive give women a culturally sanctioned and yet coded way of expressing what is for many of them an oppressingly common sense: a sense of not fitting in. A sense, as one girl put it, that "the world isn't for you."[78]

The Ritualized Agent

In this sense, girls' and women's ritualizing quests for thinness do not simply reflect a superficial acquiescence to ruling codes of femininity. They also involve an attempt to navigate the legacy of silence and invisibility that these codes embody: a legacy in which women's creative powers and aspirations have been tragically underfed. Part of what makes the pursuit of slenderness so compelling is that it seems to give girls and women what history has denied them, namely, the power of self-determination.

By deciding whether, what, or how much to eat, a woman exercises a kind of self-determination that has historically been the prerogative of men. In her daily rituals of self-surveillance, a woman gains a feeling of power that she does not experience in other areas of her life. A woman who ate and dieted compulsively explains: "Food was power and control. Food was making my own decisions about what I would eat, when I would eat, how much I would eat. Food was taking control over what I looked like."[79] Another woman juxtaposes the sense of control she derived from her teenage dieting practices with the lack of freedom she felt in relation to her changing adolescent body, the new attention she received from men, her father's "ironfisted strictness," and her parents' insistence that she grow up: "Maybe I was looking for ways to regain dominion over an increasingly out of control situation. I could direct my food intake and physicality like I couldn't direct those around me."[80]

Ironically, deliberating over whether and what to eat may also seem to free a woman from the messy, mundane realm of food and body to which females have been assigned in Western thought and culture. In her essay "Food/Body/Person," Deane Curtin observes that traditional Western philosophies have relegated food and persons associated with growing, preparing, and serving food (usually women and people of color) to an inferior realm of being, a profane and temporal realm of life dictated by bodily needs. True knowledge and freedom, this vision implies, are to be sought and found in the superior sphere of abstract ideas, a sphere untainted by contingency, particularity, and change.[81] Given the ongoing influence of this Platonic dream in America today, the sense of agency that comes from deciding whether and what to eat may intimate a woman's longing for a much larger liberty: the liberation from the realm of physical necessity, a realm symbolized by the need to eat.

How much liberation do weight-loss rituals engender? From one perspective, the sense of agency that dieting creates can be seen to reflect the relative autonomy that *some* women (mostly white and middle-class) now enjoy and that *many* girls and women have come to want. Moreover, in a society where computers, machines, cars, and other technologies have made life intensely sedentary for many persons, regular exercise and careful eating can help promote a sense of overall well-being. Surely some women exercise regularly and watch what they eat not with the primary intention of getting thin but as a means for getting and/or staying well: a means for nourishing and affirming a body-soul connection, a way of connecting with other women (in the locker room or at the gym), and even a way of tapping into a larger creative energy of life.

Forgoing exercise and eating indiscriminately are hardly adequate solutions to the sense of powerlessness and disconnection that many girls and women feel in relation to their bodies. Yet the fact that some of the primary rituals this culture proffers girls and women for cultivating a sense of agency and worth require obedience to oppressive ideals suggests the limits of the power that losing weight engenders. Like the traditional models of female holiness, such ideals affirm the "perfection" of a chosen few while ignoring the struggles of many. Although such disciplines compensate girls and women with a sense of agency and purpose, they do so by reproducing the scenario in which a woman's salvation depends on her sacrifice and submission.

Practices aimed at slenderizing the female body create their own rewards: a sense of social approval, moral superiority, physical desire, cultural identity, and self-determination. They do so, however, by rendering girls and women more subservient—in Susan Bordo's words, more "pliable" and thus more "useful" to the dominant social order.[82] Indeed, these everyday rites of womanhood are the means whereby this "order" is reproduced.[83]

From Multiple Meanings, to Common Senses, to Many Dollars

By ritualizing some of the most mundane of all human activities—eating and moving—women's diet and fitness rituals harness the power of those two resources that history seems to have granted them: food and body. Through the privileged contrasts they create, these rites generate opportunities for experiencing something more, something better, something beyond the vicissitudes of life on Earth, something sacred in a disenchanted world. In these rites, necessities become possibilities.

And possibilities become profits. In the United States today, reducing and tightening the female form is a highly profitable business, not simply because of its nearly predictable lack of permanent success but also because of the sense of direction it fosters among those who are overwhelmed by the problems of life at this historical moment.

On some level, weight-loss rituals "work" by creating simple and accessible solutions to the questions "What do I want?" and "What should I do?"—questions that have grown ever more complicated amid this culture's movements and backlashes. The industries of Culture Lite capitalize on the eclipse of Truth and the dispersion of meanings that these shifts entail by providing a host of ready-made "answers," even before any questions are raised. Such "answers" are attractive because their solutions are tangible and immediate. Promotions for diet programs often begin with the promise "In just one week . . ."[84] A television ad for *Bally's* fitness centers assures potential converts/consumers: "Twenty-four dollars is all it takes to turn your life around."

Diet industries also cash in on the changing expectations of womanhood that have emerged during the past three decades by reinterpreting the feminist assertion that "biology is *not* destiny." An article in *Vogue*, entitled "Redefining the Body," encourages women to use body-sculpting to produce a "look" that is "both strong and feminine." This technique involves "chiseling one's body fat to expose the muscle." Such a standard applies to every woman, the author warns, "no matter what shape you're born with."[85] A similar article on body-sculpting features a close-up of a woman's firmly shaped butt, grabbed by her own hand, which bears an expensive-looking ring. The copy at the corner of the page explains: "A firm fundament announces to the world that the owner controls her own destiny—and can wear an ass-grabbing thong with aplomb."[86]

The popularity of body-sculpting among economically elite women suggests the multiple ironies through which the ideal female body is ritually produced. Women, who are generally born with a higher ratio of fat on their bodies, are seen to perfect themselves in proportion to the amount of fat they eradicate from their bodies, especially those parts of their bodies seen to mark them as "female" (hips, buttocks, stomach, thighs). That breasts are supposed to stay inflated and plump while the rest of the body is flattened and trimmed underlines the unattainability (aside from surgical alteration) of this bodily ideal. Muscles, which have traditionally been associated with masculinity and working-class life, are transcribed onto female bodies to signify social privilege: these are bodies whose "owners" have time and money to spend at the health club.[87]

Women of color, who have largely been excluded from the public sphere except when their labor was needed for jobs that nobody else wanted to do, now have role models like black fitness pro Victoria Johnson encouraging them to "shape up for summer without ever leaving home." A growing portion of the $78 million that diet companies spend on advertising is now targeting black and Latina women, especially those who are believed to be upwardly aspiring and mobile.[88]

Beneath their egalitarian veneer, the promises of Culture Lite create an association between the fat-free body, material privilege, and individual self-control. A magazine ad for Nestle's dark chocolate fudge diet product called "Sweet Success" illustrates this nexus. The ad features a slender female torso wearing an elegant black dress. The figure is outlined to convey the image of a paper doll: depthless, playful, and, ultimately, headless. Given popular definitions of female "success" today, losing weight is not only a gendered practice; it is also racially, generationally, heterosexually, and economically inflected. Market research profiles of the typical dieter, a woman who is white, urban, married, employed, well educated, financially sound, and between the age of twenty-five and forty-four, underline this point.[89]

The belief that undergirds the call to slenderness, that everybody can and should get fit—"no matter what shape you're born with"—ignores women's uneven access to the cultural "goods" that the fat-free body requires. Neither the time nor the accoutrements through which middle- and upper-class bodies are trimmed (health clubs, personal trainers, home exercise equipment and videos) are easily affordable to women from lower income brackets. Even exercise that appears to be free, such as walking or jogging, is a limited option for those who live in neighborhoods where simply being outside is unsafe.[90] Commercial diet foods are expensive, and so-called healthy or low-fat products usually cost more, even though they are often cheaper to produce.[91] As it turns out, creating a fat-free female body is far from free; and despite occasional moments of color, Culture Lite is very white.

As more and more girls and women turn to weight loss as a strategy for making meaning out of the inequities and contradictions of their lives, as consumer markets encourage them to shape up and burn fat "without ever leaving home," as elite women worship and imitate an ideal defined through economic and racial exploitation, as minority females join the majority in hating their bodies, as weight-loss industries' profits get fatter by making female bodies and imaginations smaller, those with critical consciousness and religious faith need to take a serious look at what is really eing gained and lost in the saving promises of Culture Lite.

Reinventing Womanhood: "Is This a New Religion?"

A few years ago, I came across a magazine ad for Avia running shoes whose text captures the spirit of this chapter's inquiry. "Is This a New Religion?" the bold-faced copy asks its readers. The central image of the two-page ad features a young, white, taut, and sweating female body, dressed in a leotard, arms extended in a gesture that recalls a crucifix. This image is flanked by two others: on one side, the same sweating woman bent over and lifting weights, muscles and bosom accentuated by a bluish haze; on the other, a close-up of the shoes cast in the same mystifying light. Together these images form a triptych, but the religious motifs do not stop there. In the upper corners of each page, the ad addresses its own query:

> This is not about guilt. It's about joy. Strength. The revival of the spirit. I come here seeking redemption in sweat. And it is here I am forgiven my sinful calories. Others may never understand my dedication. But for me, fitness training is something much more powerful than exercise. It is what keeps my body healthy. It is what keeps my mind clear. And it is where I learn the one true lesson. To believe in myself. *Avia.*

On an obvious level, this text illustrates the affinities between contemporary diet and fitness rituals and certain terms and beliefs of traditional Christianity. More subtly, however, it suggests that women's subordination within traditional religion makes them prime candidates for this "secular" substitute. Defined through an ostensibly progressive rejection of biblical religion's most notoriously harmful features, its degradation of women and the body, this commercial alternative proffers a new ultimate point of reference, Womanhood Herself: revived and redeemed, made powerful and clear through a diligently trained and slender body. The image juxtaposes a stereotypical view of Christianity (characterized by guilt, damnation, and belief in female weakness) with a liberal vision of "a New Religion" (defined by joy, redemption, and affirmation of female strength). As such, this ad speaks to those whose needs for a sense of meaning remain unfulfilled by the promises of traditional religion and whose dreams have been further delayed or lost in the shuffle of a rapidly changing and unevenly conflicted world.

The question that the Avia ad raises is not simply *whether* women's pursuit of physical perfection constitutes a new religion but also *what kind* of religion this pursuit turns out to be. For in the end, this "alternative" salvation myth has much in common with the oppressive paradigms and beliefs it seems to replace.

The problem with this "new religion" is not that it fails to create a sense of meaning but that the meanings it generates are perniciously narrow. The fat-free female form and the ritualizing pursuit thereof reinstate both the privilege of women who are white, middle- and upper-class, young, and heterosexual and the privilege of men who, by contrast, are not "called" to identify and value themselves through their bodies. The narrowness of such ideals and practices, along with the reductive logic and controlling ethos they presume, helps sustain a sociosymbolic system that fails to nourish the diversity and complexity of humans' searches for meaning.

That the salvation myth of female slenderness fails to deliver the redemption it promises does not necessarily stifle its authority and allure. In the absence of imaginative and tangible alternatives, the symbolic beliefs and rituals that comprise this slender plan of salvation acquire an even greater significance. For girls and women who find no other way of dealing with their anxieties and longings, no alternative means for expressing their experiences of confusion, injustice, and pain, these banal beliefs and daily disciplines become exceedingly important. For them, what is lost is not weight but faith: faith in one's body and in the world, faith in others and in anything larger than the self. This loss is not merely a metaphysical eclipse of meaning. The lack of trust that some girls and women experience is so thoroughly embodied that it turns into a life-threatening loss of hope. This loss is embedded in the struggles of girls and women who become anorexic and bulimic.

Four

UNIVERSES OF MEANING,
WORLDS OF PAIN

The Struggles of Anorexic and Bulimic Girls and Women

Throughout much of Christian history, theology has been largely assumed to be the business of a select few: those who sit in ivory towers, those who put on priestly collars, those whose heroic feats or creative genius give rise to seemingly timeless questions about ultimate meaning and value. Perhaps the presumed loftiness of such queries has contributed to their ill fate in the United States today, where they are often relegated to the universe of the individual self, or treated with absolute assurances within the public sphere, or bought and sold in the interests of consumer capitalism. In this context, such questions are either too private or too general, too volatile or too irrelevant, too worthless or too profitable to merit serious and sustained reflection.

Meanwhile, many people find themselves with few resources for dealing with the vicissitudes of their lives, for mediating their griefs and joys, for formulating wonderings and living with uncertainties, for challenging dehumanizing forces and imagining how things might be different. But concerns about the meaning of life do not simply disappear when they become inaudible and unarticulated. Sometimes their burial sites become the grounds for more drastic and desperate solutions. Some who are conditioned to do so try to resolve them by doing violence to others. Those with different social training often turn against themselves.

Perhaps our inability to detect the spiritual hungers that girls' and women's eating problems intimate has a lot to do with the way we have learned to see, with what we have learned to look for. By "we" I mean especially the producers of formal knowledge, whether "religious" or "secular." We, whose primary tools for understanding ourselves and our world often presume and create an absolute distinction between religious and secular ways of knowing. Such a distinction not only obscures the symbolic and ritualizing processes through which meanings are negotiated (by both "us" and "them") but also occludes the ambiguous effects of these processes: their capacity to enhance and/or deplete the quality of life on Earth.

My analysis of the beliefs and rituals through which eating problems develop suggests that this ambiguity pervades the search for meaning beyond the scope of traditional religion. Although the salvation myth of female slenderness can foster a sense of agency, purpose, and belonging, its strategies and ideals are precarious weapons against meaninglessness and pain. Few females are totally immune to the idealization of female slenderness that permeates this culture's dominant vision of womanhood. For some, however, the narrow lines of this ideal come to signify much more than the culturally sanctioned shape of womanhood. For some, such lines delineate an extremely narrow road to salvation, providing the symbolic and ritual means whereby the spiritual yearning for something more becomes a holy crusade for something absolute.

I have argued that the symbols, rituals, and beliefs through which girls and women strive to reduce their appetites and bodies constitute a "secular" plan of salvation and that this plan draws on the patriarchal legacy of traditional Christianity. I continue this analysis now by focusing on the very serious problems to which this salvation scheme can lead: anorexia and bulimia. This analysis examines the universes of meaning that anorexic and bulimic women symbolically and ritually build and the reductive strategies for their construction.

Making Meaning Out of Meaning Making: Interlude

In July 1994, I was consumed with the task of trying to articulate some of the theoretical assumptions behind my interpretation of eating disorders. Caught in a web of concepts, categories, and theories, I was first surprised, then saddened, when a friend pointed me to an obituary in the New York Times: "Christy Henrich, 22, Gymnast Plagued by Eating Disorders." Next to the article describing the brief life and slow death of this Olympic hopeful was a picture of Henrich performing on the balance beam, one leg pulled above her head in a pose of hyperflexibility, as if her body had no limits, as if her spirit yearned to fly. Yet precisely such limits, especially the physical weakness brought on by years of struggle with anorexia and bulimia, forced her to retire from gymnastics in 1991. By the middle of 1993, she weighed sixty pounds. "Cause of death," the newspaper read, quoting hospital reports: "Multiple organ system failure."[1]

I had never heard of Christy Henrich. My surprise at reading this story and imagining her struggle was more of a recollection. I remembered what it felt like to go for days without eating, then to be unable to stop myself. I thought about the numerous accounts of girls' and women's struggles with food and their bodies that I had read and analyzed—stories of unfathomable yearnings and intense fears, of irrecoverable losses and unbelievable resilience. In a way, my attempt to understand seemed to have distanced me from my own previous experience and from the sufferings of those whose problems I deem to reinterpret. In my effort to highlight the desire for freedom and connection that eating problems bespeak (if not scream), it had become easy to forget one crucial thing: some girls and women die from them. Moreover, based on the stories I have read, those who do not die frequently experience their lives as a kind of living hell: isolated, trapped, meaningless.

Amid these stories, Henrich's battle with anorexia and bulimia seemed to me to be not entirely unique—except for the publicity it received. And such public attention is more than an incidental aside. For it points to (without pointing to) Henrich's status as part of a cultural elite, not simply by virtue of her athletic achievements but also because of her white skin and relative affluence. As with the death of the popular singer Karen Carpenter,[2] this attention obscures as much as it illuminates insofar as it circulates a picture of eating disorders as epitomized by the most extreme cases (those that culminate in death), while it inadvertently perpetuates stereotypes about who gets these problems (excessively privileged, high-achieving white girls) and why (distorted body image, low self-esteem). Perhaps most important, the language used to explain the tragedy—language that simultaneously produces its meaning—suppresses the unsettling questions that the fatal conclusion of Henrich's suffering raise. "Cause of death," we are informed: "Multiple organ system failure."

Continuums: From Healthy to Harmful, from Ordinary to Ultimate

There is a striking and in my view troubling resemblance between the search for certitude that guides many professional attempts to understand the struggles of anorexic and bulimic women and the strategies for making meaning that these struggles employ. By focusing on the symbolic and ritual processes whereby such meanings are created, my discussion thus far challenges both the quest for unambiguous explanations and the army of models and methods on which it draws. In so doing, it unsettles the common view that eating disorders are clearly defined personal pathologies that affect only a narrow slice of the female population and that are caused by certain essential and/or external forces, be they chemical, familial, or societal.

The prominence of this standard view inhibits our capacity to see and effectively respond to these problems. In the course of writing this book, friends and acquaintances frequently approached me with unsolicited anecdotes about someone they knew who suffered from anorexia or bulimia. Perhaps the most recurrent feature of these stories was the surprise people felt upon learning that someone close to them has or had a problem. "I can't believe I was so naive," a friend told me when she found out that her sister had been bulimic for twelve years. "I knew she worried about her weight and food, but so did I when I was younger. I had no idea she had a problem." Another friend told me he was "shocked and hurt" when he found out that his female partner had been bulimic for most of their three-year relationship. Like a lot of people, his surprise was coupled with deep regret for not having been able to offer support sooner.

The other sides of these stories—those told by anorexics and bulimics themselves—record the secret anguish and despair that rituals of starving and bingeing engender. Often the similarity between these rituals and those considered "normal" in this society makes it possible for women and girls to engage in them for years without calling attention to themselves. "People began staring when I hit eighty-nine pounds," an anorexic woman recalls. Even then, she saw such stares as signs of admiration and envy rather than an indication that something was wrong.[3] It is even easier for bulimics to conceal their food rituals because many of them do not lose or gain noticeable amounts of weight. A woman who vomited three to four times a day for five years recalls: "Five years I lived in shame, in my own little world, keeping secrets and telling lies to everyone I loved. . . . No one knew and I never got help."[4] The painful secrecy surrounding these "little worlds" can be intensified for those whose racial, economic, or sexual identity does not fit professional or popular stereotypes of the eating-disordered woman. A young black woman explains: "I had been suffering from anorexia with intermittent episodes of bulimia for almost two years. Because I was a dancer, people expected me to be thin, and because I am Black, no one suspected an eating disorder."[5]

Despite the tremendous suffering surrounding their practices, many anorexic and bulimic women manage to carry on with their day-to-day lives for extended periods of time. On the surface, there is nothing terribly unusual about their attitudes toward food and their bodies. And in a society where "high-achieving" women are expected to worry about their weight, it is not surprising that anorexics and bulimics typically excel in their endeavors—as straight-A students, exceptional athletes, successful career women, and so on—at least in the early stages of their illness. Indeed, the bourgeois values (such as self-control and material privilege) through which such "achievement" is defined make it possible for anorexic and bulimic bodies to pass as "healthy." A woman who reduced her 5' 7" body from 140 to 116 pounds through rituals of starving, bingeing, and purging recalls her doctor congratulating her for being " 'the only one in your family who has a handle on their weight.' " Oblivious to her health-destroying tactics, he encouraged her: " 'Keep it up! You're doing fine!' "[6]

Scientifically oriented discourse is particularly inarticulate regarding the extent to which anorexia and bulimia develop out of the symbolic codes and ritualizing practices that cultural authorities recommend as "normal" and "healthy." Remarkably, even the most celebrated experts in the field fail to see eating problems as part of a larger continuum of socially sanctioned disciplines that diminish female flesh. In her pioneering work with anorexics, the famous psychiatrist Hilde Bruch made little mention of the cultural underpinnings of the "relentless pursuit of thinness" that she believed masked her patients' "underlying problems."[7] Bruch's focus on family dynamics as the main context in which a girl's relationship to her body develops not only failed to examine the patriarchal quality of these dynamics but also prevented her from hearing the public/popular beliefs and meanings that pervaded her patients' "personal" discourses. "When I started I was not thinking of losing much weight," an anorexic woman told Bruch. "I never thought of losing as much as twenty pounds." At the time of her interview, she had lost nearly fifty pounds and was using laxatives, diuretics, and other medications to "help the weight-loss along." Despite her famished condition, this woman's recollection of the early stages of her anorexia is astonishingly matter-of-fact: "I always admired slim people," she said, "then I wanted to be slim myself. I went on a diet, and I feel very normal now."[8]

To highlight the continuity between anorexic and bulimic rituals and the eating practices of "normal" girls and women is not to erase the distinction altogether. Dieting is not the same as anorexia, however similar the reductive logic underlying these practices may be. The stories of anorexic and bulimic girls and women suggest that the transition from "healthy" to hazardous eating is marked by an increasingly involuntary absorption with food and body. For some, what begins as a "normal" preoccupation develops into an all-encompassing fixation, a kind of ultimate concern. "Five years ago, I went on a 'diet' that lasted a year and half," a woman writes:

> During that time (and, to a lesser extent, for three or four years after), I was so obsessed with controlling and limiting what I ate that my life revolved around counting and restricting calories. . . . Losing sixty-five pounds was not my original goal, but as I lost more and more weight I began not to have any goal at all: I just continued dieting and losing— until I weighed about eighty-five pounds.[9]

Variations of the phrases "My life revolved around what I ate" and "My whole life is centered around wanting to be thin"[10] permeate the stories of girls and women with eating disorders. "Food became an obsession with me," another woman explains:

> I'd sit in class and plan my meals (if you could call them that) and figure out exactly how many calories were in every bite I put in my mouth each day. . . . I was so obsessed with [food] that I thought about

it every second. I thought that I couldn't eat anything or I'd gain a pound—an ounce. If I did splurge and eat some extra mushrooms on my salad, I'd plan two hours of exercise to work it off.[11]

Despite the apparent deliberateness of self-starving, bingeing, and purging rituals, the transition from dieting to dangerous eating is at least partially marked by a loss of control. The character of this loss varies, depending on both the severity and kind of eating problem. For those whose dieting practices crescendo into anorexia, refusing to eat gives way to an inability to eat—or what is described as an inability to eat: "I just couldn't eat food anymore," one anorexic woman explains. "I can't make myself eat, even if I'm hungry," another insists.[12] Yet a closer look at anorexic women's stories reveals not so much an inability to eat as an inability to focus on anything other than the food they feel compelled to deny. In fact, the loss of control that accompanies the development of anorexia often leads to the breakdown of such extreme restrictions and the emergence of bulimic patterns.

When describing this breakdown, many anorexic-bulimic women emphasize what sociocultural interpretations of their problems do not, namely, their physical aspects. "The body gets to a point of starvation where it will autonomously eat to save itself," Marya Hornbacher explains.[13] Women often depict their bulimic rituals as responding to the insatiable hunger that years of rigid dieting instilled. "I had enough of starving myself," a woman explains, "so much that I just went in the opposite direction." The progression of this woman's problems is fairly common: "I went from starving myself, to eating normally and throwing it up, to overeating and throwing up." Such patterns became more ingrained in the course of two years: "I started off throwing up a few times a week, then once a day, then three to four times a day to finally after everything I ate . . . I really wanted to stop but I just couldn't."[14] Eventually, repetitive cycles of bingeing and purging caused this woman to regain the weight she lost during her anorexic phase, which reinforced her efforts to reduce, which led to more bingeing and purging. Part of what makes these cycles so viciously difficult to break is their entrenchment in physical processes, sensations, and rhythms. Another woman explains:

> Whenever I deviated from my planned meals by as much as a bite, or felt the slightest bit too full, I simply downed a handful of laxatives and waited for them to clean me out. What the resultant emptiness usually triggered, however, was the desire to eat again. I reasoned that I hadn't retained any of the calories so I could afford to eat again. It was an ugly catch-22 situation out of which I couldn't find my way.[15]

The self-perpetuating quality of bulimia can also add to its longevity: "Starve and binge. Starve and binge. It was the pattern of my life for so many years."[16]

Many women whose self-imposed starvation backfires into bulimia say they prefer the anorexic phase of their illness. "I distinctly did not want to be seen as bulimic," Hornbacher recalls. "I wanted to be an anoretic. I was on a mission to be another sort of person, a person whose passions were ascetic rather than hedonistic." This preference reflects a widespread cultural association between feminine virtue and self-control. In view of this association, bulimia is seen as a step down from anorexia. Having experienced both, Hornbacher reflects:

> Bulimia, of course, gives in to the temptations of the flesh, while anorexia is anointed, is a complete removal of the bearer from the material realm. . . . In truth, bulimics do not usually bear the hallowed stigmata of a skeletal body. Their self-torture is private, far more secret and guilty than is the visible statement of anoretics, whose whittled bodies are admired as the epitomes of feminine beauty.

In a society that beatifies women who rise above their needs and cravings—especially their desire to eat—it is not surprising that anorexics are often quietly held in awe, compared to bulimics, who, in Hornbacher's view, are typically seen as just plain "gross."[17]

Sometimes extended periods of food deprivation give way to out-of-control eating that is not "compensated" by purging methods or that is offset by milder forms of bulimic behavior (such as renewed dieting or exercise). While there is debate in psychiatric circles as to whether this kind of eating problem—dubbed "binge-eating disorder"—constitutes a pathology in its own right,[18] there is little question, based on women's own accounts, that binge eating can be physically and emotionally debilitating. "The psychological pain of these experiences was devastating," a woman says of her inability to contain her appetite. "My life was totally out of control and I barely felt human anymore."[19] Like many women who eat compulsively, this woman had a long history of dieting, which created what she called a "cumulative hunger." Such histories often begin when a large-bodied girl is instructed or coerced to lose weight. Years of chronic deprivation lower the body's metabolic rate, leading to rapid weight gain once the restriction is broken, compounding a woman's sense of worthlessness in a culture that demonizes obesity, and leading to further restrictive measures, which only intensify her desire to eat.[20]

If it is impossible to understand girls' and women's struggles with anorexia and bulimia apart from prevailing cultural norms and social conditions, it is also misleading to view these problems in isolation from each other. In the words of one anorexic-bulimic woman: "The events and sensations that had motivated me to consume were the same ones that incited me to go hungry."[21] Despite their symptomatic variances, anorexia and bulimia are deeply related. These problems represent the far end of a continuum of rituals, symbols, and beliefs that constitute this culture's prevailing myth of what it means to be a woman and what we must do to achieve salvation. I do not treat them separately because even when they do not physically overlap in a girl or woman's experience, they are connected by the reductive logic and controlling ethos that fund their meanings and by the spiritual crises they aim to mediate.

"Multiple Organ System Failure": When Meanings Become Meaningless

What I refer to as "spiritual crises" can be seen to play a decisive role in the transition from "healthy" to harmful eating patterns. In girls' and women's accounts of their struggles with food, these crises are not typically formulated in terms of traditional theological quandaries (such as questions about the existence of God or the nature of the Trinity). In most cases, they are articulated in terms of a profound feeling of emptiness, a sense of alienation, powerlessness, and despair. This sense points to a basic loss of meaning: an inability to experience oneself as connected and one's life as valuable.

From a theological perspective, it is tempting to interpret these crises in the classic terms of Paul Tillich. A leading voice of twentieth-century Protestant liberalism, Tillich saw the eclipse of meaning that haunts the lives of modern persons as a sign of their "tragic estrangement" from their basic spiritual ground. He referred to this ground as "ultimate concern," which he saw as the "substance" of religion, for which "God" is the name or concept. While this definition of religion enabled Tillich to see the "religious dimensions" of all human experiences and cultural creations, it also led him to overlook the socially constructed character of his own concepts and claims.[22] Tillich failed to notice that the presumed gulf between human essence and existence—between our ultimate and our everyday concerns— is symbolically produced and variously experienced by persons in diverse social locations who have unequal access to cultural resources and power. As a result, Tillich did not see the extent to which a person's spiritual crisis—his or her loss of a sense of meaning in life—is rooted in experiences that are invariably shaped by circumstance and history.

To understand the extremes to which some girls and women go in their efforts to contain their appetites and bodies, we must not only see the hunger for meaning that these efforts aim to feed; we must also recognize the social and political circumstances that contribute to their pangs. For many girls and women today, the feeling that life may not be worth living is rooted in the frustration and disappointment they experience in the face of unjust social conditions. For some, experiences of racism, sexism, ageism, poverty, and/or homophobia result in the sense of emptiness that food and body obsessions function to fill. Others, who by virtue of their social privilege can afford to buy into the dominant culture's values, may become disenchanted with the illusory rewards of their purchases. Other vexing or oppressive experiences—from the death of a loved one, to the pain of divorce, to the damages incurred through emotional, sexual, and physical abuse—can result in a loss of faith that life has meaning. Though the events and experiences that give rise to feelings of emptiness may be extremely traumatic, they are not necessarily out of the ordinary. Assaults on girls' and women's well-being, from the insidious and subtle to the downright brutal, are absurdly quotidian in the United States today.

When the circumstances of a girl or woman's life prohibit her from seeing a "bigger picture"—a view that reminds her of the possibility of something more—she may find herself resorting to whatever symbolic or ritual provisions are available to her, even if those provisions deepen the hunger they are supposed to fill. The meanings created by ordinary weight-reducing practices become toxic when there seem to be no other strategies and visions for imbuing life with a sense of meaning and when there are no communal bonds for supporting different ways of seeing and being. Lacking imaginative and tangible alternatives, some girls and women cling to the ideals and disciplines most readily available to them, even when their meanings become meaningless. For those who are unable to tap into other sources of strength and truth, those whose experiences of pain and frustration remain unspoken and unseen, this meaninglessness becomes a crisis with which many girls and women have no way to deal. "I turned to my eating disorder," Hornbacher explains, "because I had never, ever figured out how to fucking *deal*."[23]

As a strategy for dealing with pain and emptiness, some girls and women imaginatively construct their own little universes of meaning. "There was a tremendous amount of anger, pain that I didn't deal with," an anorexic women recalls. "So I just sort of went into my own little world . . . And then that world became totally about eating and weight."[24] To see the spiritual dimensions of these "little worlds" is to notice the struggles for meaning they wage in the face of suffering and confusion. Sometimes these struggles are articulated in explicitly Christian idioms and terms, suggesting a link between the imaginative worlds of anorexia and bulimia and the paradigms and values of this culture's dominant religion. But even in cases where their language is not explicitly "religious," it is possible to see both the implicit religious function that these symbolic universes serve and the dogmatic logic and controlling ethos through which they are constructed. Rather than look for an unconditioned truth, whether in the form of an experiential core or a theological ideal, my discussion below aims to analyze and assess the processes whereby anorexics and bulimics become imprisoned in the worlds they create in an effort to be free.

Transcendent Values: The Language of Perfection

The strategies used to build such worlds take their cues from popular models and practices of womanhood. For most females in the United States today, losing weight derives its value in relation to such visions and the aesthetic-moral-scientific codes of conduct surrounding them. For those who become anorexic and/or bulimic, however, the virtue of slenderness becomes less directly tied to prevailing ideals of womanhood, even though the dogmatic logic that such ideals embody provides the rules for composing much narrower regimes of truth. "I began to follow a strict diet," a woman recalls:

> I carefully counted every calorie I ate, as well as every calorie I burned. My limit was 1,000 calories, countered by a burning of 1,600 to 2,300 calories. I measured a successful day by an empty and growling stomach when I climbed into bed, safe from further temptation. A supersuccessful day meant I burned at least a thousand more calories than I consumed.[25]

By exaggerating an ordinary ritual of womanhood (calculating calories), this woman constructs an "otherworldly" system of values, an underground theater of moral meaning in which the drama of her starvation acquires an all-encompassing significance, in spite of and because of its minimizing codes.

"At first, 500 calories daily. Then 200, then 100. Then 100 every other day. Then once a week," Hornbacher narrates the beginnings of her anorexic struggle.[26] If such measures far exceed those recommended to women as "healthy," that is partially the point. By stretching the common rites of dieting into uncommon measures of deprivation, an anorexic creates what appears to be an alternative frame of reference, even as she remains within the parameters of acceptable womanhood. This frame is composed of symbols, rituals, and beliefs that extend, to the point of apparent contradiction, the standards and disciplines that orient the lives of "normal" women. Within such a frame, the desire to eschew the undistinguished plight of "ordinary" women is spoken through the belief that one is too fat: "Everybody says I'm skinny," an 86-pound anorexic woman explains, "But I'm not skinny enough. I must be just right, because I want to be a model and actress. I hate my body; it's too big. I hate food. I have to have my stomach flatter. My arm has two percent body fat, but I want it all gone. I'm just too fat."[27] Following its lines to their logical extreme, this woman's language reinstates a narrow model of womanhood even as it mocks the emptiness of this ideal. At the same time, its function is clear: the creation of a sense of transcendent value in the face of insignificance, of meaning in the mirror of an impossible ideal.

The desire for a sense of value beyond the measures and expectations of "ordinary" women is seen in another woman's story of her battle with anorexia, the language of which recalls the biblical theme of being "chosen." She refused to eat, this young woman told her therapist, because she believed that "more is expected" of her, that somehow she is "morally obliged" to give more: "Only when absolutely everything has been given, when I really cannot give any more, have I done my duty." The sense of righteousness she derived from her "undernourished and overtired" body set her apart from and above ordinary persons. "Some time ago I saw what a 'not special' life implies," she explained. "It implies that I don't need to do such hard work." Although she admitted that this "work" cost her the freedom it was supposed to gain, the sacrifice gave her a sense of moral superiority and righteousness: "Ordinary people are not trapped because they are not brilliant in everything . . . I noticed that ordinary people are more happy and carefree. To me, 'good enough' was condemnation instead of the state of satisfaction." This woman's value system is tied to her eschatological vision, her otherworldly vision of the "end of time":

> The more weight I lost, the more I became convinced that I was on the right way. I wanted to know what was beyond the ordinary living. . . . Abstinence was just in preparation for special revelations; it was like the things the saints and mystics had done. I wanted to be praised for being special . . . to be held in awe for what I was doing. I found out that it was hard to be recognized by other people as an enlightened person. . . . I didn't want anybody to know it, but I was convinced that one day I would get the mystical insight—I was waiting for the day of the great Revelation.[28]

This woman's use of religious language to describe/construct her anorexic world of meaning, though especially vivid, is not altogether unique. In her memoir, Marya Hornbacher compares the suffering that her self-starving rituals engendered with the self-inflicted tortures of medieval female saints, "their flagellums, their beds of nails, their centuries-late apologies for Eve who doomed all women to the pains of the flesh by giving in to the pleasures of that flesh. They lacerate their own flesh in penance for Eve, for the sins of the world, which they shoulder as their own." Separated by centuries of time and circumstance, Hornbacher nonetheless sees a connection between her own self-mortifying struggle and that of holy women like Margaret of Cortona (who starved herself to death in 1297). Both sought power through physical pain and penance; both made a virtue of torturing their flesh. Considering God, Hornbacher determined that "he, if they were on speaking terms, would tell her to starve for general sins," sins that entered into the world through the appetite of a woman.[29]

Not all anorexics and bulimics employ such explicitly religious references to describe and interpret the "revelations" and "holiness" that their hunger rituals engender. These women's perceptions are not generalizable. My point in examining them is neither to identify their essentially religious content nor to locate their universal meaning. Rather, I want to highlight the continuities they suggest between the salvation myth of female slenderness and certain ethical paradigms of the Christian tradition, particularly those that define female sanctity through a series of moral oppositions, creating an ideal of holiness that can be attained only through the superhuman sacrifice of a chosen few.

Traditional religious ideals of female sacrifice, suffering, and self-denigration are sometimes very thinly veiled in anorexic and bulimic girls' and women's quests for a sense of transcendent worth. One woman recalls the self-scrutinizing rituals she used to perform in front of a mirror as a teenager:

> My ribs jut forward as my stomach sinks inward, letting air out until it's almost concave, a hollowed-out sphere. I don't know where my intestines go, where my liver flees, what can be left between skin and spine. It's so spare I believe I can push right through, touching bones, muscles, my structural essence . . . oddly I feel as if I've been cleansed. . . . I wonder idly if sacrifice is at the heart of my life; if so, my body has the proper penitential look.[30]

In a symbolic system where female lack of appetite is a visible sign of invisible virtue, a woman's desire to eat signals the epitome of moral decline. "I felt that eating was a dirty, sinful act that I wanted to share with no one," a young bulimic woman writes. "When one of my parents did see me eating I would start, and, as if I'd been caught doing something wrong, I'd try to gulp down the morsels whole."[31] The shame that anorexic and bulimic women typically assign to their desire to eat—a shame that has been theologically inscribed on female appetite through the legacy of Eve—adds to the ostensibly private constellation of their moral universes. Despite their links to familiar conventions of traditional religion and their embeddedness in the language of Culture Lite, the sin of eating, the penance of purging, and the sanctity of fasting are experienced as a personal battle between good and evil, between worth and insignificance.

The social underpinnings and cultural ethos behind such "personal" battles become clear when we consider the language of "perfection" that anorexics and bulimics commonly employ. "I wanted to be a perfect, slim model size," a young woman states. "So I just cut down on what I ate." When she reached her goal of losing fifteen pounds, however, this woman decided to continue her regime, until she weighed only seventy pounds: "It wasn't that hard to lose weight," she explained, "and besides, if I got under 'perfect' I could eat everything."[32] The very banality of this quest for "perfection" masks the classic theological assumptions through which it is construed, including a notion of the highest good as set apart from the ordinary world of conflict, fragility, and flux, and a view of salvation as the compensatory reward of extraordinary sacrifice and self-denial.

If the craving for "perfection" is a recurrent idiom in anorexics' and bulimics' discourses, it is also a common theme in the literature devoted to explaining these problems. Psychologically minded writers trace an anorexic or bulimic woman's "perfectionism" to a host of underlying "distorted concepts," especially an "enigmatic" lack of self-esteem. In Hilde Bruch's view, the anorexic/bulimic woman's desire to be perfect responds to a deeper misconception: "Deep down, every anorexic is convinced that basically she is inadequate, low, mediocre, inferior, and despised by others."[33] However accurate this clinical portrait may be, its experiential focus creates the impression that perfection is the actual goal and low self-worth the driving force behind anorexic and bulimic behavior—as if the desire to be perfect were a natural response to the problem of low self-worth, as if low self-esteem were itself the original cause of such problems.

Such an analysis fails to examine the cultural legacies and conventions, as well as the cultural logic and ethos, through which the language of perfection makes sense. This language is meaningful both in relation to popular visions of womanhood that define female salvation through bodily perfection and in relation to social conditions that variously impede women's struggles for a sense of value in other arena. The language of perfection is both pragmatic and persuasive in a culture where a girl or woman must do exceptional things "to be recognized by other people as an enlightened person," to be valued for something more than her body. The very emptiness of such a superlative creates a space wherein a girl can dream of a world in which she matters. While the size of "perfection" varies in the symbolic worlds that anorexics and bulimics fabricate, its strategic aim is fairly steady: that of saving them from the common female fate of cultural insignificance. "Even now it is very difficult for me to go into a store and have to say 'Yes, I want a size 5,' " a former anorexic says, "because to me that seems so common. . . . All my friends seem to wear size 5 or 7, and I didn't like just being one of the crowd."[34]

The language of perfection speaks to both the pressure to fit in and the desire to stand out. Either way, the seemingly transcendent values it creates become tools for managing a variety of impossible, perplexing, and/or unfair situations. "I was sick of being capable, focused, competent, mature," Hornbacher recalls of the pressures she felt at an elite high school. "Part of me just wanted to stay home in bed and read books. But I was damned if I'd admit it. So I starved myself instead."[35] Another girl's anorexic discipline provided a sense of purpose amid the confusion she felt when her father died: "I was searching to find exactly what I was supposed to do, what I was here for. I felt that the way to get at it was through all this chastising yourself, being very disciplined, in a sense being 'perfect.' "[36] Still another woman depicts her refusal to eat as both a means of rebellion against her parents and a way of fending off her "sensation and experience of despair," her "fear of being alone, of feeling abandoned, sort of being like a helpless old woman, worn out, with nothing left."[37] As this last fear suggests, the seemingly transcendent sense of worth that the language of perfection creates is, in the end, perfectly compatible with the measures of the culture it means to contest.

To understand the spiritual hungers that such a value aims to fill, we must ask not simply "What does the desire to be perfect repress or represent?" but also "What practical function does such an unattainable ideal serve in the lives of girls and women today? How does an anorexic or bulimic woman's search for a sense of value and self-worth come to be oriented around such a stringent ideal? What makes the pursuit of 'perfection' so compelling for some girls and women? What alternative values does this paradigm of value conceal? Who benefits from the habits of thought and desire that this model of impossibility engenders?"

Such questions shift the focus from individual pathology to social patterns and values and to the unspoken conflicts and unmet needs that permeate their relationships. Decoding the language of perfection suggests that the "low self-esteem" that is typically seen to *cause* eating disorders is the *effect* of living in a culture that fails to nourish girls' and women's desires for a sense of something sacred. The worlds of meaning that anorexics and bulimics create in their search for a sense of ultimate value rely on a cultural ethos that turns moral authority into moral superiority, while defining salvation through promises of otherworldly perfection. The transcendent values that they construct by taking the normative measures of womanhood to their logical extreme aim to negotiate such promises, even as they end up swallowing their emptiness.

Transcendent Power: The Language of Control

The continuity between the "little worlds" of meaning that anorexic and bulimic girls and women construct and the values of the world they aim to transcend is clouded by the authority they experience in designating meanings. Their symbolic worlds thus also provide a seemingly transcendent source of power. "I was a goddess in my own little world," an anorexic-bulimic woman recalls, "meting out punishments and rewards for evil and virtuous behavior."[38] At the heart of these self-authorizing universes of meaning is a body capable of superhuman feats. "You don't notice you've entered a fantasy world," Hornbacher says. "You only know the exhilarating dizziness, the feeling that you could run, without stopping, for days." The strength she derived from her anorexic-bulimic rituals made her feel invulnerable to the needs of her body as well as the demands of others:

> You can't tell what hunger feels like anymore. You stop feeling pain, emotional and physical. If all else failed, if anyone found out I'd been faking my smarts, talents and brashness all along, at least I could say I was thin. If everyone left, I would have this. If anyone tried to control me, I could be stronger than them. No one could stop me from dying if I goddamn wanted to die.[39]

Refusing to eat or digest one's food as a strategy for exercising agency and power depends on the belief that food is exceedingly meaningful. "Food has too much significance," an anorexic woman states. "It is like a monster standing there waiting to attack me. It says 'I dare you to eat me.' "[40] However bizarre such beliefs may sound, they merely extend the terms of the salvation myth of female slenderness, especially the opposition between female virtue and pleasure that this myth assumes. This split is embedded in the binge-purge patterns of bulimics, particularly in the feelings of shame that their rituals produce. "When I was dieting," a woman explains, "I couldn't get enough food. I was too ashamed to eat all I wanted in public so I binged secretly. I couldn't stop, even when I was full, and often ate until it hurt. Because it was so hard to stop, I was afraid to start eating and would put off my first bite until late in the day."[41] This all-or-nothing approach to eating widens the gaps between a bulimic woman's "private" obsession, the popular beliefs and rituals through which it evolves, and the public world of power from which she feels excluded.

Sometimes the terms and strategies through which anorexic and bulimic women seek a transcendent source of power explicitly reference the models and tactics of traditional religion. One woman depicts her anorexic struggle through the Christian convention of martyrdom, with its nexus of suffering, righteousness, and power:

> The whole life is like you are carrying a cross—something heroic, something that is very difficult and demands admiration. I felt [that] doing something that was not hard was quite inconceivable; it would be lazy and despicable. Life was like the labors of Hercules—things he was forced to do though he didn't like them. That's what I felt life was—everything was a heavy duty thrown onto me.[42]

Although the protagonists of such spiritual heroism have traditionally been men, the sacrifice they are called to perform has been theologically inscribed as feminine. To paraphrase an insight of Jennifer Manlowe, the qualities that have been seen to make a good Christian, such as self-sacrifice and submission to authority, are the very qualities that define the conventional ideals and rites of womanhood.[43] At the same time, as the work of Nancy Jay suggests, ritual sacrifice has traditionally served a specific kind of religious function, namely, "as remedy for having been born of woman."[44]

The ambiguous quality of religious submission and self-denial as a means for exercising authority and obtaining public influence has a long history among women in the Christian tradition. Self-starvation and other ways of mortifying the flesh provided avenues for women who sought to exercise spiritual authority and experience supernatural power. This legacy echoes in the story of a present-day anorexic-bulimic woman:

> Now checking in at ninety-one pounds, I thrived on hunger, uneased when I was not satiated with my one-hundred calorie meal. I felt weightless, hollow, as if I could pass through tangible objects like a ghost. I was supernatural; removed from the cruel world, untouched by reality. I had conquered reality.[45]

The power produced through such ritualizing self-denial is the power to transcend the conflicts and cruelties of life in and from the female body. The sacrificial subtext of self-starvation appears in another woman's poetic rendition of her anorexic-bulimic struggle: "My body is too huge to heft up on the cross," the first stanza of the "crucifixion" begins. The ultimate sacrifice is complete when her "too huge" body has been "purified": "Clipped, spayed, and paper thin, / I glue my body to the cross. / Now then—a perfect fit."[46]

Such explicit Christian references point to the affinities between traditional models of female piety, on the one hand, and the beliefs and rites of contemporary anorexic and bulimic women, on the other. These affinities further suggest similarities between the model of power that shapes the anorexic-bulimic struggle and the dominant paradigm of patriarchal religious authority. In particular, the model of power that the salvation strategies of anorexic and bulimic women employ resembles the classic theological view of ultimate power as omnipotence: as a transcendent, invulnerable governing force that rules (by coercion if need be) over all that threatens its (or "His") dominion. Religious feminists have characterized this hierarchical form of power in various ways. Starhawk calls it "power-over"; Sallie McFague refers to it as "monarchical."[47] Though in its earthly forms this dominating kind of power has historically been reserved for those whose rules and methods it most closely resembles (elite males), its omnipresence has made it a pervasive if vacant dream of many who long for a greater sense of agency and purpose.

In the stories of anorexic and bulimic girls and women, this hierarchical model of power is apparent in the language of control. One woman's statement that refusing to eat "was the only thing I felt I could control in my life" echoes repeatedly in these narratives. "I felt like I had control of what I ate and what I did," another woman explains, "and that nobody was telling me what to do."[48] Still another woman recalls: "I felt powerful as an anorexic. Controlling my body yielded an illusion of control over my life. . . . I had reduced my world to a plate of steamed carrots, and over this tiny kingdom I proudly crowned myself queen."[49] A view of power as domination also shapes the struggles of bulimic women, despite the loss of control surrounding their cycles of bingeing and purging:

> Finally there was nothing left but bitter green bile. With a feeling of relief and accomplishment, I flushed the toilet and turned to the sink to wash my hands, splash cold water on my face and rinse the bile from my mouth. Meeting my own gaze in the mirror, I told myself Everything is under control.[50]

Such rhetoric does not simply defy the bulimic woman's reality, any more than it mirrors it; it *makes* that reality, wishing it into being, if only for an instant, along with the illusory agency it offers.

The desire for control that permeates the struggles of girls and women with eating disorders garnishes a lot of attention among experts in the field. Again following the lead of Bruch, psychological literature tends to depict this desire as a response to feelings of "helplessness" that anorexics and bulimics report.[51] Feminists offer more nuanced views of this desire as a logical reaction to the powerlessness women feel in a patriarchal culture. Insofar as they focus on the experience of wanting control, however, these views tend to rationalize, rather than problematize, the logic that eating problems employ: as if "control" were an actual, attainable end, as if the quest to conquer were a suitable solution to feelings of helplessness, as if such feelings themselves were the cause of eating problems.

By focusing on anorexic and bulimic girls' and women's experiences of wanting to be in control, both conventional and feminist analyses tend to overlook the practical functions and cultural paradigms that make this desire so meaningful. In this culture, the power of female starving, bingeing, and purging is the power of any language: the power to create reality, to wield meanings, to influence others. This power becomes precariously precious for those who have no other way of speaking and contesting the restrictions they experience: "As long as I didn't feel I could rebel in any other way," a bulimic woman explains, "the bingeing and purging was a violent release of my fears, frustrations, and anger."[52]

Young girls in particular have few words to name, much less question, the social norms that limit their freedom. "I can't think of anything that really made me angry," an anorexic woman says, describing her childhood to her therapist. Eventually, however, she remembered how voiceless she felt as a little girl:

> This was when I was much younger, and I'd sit at the table, you know, a little girl should be seen and not heard, and I'd sit there politely, and then there would be the discussion about business matters, and then they would start to argue and bicker. I would try to do anything to divert their attention.[53]

Eventually, "anything" included refusing to eat, an action that was supposed to speak louder than words, except that it blended so well with the grammar of upper-class femininity already in place within this girl's family system.

According to standard psychiatric literature, the desire for control is typically manifested in anorexics' "manipulative" behavior, particularly in their profuse displays of docility. Conventional wisdom follows Bruch's picture of anorexic girls as having "overcompliant" personalities, a result of their poorly developed "self-concepts." Some women do interpret their eating disorders as reflecting their intense desire to please: "I have this great unbelievable fear of people not liking me," an anorexic woman admits.[54] But to see this desire as rooted in a manipulative or docile personality is to ignore this culture's dominant iconographic and philosophical traditions, which define female pleasure as the art of pleasing others. Such an interpretation also discounts the experiences of some racial and ethnic minority females who are socialized to be assertive and self-directive within and beyond their family systems.[55] For these women, what appears to be obedience or assimilation to dominant (white) cultural norms of female slenderness may in fact mask an aggressive strategy for survival in a society marked by racial hierarchies and divisions.

What seems on the surface to be overcompliance may also function to disguise a history of unspoken injustices and failed resistances. "It's just that there wasn't any fairness," an anorexic woman remembers. "It just wasn't fair as a little girl. There wasn't any way of winning." Like many young girls, she lacked a vocabulary for linking this sense of unfairness to a wider social system, and her attempts to name and protest the injustice were also undercut by her family's (this culture's) hierarchical approach to authority: "You were wrong before you started. . . . Eventually I just didn't say anything. You wouldn't be accepted from what you said, or you'd be wrong and then you could be forced." As an adult, this woman developed anorexic rituals that gave her relief from feelings of helplessness and being misunderstood: "Now I have chosen the life I live. . . . I am really very disciplined, and if I believe something I really work hard at it. How much, how very much I enjoy the streamlinedness of it, the simplicity."[56]

Girls' and women's use of starving, bingeing, and/or purging as a means for exercising agency and authority must be seen against the backdrop of a society that continues to restrict their access to public voice and power. Indirectly, their historical exclusion from formal realms of religious power contributes to their role as priestesses, goddesses, and queens in their own imaginative counterparts. While girls and women are still generally (though variously) prohibited from making the laws that govern the social body, most of them are aptly positioned to manipulate the codes for ruling their own.

To understand the spiritual dimensions of anorexia and bulimia, we must ask not simply "Why do anorexic-bulimic girls and women want to control their bodies?" but also "How has the language of control become the most viable idiom for exercising agency and resisting domination?" This question suggests that neither the desire for control nor the sense of helplessness to which it responds is the *cause* of eating problems. These feelings are best seen as the *effect* of living in a culture that is guided by a logic of domination: a way of thinking-feeling-being that reduces power to control. Insofar as they embody this logic, women's searches for a deeper source of power and meaning perpetuate the painful legacies they mean to contest.

Transcendent Order: The Language of Body/Mind Division

The "streamlinedness" of the logic whereby women ritually starve, binge, and/or purge themselves into another world of meaning contributes to the rigid order of the universes they construct. This order is not simply the

product of an anorexic or bulimic woman's ideas; the contours of her imaginative world are established through rituals of bodily observance: "Discovering and rediscovering the flat, smooth lines of the flesh over my hips,
pelvic bone, ribs, thighs became an obsessive ritual, the first thing I did on
waking, the last thing before I slept."[57] Another woman describes similar
rites for mapping and securing the borders of her anorexic-bulimic body/
world:"I devised my own fat tests. I would look at my wrist and see if the
bone on my wrist was as prominent today as it had been yesterday. I mean
people would actually be thinking that I was in a conversation with them
and there I'd be measuring my fat."[58]

If the proximity of a girl's own body makes it an easily accessible resource for defining her own "reality," the cultural legitimacy of her bodily
focus makes it a permissible means for cultivating her own sense of order.
The concrete, empirical quality of these measures masks their imaginative
basis and symbolic function:

> One day, after a binge and purge, I went to the gym in search of a
> scale. Seventy. I got off the scale. I took off my belt and my shoes and
> got back on. Sixty-seven. I stood sideways, naked in the mirror, and
> realized that I literally had almost no flesh left. Where my rear used to
> be was a pointed bone. All of my ribs stuck out; I thought it was
> perfectly beautiful.[59]

At some point in her endeavor to eliminate her body, the "beauty" that an
anorexic or bulimic woman sees seems unrelated to the aesthetic ideals of
femininity that ordinary women emulate. "Outwardly," one anorexic woman
admits, "I readily acknowledge that I am thin, tired, physically unattractive,
and that I should gain some weight."[60] Inwardly, however, she finds
"beauty" in the "order" of her hungry body. "You are depriving yourself,"
another woman explains. "You are starving to death—and you tell yourself
it is beautiful."[61] The very extremity of this "alternative" aesthetic hides its
links to the popular myth of female slenderness, in which a woman must
deny her appetite if she wants to be beautiful-loved-successful-free.

Such links are implicit in one anorexic-bulimic woman's belief that female bodies are ugly and inferior: "The way the female body is built," she
exclaims, "it has pads in places that do look like bulges . . . From childhood
on I had a negative association, felt it was not nice to look like a woman."
For this woman, gaining weight means having "the kind of body females
have."[62] At least in part, the anorexic-bulimic woman's fear of her own flesh
is shaped by ideologies of gender that imprison women in their bodies by
identifying them with the mundane, messy realm of the flesh. In an attempt
to escape this realm, "we claim a loss of appetite," Hornbacher explains, "a
most sacred aphysicality." By abstaining from food, starving women become
"superwomen": women "who have conquered the feminine realm of the
material and finally gained access to the masculine realm of the mind." In

this light, Hornbacher sees her own anorexic-bulimic body as expressing "both an apology for being a woman and a twisted attempt to prove that a woman can be as good as a man."[63]

The desire to transcend the prescribed limits of life in a female body and to enter the hallowed, male-defined sphere of ideas is a common theme in the stories of anorexic girls and women. One woman insists that she does not need "physical, earth-plane nourishment," that unlike most women, she can live on air and pure ideas. The reductive logic that underwrites this Cartesian ordering of existence is clear: "I wanted to make it as simple as possible. I believe in simple things and I finally got my diet down so simple . . . that I might have felt comfortable in my head—and that matters a lot. Whether something is comfortable in my head."[64] In the tidy realm of ideas, in the seemingly simple purity of thought, anorexics and bulimics seek refuge from the changes, vulnerability, and needs of embodiment: "I had no patience for my body," Hornbacher recalls. "I wanted it to go away so that I could be a pure mind, a walking brain."[65] Another woman says that her anorexia enabled her to live apart from the hassles of the material world: "The richness of my life consisted at the time of ideas, not of concrete things, certainly not of people. I had made a point of being 'independent' of the world, so to speak."[66]

Despite their conceptual apparatuses, the work of building these "independent" realities is no more metaphysical than the crises of meaning they aim to address. Their order is established through the physical sensations that starving, bingeing, and purging produce. In a culture where female slenderness functions as a sanctimonious ideal, a woman's growling stomach confers as it confirms the presence of meaning. The denial of hunger is a strategy for intensifying the "truths" that anorexics and bulimics tell themselves. "I can't make myself eat," a woman insists. "I'm afraid to gain weight and then I hate the way I look." Despite such claims to the contrary, anorexics are in fact extremely hungry: "You are constantly preoccupied with food, [and] also what you look like," another anorexic woman admits.[67] The disjuncture between an anorexic's reality (hunger) and her rhetoric (denial of hunger), its lack of "common sense" within the ordinary world, is crucial for the maintenance of meaning beyond this world.

Some anorexic and bulimic women use the language of Christianity, most notably asceticism, to articulate their search for an otherworldly order of existence. "There was a period when I was very ascetic," one woman recollects, "and I believed the mind should control the body completely. That is what I discovered when I had those three days of not eating, that I could go on perfectly well without eating. I got convinced that the mind could do anything with the body that it wanted to."[68] Seen in the tradition of asceticism that this woman's story calls to mind, refusing to eat may represent not merely a rejection of the body, as Margaret Miles has pointed out, but also a means for reorienting desire.[69] Still, this reorientation is directed away from the flesh, creating a mind/body division: "If I have to suffer pain," an anorexic woman explains, "I should be able with my mind to disconnect this pain from my mind's activity."[70]

To highlight the ascetic overlays of some women's depictions of their eating problems is not to identify a religious core in their experiences. My aim here is to underscore the dualistic logic that links contemporary anorexic and bulimic rituals to the patriarchal tactics of traditional religion. Though Christian authors prior to Descartes described the distinction between body and soul in terms that implicitly presumed their interdependence, this distinction has been historically misperceived and construed in terms of radical separation.[71] In the view that became dominant in Christianity, a dualistic logic shapes a vision of human life wherein flesh and spirit are hierarchically divided and mutually opposed. This pattern of separating and ranking various aspects of human existence defines the order of meaning both within the worlds of anorexia and bulimia and between these imaginative universes and the society they seek to transcend.

Perhaps the most notorious expression of the dualistic order of these worlds is seen in the language of mind/body division. This split provides a prominent idiom in the accounts of anorexic and bulimic women. One woman explains that her starving and bingeing rituals stemmed from her belief that "the corporeal didn't really matter."[72] Another woman says that she "always felt like [her] soul was skinny": "My soul was free. My soul sort of flew. It was tied down by this big bag of rocks that was my body. I had to drag it around. It did pretty much what it wanted and I had a lot of trouble controlling it. It kept me from doing all the things I dreamed of."[73]

The tenacity of the mind/body split in the struggles of women with eating disorders has not escaped the notice of professionals in the field. One leading expert, for example, depicts anorexia and bulimia as "psychosomatic illnesses in which body is pitted against the psyche."[74] However sensible this observation seems, it conceals as much as it reveals insofar as it presumes the very distinction it identifies as the problem: as if it were possible to know where the "body" ends and the "psyche" begins, as if this division were in fact an experiential given. Unwittingly, such analyses reinstate the very dichotomy they mean to criticize. Insofar as they assume that an anorexic or bulimic girl's references to her "mind" and "body" imply the actual existence of such a split, they fail to interrogate both the logic through which this polarity is produced and the cultural systems that feed off its meanings.

If instead we see the mind/body antagonism to which anorexics and bulimics appeal as a product of language and culture rather than an experiential given, we can recognize its strategic function in their imaginative worlds of meaning. Pragmatically speaking, the symbolic beliefs and rituals whereby an anorexic or bulimic woman separates her "mind" from her "body" can serve to remove her, however fleetingly, from the unbearable weight of a disordered world.

For a disproportionately high number of girls and women with eating disorders, the oppressive weight of this world is violently inflicted through physical and sexual trauma. Feminists like Jennifer Manlowe and Becky Thompson have explored the connections between the mind/body split that bulimics and anorexics describe and the histories of sexual trauma that eating problems mask, histories that are frequently overlaid with other experiences of exploitation, including racism, poverty, and homophobia.[75] Thompson suggests that the dissociation that fasting and bingeing induce can serve as a means for abdicating a body that has been sexually violated. For some women, "leaving the body" through bingeing or fasting parallels the experience of leaving the body during sexual abuse. Starving, gorging, and/or purging can thus be seen as "survival strategies" through which women cope with the anguish and loss brought on by sexual abuse.[76]

In the language of anorexia and bulimia, girls and women try to say what is not permitted or not possible within the symbolic terms and practices currently available to them. Through a network of rules, idioms, rituals, and signs that are at once foreign and familiar to those outside their little worlds of meaning, they vie to make sense of the senseless violations, inequities, and deferred dreams of their lives. As with other linguistic systems, however, the language they use does not simply mirror, it also shapes, the reality it seeks to name. More precisely, it re-creates the damages it tries to speak. Even so, the pain that the language of starving, bingeing, and purging produces can seem less gnawing than the hunger for meaning it tries to fill. By refusing to eat or digest her food, a girl or woman enacts a drama in a world where she cannot find or tell her story. The apparent duplicity and eventual extremity of her plots and methods—starving-gorging-purging all in the name of slenderness—mask the will to survive a life without meaning.

To study the strategies and question the paradigms of the worlds of anorexia and bulimia is to shift the analytic focus on eating disorders from causes to processes, from reasons to functions. This shift requires that we ask not simply "Why do women despise their bodies?" but also "How has a vision of humans as fundamentally divided both within ourselves and from each other become such a compelling if subtle dream?" In the United States today, this dualistic vision of "reality" is so deeply entrenched in prevailing methods for creating order out of confusion that its divisions (such as mind/body, male/female, black/white) are taken for granted even when they are being loquaciously critiqued. Perhaps not surprisingly, the reductive logic of separation provides a powerful tool for organizing an anorexic or bulimic girl's universe of meaning, even as the alienation it creates ties her ever more tightly to the troubled world she seeks to transcend.

Transcendent Comfort: The Language of Addiction

Amid this troubled world, anorexic and bulimic women's food and body rituals provide an invaluable source of comfort. Rituals of deprivation and satiation create a sense of solace by romancing the possibilities of pain, pleasure, and relief. Refusing to eat represses a woman's appetite, but it also stimulates its cravings, heightening the potential for satisfaction. An anorexic woman explains:"I find it impossible to describe the pleasure I would get out of a cup of coffee which I permitted myself late at night, when I had the lights dim. It was warm and made me feel better because I felt cold— the pleasure was so great that it is indescribable in words; it was like real ecstasy."[77] The comforting sensuality of food is also experienced in rituals of compulsive eating:

> I have lusted after Oreo milkshakes, been consoled by bologna and cheese sandwiches, tasted of the dark chocolate candy of life and drunk deeply of the egg cream in remembrance of holiness. Eating is sensual, every flavor, every texture a delight, a moment in paradise which I would freeze to stay there forever if I could.[78]

The discomfort of feeling starved or stuffed becomes tolerable, even enjoyable, when it serves as a pretext for (or postscript of) a "real ecstasy," a temporary feeling of intense satisfaction that transports a woman out of her pain and emptiness.

Among anorexic girls and women, the pain/pleasure of starving and eating and the process of making meaning are mutually enhancing, even when they are mutually restricting: "I get my only happiness from eating a cookie," a young anorexic woman says with regret.[79] Girls and women with eating disorders exaggerate the link between eating and making meaning that is dormant in every person's encounter with food. A woman who eats compulsively describes her overdetermined relationship to food:

> Every day, I see people treat food as a tasty, nourishing part of life. It is not magic for them, not dangerous, not mythical, not a ritual to torture or ease their souls. It has meaning for them but meaning in its proper place; it is not an idol, neither a god to worship nor a demon to fear.[80]

Similarly, an anorexic girl assigns significance to every detail of her eating ritual:

> If it's not a game I'm not going to eat. I mean, how do you think I eat a bowl of vegetable soup, bite by bite? Heavens no. I pick out the corn first, then I pick out the peas, then I think—Hmm now I'll pick out the alphabet letters. If I can't play with it, it's no fun. I'm not going to eat something just to eat it.[81]

The playful quality of such eating rituals makes them both pleasurable and meaningful. But this playfulness also masks the dangers that refusing to play the game can unleash. Such dangers are depicted in an anorexic-bulimic woman's account of her family's Thanksgiving ritual. "Fat was lurking every-where," she writes.

> I tried not to inhale too deeply, because I felt certain that even smells this rich would be enough to put cellulite on my thighs. . . . I proudly surveyed the slender dancer's body I had worked so hard to create. Just a little more to lose. As I dressed for dinner, I imagined each item that was to be served as a pile of lard.[82]

Part of what makes such imaginative beliefs seem so real is the tangible quality of the comfort they provide. The pleasure of bingeing or starving is fast and physical. "When I felt rejected," a woman writes, "a peanut butter sandwich made me feel less so. Maybe it was the way it stuck to the roof of my mouth, making me feel a little less alone."[83] For another woman, the comfort of overeating was followed by the relief she felt after purging, a pattern that intensified her need for ever-greater deliverance:

> Ex-Lax is a good trick. You can eat all you want, as long as you keep taking Ex-Lax. . . . I became more weight obsessed and neurotic than ever. Any meal that I had not expelled within an hour had me worried, almost frantic. I took more little red pills. I sat in the bathroom and waited. I spent half my waking hours in those days on the toilet.[84]

Though such rites seem to transgress prevailing codes of feminine health and beauty, they merely extend the myth of slenderness, in which no price is too high to pay for the saving grace of being thin.

Sometimes girls and women describe the solace they derive from their bulimic and anorexic rituals with the conventions and language of biblical religion. In some accounts, food obtains a significance traditionally reserved for that of a providential creator. "Food was my mainstay, my rock," a woman says. "It had always been the one thing which never disappointed me." Another women echoes this theme: "Food is my most passionate lover, my oldest friend, my solitary vengeful and loving God."[85] The connection between these relationships of "absolute dependence" and the rhetoric of modern Protestant liberalism is lucidly depicted in one woman's parodic comparison between compulsive eating and religious devotion:

> Anguished and alone, I eat and pray and cannot tell one activity from the other, aching to be nearer my Kraft Macaroni and Cheese to thee. . . . And though evil shall tempt me, I am not afraid, for food is my guide as I walk through the world, the cans of Spaghettios and cups of pudding my signposts and markers. Here is familiar territory, what-ever else may be foreign and threatening.[86]

This rhetoric suggests that the patterns whereby bulimic and anorexic women seek comfort in food parallel the ways that Christian women have been encouraged to seek redemption, namely, by depending on forces outside of themselves.

Relationships of salvific dependence also define the symbolic worlds of women who refuse to eat. Despite their abstinence, anorexics are no less dependent on food as a source of meaning and a means for altering reality. The trancelike state that prolonged fasting engenders resembles the dissociation that eating compulsively can induce. "You are in a constant daze," a woman describes the anorexic stage of her illness: "You do not feel as though you are really there. It came to the point that I doubted the people around me; I was unsure whether they truly existed."[87] Other peoples' insistence that an anorexic woman eat only strengthens the narrow vision that her rites produce:

> Everybody presses you to eat more . . . and that is when your tunnel vision comes in. . . . You are living like in a trance. . . . You lose sight of what you are really like, though with other people you can see exactly what is going on. It is just like this: you are safe in your narrow tunnel, but nowhere else.[88]

The escapist strategies that anorexics and bulimics use to build and secure their little worlds of meaning resemble certain features of Christian theories of salvation, especially those that orient the quest for fulfillment through an otherworldly ethos. In both schemes, such an ethos fosters either passive acceptance or denial of human suffering and the conditions giving rise to it. Throughout Christian history, a belief that redemption takes place in another space and time overshadowed an alternative view of salvation as the transformation and healing of life in *this* world.

The links between an otherworldly approach to salvation and the reality-altering strategies of anorexic and bulimic women are evident in their descriptions of the medicating or numbing effects of their eating rituals. Describing her problem with compulsive eating, one woman explains: "Food is the drug of choice when I need to be anesthetized against the onslaught of unacceptable emotions, emotions that I don't want or know how to handle."[89] Another woman echoes this theme: "Food has served as my blanket, my succor. . . . I have used food to dull my feelings, to divert my restlessness."[90] Still another says she is "addicted" to food:

> I am almost constantly thinking about my next meal. . . . Just as soon as one meal is over I begin planning, fantasizing, worrying about the next. I plan my days around eating and the food I want to eat. I plan social engagements around food. I turn down social engagements in order to stay at home and eat secretively.[91]

Women's reports of the druglike effects of their anorexic and bulimic practices are undoubtedly influenced by recent trends in popular and professional discourses on women and food. A view of eating disorders as addictions has gained considerable influence in therapeutic communities, but the popularity of this paradigm is largely indebted to the twelve-step program Overeaters Anonymous (OA). Based on a disease model that was initially developed to help white, middle-class, male alcoholics stop drinking, OA literature depicts food addiction as stemming from a woman's inability to cope with difficult emotions and her corresponding failure to trust a power higher than herself. This approach seems to be more sensitive to women's own accounts of their eating problems than many formal analyses. However, by locating the source of an anorexic or bulimic woman's illness in her "addictive personality" or "character defects," this program tends to naturalize the problems it means to solve.

A different picture emerges if we examine both the cultural ethos that the desire to anesthetize oneself embodies and the pragmatic function that this desire serves among diverse girls and women. The social, symbolic, and strategic basis of "food addiction" is implicit in the story of a woman who began losing weight to become "more attractive" but who intensified her discipline when the rewards of her achievement disappointed her. Starving and bingeing became a method for "getting through" the "empty spaces" of her outwardly successful life. "I became so anxious and nervous today," she told her therapist, "and I know it is simply due to the fact that I started to eat. . . . I had more salad dressing than I should have had, and I had butter. And now I am so terribly anxious and upset about it." When her therapist suggested that her concern about salad dressing and butter is "completely trivial" compared to her underlying problems, she agreed but insisted that "right now to me it is the whole world."[92]

To understand how things as "trivial" as salad dressing and butter can acquire an ultimate significance, we must do more than explain their hidden significance. One woman's poetic reflection on her eating problems illustrates the insufficiency of such an explanation:

> This [food] is so deeply satisfying
> that I do not care
> if it stands for something else,
> I am content to crave
> the readily accessible.
> Later, distressed, distended,
> I cup my aching belly with empty hands
> and could cry for reasons
> I cannot fathom.[93]

Insofar as the unfathomable reasons why girls and women starve, gorge, and purge themselves are too multiple and too complex to be spoken directly within the ritual and symbolic provisions available to them today, it is crucial to ask not simply "Why?" but also "How?"

Pragmatically speaking, food is one of the most reliable, legal, and easily accessible substances that girls and women have for altering their realities. "I revel in the convenience of using food for stress relief," a woman says.[94] This "convenience" applies to not-eating as well: "How easy it was to set yourself against food," a woman muses. "Just one powerful no, instead of a zillion daily decisions, a zillion daily capitulations."[95] Another woman recalls the ease of her bulimic rituals: "The binge no longer threatened my body. I could quickly walk to the bathroom, bend over the toilet, and with ease the binge would come up in one mass."[96] The practicality of food as a remedy for pain is compounded by the reliability of its comforting effects: "I trust food as I trust no person: to be there, to understand me, never to make demands. . . . Food is dependable; should the world crumble, should everyone I know walk away, there will still be coffee yogurt and chocolate chip cookie dough."[97] Being thin can serve a similar function. A woman explains: "I also decided that if everything else went wrong I could always be skinny."[98]

The fragile shelter that the narrow worlds of anorexia and bulimia create provide temporary escape from real-world experiences of disappointment, frustration, and pain. A lesbian woman, for example, recalls how her bulimia gave her a way to avoid this culture's heterosexual imperative: "I ate because I didn't care for men . . . and because I didn't know yet that loving women was an option, even though I knew I loved them."[99] Another woman tells how she began to build her anorexic universe when her parents divorced, her father disappeared, and her mother remarried and sent her to live with relatives:

> The bathroom scale became my sanctuary. . . . I devoted all my thoughts and energy to food, or the lack thereof. By the end of the week, I had dropped to 95 pounds, now adhering to 600 calories a day, tops. My days were spent with eyes fixed on the clock, anxious for my next permitted meal. In raving pursuit of thinness, I stopped chewing gum as dessert after learning it had eight calories a stick.[100]

Still another woman recalls that as a girl she retreated into her "own little world" of anorexia to escape her father's emotional abuse—his "pointless criticisms" and "steel blue looks" that seemed to say: *How could you be so stupid? What a disappointment you are.* Before long, this girl's anorexic world became her haven from "all that went wrong in my life, all the small disappointments, the anger I felt, any emotion I could neither express nor understand."[101]

The silent sufferings, the unspoken exclusions, and the impermissible passions that circumscribe the lives of girls and women are not so much the "causes" as they are the contexts from which some of them build their deadly alternatives. "I eat to be redeemed, and I eat out of fear that there is no redemption," one woman explains; her story blurs the lines between reasons and functions, between solutions and problems, between banal and ultimate salvation:

> I eat because I hate the world I live in, and am afraid I can neither fit into it nor change it. I eat because I love the world I live in, and am afraid it will be taken away from me. . . . I eat to make the world go away, and the world doesn't go away and I eat more. I eat when I am reminded of how unfair life is, and how regularly people are hurt and hurt each other, of how mundane evil has become. . . . I eat when people look at me and immediately write me off, when people do not take my intelligence seriously because I am a woman. . . . I eat because I do not cry about AIDS deaths or crack babies or drive-by shootings or the S & L scandal or the million other daily outrages. And I eat because I am afraid the world will go merrily on its way to hell in a handbasket without my being able to make a difference or turn the tide.[102]

The dynamics whereby women starve, eat, and purge themselves more deeply into the world they long to transcend are not reducible to individual defects or addictions. To understand these dynamics is to recognize what musician Amy Ray refers to as "the numbing of America."[103]

We live in a society that seems increasingly numb to the causes and effects of human suffering. A "culture of numbness" makes it easy to demonize a woman's eating, even as other forms of conspicuous consumption are encouraged, envied, and praised. This same numbness leads us to revere female hunger, even as other forms of self-sacrifice—such as volunteer service or community organizing—lack adequate social support. The numbing of this society is both cause and consequence of the unacknowledged pain and loss of meaning that eating disorders embody. It is reflected in the escapist strategies of anorexic and bulimic girls and women, in the universes of meaning they create, and in the worlds of pain they aim to flee.

When Salvation Hinges on Destruction

In *The Golden Cage: The Enigma of Anorexia Nervosa*, Hilde Bruch describes a conversation she had with a young woman she called "Nora." Looking back on her problems, Nora told Bruch that the anorexia she created when she was sixteen was a kind of parody. More specifically, Bruch recounts, "she compared it to the devil's creation of Pandemonium in Hell, the way it is described in Milton's *Paradise Lost*." Nora's own description follows:

> *They have lost Heaven, and they want to rebuild it. They don't mean to create a parody [of Heaven]—they want to get away from suffering, not to construct its locus. They create a city which materially is beautiful—of rich*

ores and jewels and craftsmanship and yet which, lacking the spirit of Heaven, is an absurd and tragic grotesquerie.

Similarly, I wanted to avoid anxiety, emptiness, disconnectedness, suffering. Anorexia nervosa isn't an attempt to make yourself suffer; it's an attempt, from a postlapsarian vantage point, to recapture Eden by revealing it; with the pain you feel, with shivering cold, warmth becomes real and wonderful again. Food becomes delicious and gratifying. Everything becomes ordered, organized, compact, and can be fantasized about in ordered sorts of ways [italics in original].[104]

As Nora's analogy suggests, the worlds of meaning that anorexics and bulimics create and inhabit are, in the end, not very transcendent at all. They not only lack "the spirit of Heaven"; they also inadvertently deepen the void they seek to fill. Ultimately, the values, power, order, and comfort they provide merely extend—rather than challenge or change—the cultural and religious legacies that fail to adequately nourish girls' and women's hungers for a deeper and larger sense of meaning.

Despite this failure, the meanings that these worlds construct can become so compelling that some girls and women are quite willing to die for their truths. "I'm so scared to put any weight on," a young woman explains. "If anybody ever said, 'Gee, Helen, you look fatter. Your face looks better . . . ' you might as well kill me. . . . I am so afraid of these words."[105] What is toxic is not these words themselves but the reductive logic that gives them meaning—the all-or-nothing mentality that makes this woman believe her life is worthless if she is not supremely thin—and the culture in which this mentality finds ample support. Lacking alternative strategies and visions, the struggles of girls and women with eating disorders signal not a wish for death but a hunger to live more fully than is possible within the current social order.

To see the spiritual hungers that eating disorders intimate is to recognize that the self-destruction that these problems entail masks a search for self-preservation. By starving, bingeing, and purging herself, a woman endangers the life she means to save. In so doing, she becomes imprisoned by the very terms that are supposed to set her free.[106] In her little world of meaning, salvation and damnation are intertwined: "While I did not establish the laws that I use to judge myself," a bulimic woman reflects, "I am the strictest of judges, as though I could save myself by destroying myself before anyone else does."[107]

The food and body prisons of anorexia and bulimia give flesh to a cultural-religious legacy wherein a woman's hunger for meaning and wholeness has been tragically malnourished. In this legacy, a woman's creativity must be tied to her suffering, her power exercised through submission, her redemption achieved through self-annihilation. To be sure, the atonement strategies of present-day anorexic and bulimic women vary. For some, chastening is accomplished through rituals of self-denial: "One reason why I lose weight is because I think, I really do think, I'm trying to punish myself."[108] Others are sentenced and sentence themselves by eating compulsively: "I judge myself with food, deliver the verdict with food, carry out the punishment with food. . . . Food is poison. I eat it in silence, in fear, in repentance."[109]

Invariably, however, one of the most devastating effects of these punitive/saving measures is the solitary confinement they construct and impose. "You create an artificial wall between you and the rest of the world," an anorexic-bulimic woman explains: "The trouble is that it is so hard to break. It should have been broken down before the mortar got fixed, and now that it is fixed I kick against it and it won't budge. You erect a kind of temporary wall, but instead of staying loose it gets mortarized and becomes indestructible."[110] Another woman describes the isolation of her anorexic world by comparing herself to the Statue of Liberty: a woman stranded on an island, "untouched and untouchable, with no relationship to anybody or anything."[111] Devoid of all connections, free from the chaos and conflicts, the yearnings and frustrations, the fragility and changes of life in this disorderly world, an anorexic or bulimic woman tries to save herself from her biggest fear of all: "I was an anoretic," Marya Hornbacher concludes, "because I was afraid of being human."[112]

As solutions to the problem of being human—a problem that at some point comes down to the question of life's meaning—anorexia and bulimia deepen the hungers they are so carefully designed to fill. The salvation they offer tries to control or escape, rather than recognize and transform, the daily-messy-unfair-painful-present-puzzling-needy-dreaming-itching-ultimate gravity of life on Earth. In the end, the affinities between the symbolic universes that anorexic and bulimic women construct, the popular salvation myth on which they draw, the explanatory gazes of those who treat them, and the idioms and paradigms of patriarchal religion point to the need for different ways of thinking and being. If the quasi-religious functions of these imaginative worlds can be inferred from the role they play in generating a seemingly ultimate source of meaning, the spiritual hungers they bespeak suggest the need for more genuine alternatives.

Five

A DIFFERENT KIND

OF SALVATION

Cultivating Alternative Senses,
Practices, and Visions

To see the spiritual dimensions of girls' and women's struggles with food and their bodies is to recognize the search for meaning and wholeness that these struggles intimate. Girls and women are not merely starving to be thin. They are starving to be well. Literally and figuratively, they are hungering for a sense of fulfillment and well-being—what theologians have traditionally referred to as "salvation."

Classic Christian references to "salvation" are tied to notions of human sin—humans' alienation from God as mythically depicted in the story of the Fall from Eden. In this story, sin is unleashed into the world by the act of a woman eating. For centuries this scenario has been used to justify women's subordination to men and their confinement to the physical realm of cooking, cleaning, and bearing children. In this scheme, a woman is "saved" either by accepting her relegation to the flesh by becoming an obedient wife and self-sacrificing mother or by taming and transfiguring this flesh by denying, mortifying, and ultimately transcending its unruly cravings. Either way, a woman's "salvation" presumes her shame and requires her self-alienation: her transgression is absolved when she forfeits a sense of agency and a feeling of peace with her own body.

This view of female sin and redemption obscures an alternative notion of "salvation" within the Christian tradition, one that reflects its Latin ties to the term *salve*, which means "to be in good health." What does it mean to be healthy and well? The dangerous quest for transcendence that women's

125

eating problems embody suggests that "health," "wholeness," and "well-being" must not be defined as a state of otherworldly, invulnerable perfection. The problem is not just that there is no return to the Garden but that there may be no Garden to which we can return. The "good health" of "salvation" must therefore be seen as a journey, an embodied process of healing and well-being. "Good health" is a physical-spiritual movement in which there are few short cuts, perhaps because there is no fixed destination.

Ultimately, the challenge of health and healing is the challenge of living fully in the midst of life's pungent mixture of suffering and joy, disappointment and hope, injustice and freedom, knowledge and uncertainty. As Buddhist feminist Joan Iten Sutherland suggests, "good health" and "healing" are best understood "not as the elimination of disease, but as a falling in love with the poignancy of being alive."[1]

For girls and women with eating problems, the transformative movement into better health and well-being is neither random nor predetermined, neither passive nor controlled. To put the matter in religious terms, liberation and healing from these problems and the sufferings surrounding them is not obtained by faith alone. But neither are they earned by doing all the right things. Classic oppositions between these two roads to salvation—faith-versus-works, believing-versus-doing—obscure the interdependence of struggle and process, action and acceptance, practice and vision that getting better requires. An alternative perspective recognizes this interdependence as well as the different kind of salvation it offers.

Beyond the Search for Causes and the Politics of Blame

This perspective shifts the focus of conventional treatments of eating disorders. Psychological, biomedical, and sociocultural treatments tend to be oriented by a seemingly unavoidable question: What *causes* these problems? Such causal models imply a view of eating-disordered girls and women as passive victims of external or essential forces, rather than variously constrained agents who draw on the symbolic-ritual resources most accessible to them to help them cope with the inequities and losses of their lives. Oriented by unambiguous explanations, most traditional approaches to treating eating disorders not only unwittingly reinscribe the reductive logic that these problems embody; in so doing they also divert attention away from what may be more fruitful questions, such as, "How do these problems work?"

The question "How?" brings into focus the function that eating problems serve, especially the role they play in providing a sense of purpose and meaning amid suffering, injustice, and uncertainty. But the process-oriented question "How?" is not unrelated to the causally focused question "Why?" To examine the spiritual aspects of eating problems is not to deny the importance of the sociocultural, biological, and psychological influences on their development. My analysis simply complicates the significance of these influences by seeing them as *both* causes *and* effects and by viewing them in relation to girls' and women's searches for a sense of value and fulfillment in a world whose ultimate meaning is a mystery.

This conceptual shift moves beyond the politics of blame and denial that frequently, if implicitly, shapes conventional searches for a definitive cause and solution. The politics of blame can be seen in the etiological narratives of therapeutic literature that blame "the mother" for the struggles of her anorexic or bulimic daughter. Similar explanatory tactics shape feminist analyses that vindicate the mother and accuse "patriarchy" as the penultimate villain. Biomedical theories often remove the burden of guilt altogether by indicting forces beyond human volition (such as neurotransmitters or hormones). Popular discourses enlist elements of all three models to blame women themselves for their troubled relationships to their bodies and food.

Despite their obvious variances, these approaches commonly rely on the very way of thinking that leads some girls and women to believe they must destroy themselves in order to save themselves from the senselessness of their pain and oppression. The blame that these discourses either affix or efface may give those affected by eating problems a sense of relief. It does little, however, to challenge the cultural logic and ethos (the reductive ways of thinking and the controlling ways of being) and the historical legacies (the anti-body, antiwoman messages of patriarchal religion and culture) through which these problems make sense in the minds and bodies of those who struggle with them.

Locating the cause and assigning the blame are no substitute for paying attention and advocating change. To effectively challenge the worlds of meaning that anorexic and bulimic women symbolically and ritually construct, we must not only recognize the search for wholeness embedded in them. We must also question the dualistic paradigms and values that give them meaning, along with the popular salvation myth that circulates their narrow "truths," and the patriarchal religious legacies that support them. At the same time, we need to develop and make accessible different models and modes for creating value and seeking wholeness outside the illusory security of the Garden.

To articulate such alternative paradigms and practices, to rethink the meaning of "salvation," we must return to the question "What does it mean to be 'well' "? In particular, what does it mean to "heal" or "recover from" an eating problem? Even more specifically, we need to ask; "What does it take to be 'healthy' in a culture that is, in many ways, very sick?" In practice, these large questions break down into a number of tangible queries, such as: What is "healthy" eating? How much food does the body need? How much exercise is too much? Too little? How much weight loss or weight gain is "unhealthy"? Where is the line between caring for and obsessing about the body? Since eating problems develop on a number of levels, questions pertaining to good health and healing are likewise multifaceted.

Certain scientific theories and measures may provide some clues for addressing these questions. For example, medical concepts like the "set point" for body weight underline the physical hazards of extreme weight loss or gain. This theory (see chapter 1) not only presumes a variety of "normal" body sizes but also helps explain the compulsion to binge that follows periods of deprivation, and it therefore suggests a balanced approach to eating that satisfies the needs of a particular body. But not all scientific theories affirm the diversity of female body sizes and needs. Many define their norms for wellness according to a single standard of physical health, marking those who deviate from this scale as "sick." Moreover, even the more flexible medical theories tend to ignore important aspects of experience (social, psychological, spiritual) that add to or subtract from a woman's overall health.

Like some areas of scientific discourse, girls' and women's own experiences of struggle with their bodies may provide some wisdom for the journey of health and healing. For example, the physical and mental disturbances that women report as a result of bingeing or starving suggest guidelines of balance and moderation. Moreover, the diversity of women's experiences of their bodies points to the fluidity of the meaning of terms like "wellness." While some women who are "overweight" by society's standards feel perfectly content with their body sizes, other large-bodied women are considerably distressed by their girth. The varying degrees to which women are comfortable with their own bodies must be taken seriously when considering questions of health. Even so, such experiences do not suggest a clear-cut norm. That some women who are severely underweight report that they feel "too fat" illustrates the limits of personal experience as a definitive key for understanding and seeking well-being.

Despite the important clues they provide, neither the "objective" codes of science nor the "subjective" rules of experience are a sufficient basis for developing an alternative approach to health and healing. To put it simply, both are influenced by social norms and values that tend to undermine rather than foster female well-being. Both scientific and experiential discourses are often unaware of the ways that for women, simply asking pragmatic questions about what or how much to eat can perpetuate the cultural paradigms (the do-and-don't mentalities) and historical associations (woman equals body) that make eating problems seem like viable solutions to the crises of meaning they bespeak.

Raising practical questions about female health and eating is tricky business in a society that is all too willing to give its blessing to women who fret about food and their bodies. Yet not to do so is to stay stuck with the answers already in place, "answers" that are often damaging at best. Practical questions about food and women's health thus need to be explored from a perspective that opposes the mentality and transforms the legacies that give eating problems their meaning.

Moving out of the prison of an eating problem depends on the creation of more integrative ways of thinking and being, ways that foster the movement of self, social, and spiritual transformation. This movement depends on (1) the development of critical and embodied awareness; (2) participation in countercultural communities; and (3) commitment to ongoing spiritual growth and vision. These revolutionary movements of personal-political-spiritual change suggest tools for creating alternative worlds of meaning, worlds in which girls' and women's creative powers are adequately nourished.

Developing Critical and Embodied Awareness

By the time I was sixteen, I wondered whether I was going to spend the rest of my life trying not to eat, obsessing about food, wishing I were thinner, and looking for the nearest bathroom in case I had to purge. My anguish at such a prospect was compounded by a fear that I did not know how to live outside the cage I had unwittingly managed to create. By the time I was a sophomore in college, however, I started noticing a connection between my "personal" body-hatred and a larger cultural obsession with keeping female bodies thin. This awareness was initially sparked by a film I saw that year, Jean Kilbourne's *Killing Us Softly,* which interrogated social expectations for feminine beauty. The next semester, my philosophy professor, a Benedictine priest, encouraged me to write a paper on Simone de Beauvior's *The Second Sex.* This book's analysis of "woman" as "the Other" helped me understand and question not only my experiences of marginality as a woman but also my negative attitudes toward my body. Gradually, I began to perceive the links between my stereotypical gender training, my feelings of bodily inadequacy, and the narrow ideals and disciplines that had somehow given me a sense of purpose.

The process of moving beyond the universe of meaning that an eating problem constructs varies irreducibly among different girls and women. Broadly speaking, however, this movement involves a *shift in consciousness*, a change that starts when a girl or woman begins to recognize and name the sense of disconnection and emptiness that her unwanted eating patterns cover. Articulations of this sense vary. Women speak of the "void," the "hollowness," the "bottomless hunger," or, as one woman put it, the "big, empty cavity waiting to be filled. Hungering to be filled. Urging me to fill it."[2] Such references signify the spiritual malaise—the crises of meaning—surrounding girls' and women's struggles with food and their bodies: their loss of faith in and connection to a larger sense of value and purpose.

Giving voice to these crises helps girls and women see that they are not inherently bad. Rather, they can be seen as *turning points*, as junctures where the critical awareness that is crucial for good health begins to grow. Naming such crises depends on the availability of a language that can render them intelligible and point to possibilities for transformation. In the United States today, such a language exists in the countercultural discourses of feminism, prophetic religion, and other liberation movements whose terms and paradigms call into question dominant cultural values and norms.

The shift in consciousness that getting well entails involves a movement from experiences of alienation into a new mode of awareness: a way of thinking that questions the authority of prevailing norms, recognizing the emptiness of their substance and the relativity of their value, while creating alternative systems of meaning and ways of seeking truth.[3] Former anorexic and bulimic Abra Fortune Chernik describes this movement: "I had looked forward to rejoining society after my years of anorexic exile. Ironically, in order to preserve my health, my recovery has included the development of a consciousness that actively challenges the images and ideas that define this culture."[4] Some feminist theo(a)logians describe women's movement from self-alienation into critical consciousness as a kind of religious conversion, an awakening to a bigger picture and a different way of seeing.[5]

Since the loss of meaning and sense of disconnection out of which critical consciousness is born is experienced in the body, cultivating a new awareness means paying attention to its embodied basis. The process of healing is a process of becoming physically and mindfully aware of uncomfortable feelings of dissonance and loss—not to get rid of them, but to use them by transforming them into resources for questioning the cultural ideals and practices that have failed to nourish them. Developing critical awareness thus enables a woman to see the connections between her "personal" anxiety about her body and the sociopolitical matrix in which she lives.

From this vantage point, becoming well means not so much eradicating all traces of conflict or emptiness from one's life. Rather, the "good health" of salvation involves an ongoing process of recognizing the relative emptiness of all cultural constructs—their lack of actual substance—while nonetheless working to shape a world that is more meaningful and humane. Such recognition pivots on the possibility of converting one's sense of nothingness into insights that foster more life-enhancing ways of being.

This process of conversion is not purely or even primarily intellectual. Bodies that are severely malnourished are ill equipped for the work of radically mindful embodied thinking. Dismantling the narrow universe of an eating disorder depends on developing eating patterns that sufficiently meet one's nutritional needs. One woman explains: "Once my hunger for food was truly satisfied, my other hungers emerged: hunger for meaningful work, hunger for satisfying relationships, hunger to make a contribution, hunger to know who I am."[6] Learning to live outside the quarantine of an eating disorder is difficult because it depends on the creation of new strategies for dealing with appetite and food, even as its aim is to make eating *less* central to one's search for a sense of satisfaction and meaning.

To recognize the embodied basis of critical awareness is to honor the diversity of girls' and women's experiences of their bodies and the need for a variety of practical measures for healing. Outside the logic of reduction, there is no generic standard for gauging a woman's "ideal weight," no universal norm for defining "healthy" eating. Practical guidelines must therefore be context-specific. Learning to eat in a way that fosters one's ability to engage in meaningful work and satisfying relationships means something different for a woman who is used to starving herself than it does for a woman who is hooked on bingeing and purging. Whether health requires eating more or eating less depends on a girl or woman's particular eating patterns and history.

"Good health" and "healing" are also partially determined by social location. Broadly speaking, deconstructing the myth of slenderness is crucial for moving beyond the anorexic or bulimic frame of meaning. But this may be especially true for socially privileged women, whose weight-loss efforts may be unwittingly tied to imperialist ideals of white femininity. Questioning the cultural associations between female slenderness, cultural superiority, and personal success is crucial for developing critical and embodied awareness. "Am I thin yet?" a woman who gave up dieting asks: "No, but hey, I'm a heck of a lot happier now than at any other point in my life. Even at slightly under 200 pounds, I am able to look at myself in the mirror and see someone I could genuinely like—even love."[7]

For some women, weight loss or maintenance may be integral to better health, but only as the *result* rather than the *goal* or *starting point* of a larger healing process. In her essay "Coming Home: One Black Woman's Journey to Health 'and Fitness," Georgiana Arnold describes how her health-destroying, single-minded pursuit of thinness lost its power as she found ways to confront the traumas and disappointments of her life, including the internalized racism that fueled her sense of helplessness. The inner growth that these confrontations set in motion enabled her to maintain her weight at a level where she felt empowered.[8]

Still, in a culture where female slenderness is an ideal through which an assortment of cultural inequities are circulated, the relationship between weight maintenance and the maintenance of critical consciousness is irreducibly uneasy. Describing this tension, one woman writes:

> By succumbing to cultural pressure to lose weight, I sometimes feel I've betrayed my feminist self, bought into the "beauty myth," failed to rebel against patriarchal standards of what women should be. Yet I know I'm healthier than when I couldn't haul a bag of (fattening) groceries up the stairs without running out of breath.[9]

While developing critical consciousness gives one tools for interrogating ruling definitions of "health" and "healthier," the diversity of women's experiences of healing suggests that such consciousness must not be defined in ways that create new orthodoxies.

Using a logic of interdependence and guided by an ethos of accountability, competing visions of what it means to be well can be situationally and systemically assessed: *situationally* because the practices that promote one woman's health may differ from those that foster another's; *systemically* because health and healing depend on resistance to prevailing social norms and conditions, which variously threaten the well-being of everybody. One woman's method of caring for her body must not negate, but should enhance, the possibilities for wholeness among other girls and women. The relative truth of one woman's sense of well-being can therefore be measured by its capacity to affirm, however implicitly, the diversity and dignity of others.

Participating in Collective Struggles to Transform Injustice and Suffering

Even after I began to make connections between my eating disorder and the mandates of society, it took a long time to stop believing in the ideals and promises that had given my life such clear direction. Letting go of the dream of thinness became possible only as I began to speak with other women who were paralyzed by the disgust they felt for their bodies. The more I spoke, the more I heard, the more my despair turned into anger. The more I shared my struggle with others, especially other critically awakened women and men, the more I came to believe that it was not my body, but the prevailing cultural authorities, that needed to lose some weight. Over time this insight became part of an awareness that inspires my desire to change the structures of the social body, rather than the outlines of my own.

Developing critical consciousness is like learning to speak another language. There is an abiding temptation to resort to more familiar terms, more comfortable patterns for making meaning, especially when a majority of people show little interest in trying to say and see things differently.[10] Given the paucity of critical vision within this culture's mainstream, participating in countercultural communities is an indispensable part of the journey of health and healing. Whether formal or informal, imagined or tangible, such communal movements need to be organized not simply around the identities that persons are assigned by the ruling culture's dualistic ideologies (black or white, male or female, etc.) but, more important, around the quality of vision they share: a judicious awareness of and commitment to change the social conditions and values that support the culture of eating disorders.[11]

Participating in such communities is vital to the pursuit of a different kind of salvation because most girls and women need more than "accurate information" to let go of the temporary power that controlling or gorging their appetites creates.[12] In a culture whose most visible ideals of womanhood show and tell us that "a woman can never be too rich or too thin," relinquishing the promise of thinness and developing new models for making meaning is not easily accomplished in isolation. "Individual" experience does not provide enough distance from the ideals through which a girl learns to mistrust her body in the first place. Moreover, the gravity of familiar habits makes reentry into the bulimic or anorexic world of meaning an ever-present possibility. Alternatively, communion with those who reject this narrow plan of salvation provides greater "objectivity" for recognizing the effects of female socialization, while it enables a woman to share and practice different strategies of resistance.

Emphasizing the communal dimensions of good health and healing opens avenues for developing critical consciousness among those who lack access to more privileged formats for consciousness-raising (such as progressive education). While long-term responses to eating problems must include a revamping of educational systems so that critical thinking becomes an integral aspect of all formal learning, "meanwhile" strategies include the formation of grassroots networks that support the process of "hearing each other into speech."[13] Some feminists have criticized the consciousness-raising groups of the 1970s for the "will-to-unity" they seem to presume. However, these critiques tend to prioritize theoretical purity over pragmatic needs, effects, and accessibility.[14] The belief that consciousness-raising groups are an outdated mode of critical practice may be a product of the educational and/or generational privilege of those who are already fluent in the language of critical awareness. This view ignores the institutional barriers, especially the class structures of liberal education, that make education for liberation the fortune of a lucky few. It also forgets the powerful connection between learning to speak and feeling heard that alternative, grassroots networks foster.

Insofar as the process of healing depends on the support of communal ties, one of the more popular means of "recovery," the twelve-step program called Overeaters Anonymous (OA), presents a limited possibility. This program offers the kind of communal context that is vital for those who have spent days and years dwelling in the exile of their imaginative constructions. Overeaters Anonymous meetings create a space where women discover they are not alone in their food and body prisons. The fluid structure of most meetings (leadership is rotating) and the give-what-you-can price of admittance (a voluntary collection is taken at each meeting) make OA a potentially democratic forum for healing. In addition, some of the "tools" for recovery that this program advocates (making phone calls, keeping a journal, having a sponsor, going to meetings) can provide effective methods not only for forging new eating patterns but also for creating more honest relationships both with oneself and with others. Finally, this program represents one of the few approaches to eating problems that recognizes and probes their spiritual dimensions.[15]

Yet the kind of spirituality that OA promotes points to its limits as an alternative path of wholeness and healing. Some of this program's most central beliefs harmonize perfectly with social norms and religious attitudes that support a culture of domination. The notion of a "Higher Power" at the heart of twelve-step discourse envisions divinity as separate from and hovering over the world of human experience. The model of "power-over" that this concept assumes implicitly sanctions a vision of human life and society as structured through hierarchical divisions (mind/body, male/female, etc.), divisions that foster the very feelings of alienation to which eating problems respond. And while the concept of a "Higher Power" is not supposed to be tied to a specific denomination, its Calvinist underpinnings are evident in the confession of "powerlessness" that "recovery" requires. At its worst, the language of turning one's will over to the care of a "Higher Power" (however "He" is understood) not only sacralizes a cultural-religious legacy that encourages female dependence but also tacitly ends up blaming individual girls and women for their sufferings.

If it is at least partially true that language produces (rather than simply reflects) the realities it seeks to name, the rhetoric of helplessness is probably not very effective for moving girls and women out of their symbolic enclosures of food and body. Such movement depends on the support of radical friendships and communities that protest rather than profess the myth of divine/male omnipotence and female helplessness. Such bonds can foster experiences of power beyond the pseudo-autonomy that rituals of starving, bingeing, and purging engender, an empowering power defined by a sense of accountability and connection rather than control.

An alternative approach to salvation pivots on this different conception of power. To fight domination with domination, dependence with dependence, denial with denial is to increase the very suffering that an eating disorder implicitly aims to alleviate. An alternative perspective sees power not as the ability to exercise absolute control but as the process of becoming empowered and accountable in relation to others. From this view, bourgeois visions of the modern, "independent woman" who is "master" of her own destiny present a vacuous answer to medieval models of female sacrifice and submission. Even feminist rhetoric that insists on women's right to "control" their bodies runs the risk of playing into a larger cultural ethos that seems incapable of conceiving of power apart from domination. To define power in terms of strength and responsibility rather than dependence and control is to see how the pursuit of "personal" health and healing connects up with a larger task, what Jewish feminist Judith Plaskow refers to as "the repair of the world."[16]

The connection between individual experience and social life that critical consciousness brings into view suggests that repairing the world and healing the self are two dimensions of the same challenge that girls and women with eating problems face. Strategies that effect change on both these levels are tremendously powerful. For example, a group of Boston-area girls and women made up of former anorexics and bulimics, along with their therapists and their mothers, formed a coalition called Boycott Anorexic Marketing (BAM), which successfully pressured the Coca-Cola company to withdraw its ad for Diet Sprite that featured a gangly young woman called "Skeleton." Therapist Mary Baures, who started the group, says that its aim is not simply getting anorexic advertising repealed but also giving women and girls who feel "powerless" a way of "talking back."[17]

Organized protests and informal conversations, women's support groups and grassroots publications, scale-smashing rallies and national boycotts are just some of the ways that the feminist movement has enabled women to interrogate and "talk back" to oppressive norms and authorities more directly. As bell hooks suggests, such questioning and back talk are vital skills for those who seek healing and wholeness from the margins of mainstream society.[18] These strategies suggest how girls' and women's hungers for freedom and meaning might be more satisfyingly fed through their engagement with others in a shared effort to challenge the "disorder" of this society.

Commitment to Spiritual Growth and Vision

My exodus out of a world circumscribed by calories, refrigerators, mirrors, and scales has been far from linear, but it has been far. It took years for me to realize that leaving this penitentiary did not mean that my life was going to be smooth and easy. There would still be, and there still are, dreams and disappointments, "good" days and "bad" days, confusions, losses, and longings. The difference is that now I also have a variety of ways and means for moving through rather than beyond these vicissitudes, for getting a glimpse of a bigger picture, for transforming rather than trying to transcend frustration and despair.

Sometimes transformation comes from spending time in the woods: walking, breathing, being with trees. Sometimes it is fueled by my sense of belonging to a larger network of people who are working to alleviate suffering and oppression around the globe. Sometimes it comes from immersing myself in the world of art: drawing, painting, seeing the intricate beauty of ordinary things. Sometimes it means studying and reinterpreting the history of my religion, its atrocities and silences as well as its wisdom. Sometimes transformation comes from seeing a movie, or reading a book, or listening to music, or even playing my own guitar. Sometimes it happens when I pray, and sometimes when I'm practicing aikido. Sometimes when I'm drinking coffee or sharing a meal with friends. Sometimes teaching. Sometimes learning. And sometimes just being.

There is no universal formula for healing: no magic key to make things better. My own experience is hardly a rule, soaked as it is in the privileges of life as an educated, middle-class white woman. Many girls and women have limited or no access to the worlds of art, nature, or education. Many do not have safe neighborhoods to walk in or nutritious food to eat. Yet reconstructing and telling our stories to each other, listening for lines of conflict and connection, may be one way of seeing how the world itself needs to change if the diversity and complexity of women's spiritual hungers are to be more adequately fed. Such tellings and listenings may not only help relocate the search for meaning that eating problems intimate; they may also provide visions of hope and rituals for seeking a different kind of salvation.

Such visions and rituals are necessary because the spiritual wounds and eclipse of meaning that eating problems both camouflage and deepen make it very difficult for women to leave the pseudohavens that these problems provide. Although recognition of the sociopolitical underpinnings of anorexia and bulimia is crucial for this movement, taken alone it is often not enough. "I know the literature on eating disorders," a woman explains:

> I understand the ways in which women are rarely free in this society to relate comfortably to food. I have seen the movies, have read the books and articles. I can offer an academic account of the economy of food, of the structure of the diet industry, of the prejudice and discrimination against fat women, of the unconformity of the anorexic. I eat anyway. The more I know, the more I eat. I eat, in part, because I know—and because, knowing, I am angry and afraid. . . . I am afraid that, confronted with the truth of my pain, I simply would not be able to live.[19]

While most feminist analyses of eating disorders rightly deplore the social norms that reward women for doing violence to themselves, few attend to the spiritual aspects of these struggles and the issues they raise regarding the prospects for health and healing. "I read feminist critiques," another woman says:

> They make sense. It does seem that our misogynist culture has taught me to despise my body, and to hanker after impossible images of beauty. I decide with grim determination that I will forgo diets and learn to love my body as it is. But grim determination does not lead to love.[20]

"Love" is not a very popular term in feminist discourse today, at least not among its more critical voices in the public sphere. There are good reasons for its disrepute. More often than not, this term is used to sanctify relations of domination and abuse. All too frequently its "truths" are felt in a host of violations against women and other marginalized persons, outrages that the promise of "love" functions to conceal. On screens and in airwaves, "love" is drenched in the salvation myth of heterosexual romance, showing and singing the ultimate fulfillment that the "opposite sex" is supposed to bring. On streets and in bedrooms, this term is invoked to authorize a variety of violences: unspoken threats and unspeakable assaults, all in the name of love. In short, it is little wonder that "love" has all but lost its legitimacy as a countercultural value.

Yet what do good health and healing entail, if not the capacity to love and be loved, including the ability to love oneself? It is an old idea, but one worth pondering, I think, especially since the values that underwrite women's troubled relationships to their bodies ("self-control," "perfection," etc.) suggest the dire need of an expanded moral vocabulary. Perhaps what is needed more than liberal embarrassment at or renunciation of traditional religious ideas such as love (and its corollaries, such as faith and hope) is critical discussion and redefinition of the truths such values potentially illumine and conceal. Keeping the idea of love afloat (but not anchored) in struggles for self and social transformation, struggles in which meanings can be tested for their pragmatic effects, may help prevent our revolutions from collapsing into politics as usual (fighting domination with domination). Putting spiritual values on the agenda of political progressives may not only serve to de-monopolize the conservative use of religious rhetoric by the already privileged cultural elite; it may also help keep critically minded folks aware of and interrogating the "something more" to which our present efforts point.

In the long run, addressing the spiritual brokenness that eating problems manifest and conceal requires more than keen political awareness. Insofar as women's struggles with food and their bodies bespeak a profound loss of faith, some kind of spiritual vision and practice is essential to the process of getting better. Such practice and vision can serve as tools for converting a sense of emptiness and violation into nourishment for struggles that are life-enriching. The spiritual belief in something greater than the individual self can help inspire a woman's movement beyond the quarantine of food and body, enabling her to break the walls of silence that separate her from others, to begin creating and telling and hearing another story of salvation within which to grow and flourish.

There are important caveats to this suggestion. First, as Elisabeth Schüssler Fiorenza points out, "spiritual vision becomes illusion when it refuses to be challenged by and confronted with reality."[21] In contrast to the universes of meaning that anorexics and bulimics construct, the spiritual vision of critical thinking sharpens rather than clouds one's ability to respond effectively to the sufferings and needs of the tangible world. Second, as authors like bell hooks, Audre Lorde, and Cornel West make clear, to assume that the call to spiritual insight and creativity is the prerogative of those who are white and middle-class is to overlook both the histories and the current needs of persons who are most damaged by the exploits of ruling cultural regimes.[22] The belief that some people in this society have spiritual needs while others are more or less preoccupied with material concerns for survival reinforces the inequities that such dualistic thinking creates.

Commitment to spiritual growth is important because becoming well is both a struggle and a process. Unlike the dogmatic way of thinking it seeks to undo, this struggle/process is unstable and shifting, ongoing yet unpredictable. Even as an anorexic girl opens her mouth to eat, even as a bulimic woman decides to digest her food, even as health begins to return to their haggard minds and bodies, the problems of life and the hunger for meaning do not disappear. "I have not, nor will I ever, completely lose the longing for that something, that thing that I believe will fill an emptiness inside me," Marya Hornbacher reflects. At the same time, she attests, it is possible to live with this yearning for "that something" in ways that are not self-destructive: "I have learned to understand the emptiness rather than fear it and fight it and continue the futile attempt to fill it."[23]

The inner calm of wholeness and healing is not a final destination. There is no state of being cured. In fact, when an anorexic or bulimic woman begins to get well, health itself can feel wrong or uneasy: "It will make you dizzy," Hornbacher warns. "It will confuse you, you will get sick again because sick is what you know."[24] For many women, recovering from an eating disorder is a process that moves "two steps forward and one step back." A woman explains:

> When you get to a new point in healing, going back is familiar. Even when you know it is bad, it is familiar. That is a really lonely place in your growth. You get to a place in healing, in spiritual growth, where you recognize these patterns. . . . You don't want to go back but that is what is familiar.[25]

Forging new patterns of thought and action requires both courage and patience, as personal and cultural backlash—the inertia of habit, the weight of tradition, the attraction of what feels safe and familiar—complicate the creation of new ways of thinking, feeling, and being:

> I could tell you there's been a magical cure, but there hasn't. Voices in my head still hiss at me: Don't eat, you're fat, you're weak, lazy, greedy, a burden, too big for a space in the world. The difference is that now, most of the time, I can shout them down. Sometimes I scream. Sometimes it takes me a couple of tries to make dinner—and sometimes dinner is oatmeal. When that's the best I can do, then it is. . . . But I eat. And you think: How hard can it be? Some days, harder than anything I've ever done in my life.[26]

Envisioning salvation as an ongoing process, rather than an eternal state of blissful perfection, enables a woman to exchange the illusory security that anorexic and bulimic rituals engender for the ongoing challenge of "talking back"—sometimes shouting—at the social/internalized voices that block creative and healing movement.

Ultimately, the process of becoming more critically aware in a culture that rewards denial demands that one join with others who are facing, rather than trying to outrun, the challenges of a world in disrepair. Spiritual vision that is steeped in utopian longings for a carefree existence only replicates the commodity spirituality, and by implication the patriarchal religious values, that feed the culture of eating disorders. An alternative way of making sense and finding value amid the poignancy of life must enable girls and women to speak and nourish the complexity of their yearnings here and now.

Resources for Meaning and Wholeness within and beyond Traditional Religion

Cultivating alternative senses, practices, and vision(s) depends on the availability of alternative spiritual resources, particularly those that transform the legacies of patriarchal religion. Such resources must challenge images that efface, reduce, and/or subordinate girls' and women's spiritual hungers while empowering them to articulate and address their myriad searches for meaning and well-being. More specifically, those who seek to leave the imaginative worlds of anorexia and bulimia need alternative symbols, stories, practices, and beliefs with which to renegotiate their relationships to their bodies, to others, and to their longings for something more.

Even a preliminary consideration of such resources must begin by recognizing girls' and women's vastly divergent relationships to organized religion: from strong connection, to partial estrangement, to tacit indifference, to all-out defiance. Honoring the range of these sensibilities suggests the need for a variety of spiritual resources both within and beyond the parameters of traditional religion. For some women, reclaiming the subversive threads of their religious traditions may be the best strategy for transforming the damages of their oppressive currents. For others, venturing beyond the horizons of organized religion may provide more suitable means of seeking and building a sense of wholeness. Still others may find it most fruitful to engage both traditional and nontraditional forms of spirituality.

The belief that what is sacred can be narrowly defined, pinned down, and reserved exclusively for those who have the correct outlook or faith is a product of the dogmatic way of thinking that eating problems incarnate. To suggest that only one set of symbols and rituals can feed a complicated variety of spiritual hungers is to use an anorexic logic, wherein eating only one kind of food is permitted in the name of purity. Yet to suggest that any image, rite, or belief will do is to assume a bulimic mentality that forfeits the burden of decision that freedom requires for the sake of temporary relief. In searching for spiritual resources both within and beyond traditional religion, what is needed is not simply principles of moderation, as the "experts" recommend, but strategies of discernment, as critical consciousness suggests.

Retelling the Stories and Resurrecting the Silences of Biblical Religion

In her classic work, *In Memory of Her,* Elisabeth Schüssler Fiorenza illuminates two conflicting visions of salvation that circulated during the common era. The first of these visions was part of an alternative prophetic renewal movement within Israel and was preached and practiced in the ministry of Jesus. The integrative symbol of this movement was the *basileia* or "reign" of God: an inclusive vision and humanizing praxis wherein all persons, even and especially the most socially despised, are empowered into health and wholeness. In the gospels, an image of the *basileia* is depicted in stories of Jesus sitting down to share a meal with his friends and followers. Schüssler Fiorenza writes: "The power of God's *basileia* is realized in Jesus' table community with the poor, the sinners, the tax collectors, and prostitutes—with all those who 'do not belong' to the 'holy people,' who are somehow deficient in the eyes of the righteous." By suggesting that salvation is available here and now (and not as a consolation prize in the hereafter), that it is experienced in the flesh (in the food and friendship of a banquet), and that it is present where it is least expected (among women, the poor, and other social outcasts), the *basileia* vision sharply conflicted with the ascetic "holiness" of the religious and cultural elite. The symbolic image of the *basileia*, that of a festive meal to which everyone is invited, radically opposed the pyramidical order of the society in which it emerged.[27]

Retelling the story of Christianity in ways that illumine the competing views of salvation within this tradition is one way of unsettling the authority of its patriarchal influences. The vision of wholeness that the *basileia* symbolizes challenges views of salvation that require the suppression of desire and the subordination of "unholy" persons. This vision also opens up a view of women in Christianity not simply as victims of oppression but as persons who actively sought and seek a different way of being in the world. The active intelligence of these women's spiritual struggles is depicted in Schüssler Fiorenza's retelling of the gospel story of an unnamed foreign woman, who interrupts Jesus' retreat from the crowd, ignores his disciples' complaints that she is being obnoxious, and enters into a theological debate with him for the sake of her daughter's well-being.[28]

Using a similar reconstructive strategy, Judith Plaskow suggests that giving voice and vision to the spiritual searches of her Jewish foresisters begins with hearing the silences of their experiences within their tradition. Such hearing calls for a radical revision of the major aspects of traditional Judaism (God, Israel, and the Torah)—a revision that more aptly reflects and orients Jewish women's struggles for social and spiritual change. For Plaskow, the image of "women's Godwrestling" is an interpretive key for this revision because it illumines a process of seeking, imagining, and experiencing an ultimate reality that is ultimately unimaginable.[29] Like the vision of the foreign woman arguing with Jesus for the sake of her daughter, the idea of "wrestling" with God in the context of community suggests an alternative model of female salvation: one that articulates the presence of divinity in women's struggles to become more whole amid a history that has largely betrayed their interests and yearnings.

Spiritual resources for contesting the silences and suppressions of patriarchal religion are also found in the writings of Womanist, Mujerista, and Asian women theologians. Even a few examples of these works illustrate models and strategies with which those who are multiply injured by the cruelties of racism, sexism, and poverty might defy injustice and envision wholeness. Arguing that the religious motif of "servanthood" has been employed to reinforce the servitude of black women, Jacquelyn Grant proposes an alternative model of Christian self-understanding and community built around the concept of discipleship.[30] Womanist theologian Delores Williams draws on the biblical story of Hagar, the slave of Sarah, to reconstruct a female-centered tradition of African American religion defined by a struggle for survival/quality of life.[31] Korean theologian Chung Hyung Kyung explores the popular religiosity of Asian women as a source for reinterpreting the meaning of God, Christ, and the Virgin Mary.[32] Similarly, Mujerista theologian Ada Maria Isasi-Diaz articulates Hispanic women's everyday religious practices and experiences as tools for their political empowerment and spiritual enrichment.[33]

In many ways, the task of reconstructing the stories and symbols of biblical religion parallels the process of giving voice to the spiritual struggles of girls and women with eating problems. In both cases, tremendous power resides in that which has not been spoken. To transform what has been silenced into speech is to upset the monopoly of influence that patriarchal religion has accumulated through time and habit. For girls and women who claim some connection to the heritages of biblical religion, challenging such influence by retrieving and renewing the radical insights and subversive undercurrents of their traditions may offer what few "secular" salvation myths can, namely, a sense of history.

The potential importance of this historical sensibility is multifaceted. On one level, it may serve as a corrective to the anorexic-bulimic attempt to live beyond change, conflict, contingency, and finitude, that is, beyond embodiment and outside of history. On another level, it may enable women to contest the legacies that tell them they have no spiritual needs and no religious stories of their own. Finally, to situate oneself meaningfully within a historical tradition is one way to assume the kind of accountability that genuine freedom and wholeness require. Drawing strength and wisdom from the struggles of our historical foresisters may not only help some of us navigate the nihilism of the present; it may also keep us mindful of girls and women we have never met, including our great-great-great-great-grandmothers and granddaughters, both by blood and in spirit.

On the Margins and Beyond the Boundaries of Biblical Religion

The alternative vision of salvation that Schüssler Fiorenza reconstructs is part of an important but historically marginal current within biblical religion. In her book *Sexism and God-Talk*, Rosemary Radford Ruether refers to this current as the "prophetic tradition." This tradition represents a countercultural strand of biblical religion. Its values and visions are most clearly articulated in the Hebrew prophets' cries for justice and in the radical ministry of Jesus. In Ruether's synopsis, the prophetic tradition has four basic themes: (1)

God's defense and liberation of the oppressed; (2) a critique of dominant systems of power; (3) a vision of an alternative social order, characterized by peace and justice; and (4) a critique of ideologies and religious systems that sanctify injustice.[34] Although feminist critiques of the prophetic tradition reveal how its patriarchal metaphors indicate its failure to live up to its iconoclastic message,[35] the self-critique that is internal to its vision makes this tradition a viable resource for contemporary social analysis and cultural critique.

In recent years, the religious philosopher Cornel West has appealed to the rubric of prophetic religion to analyze the political and spiritual crises of our times. These crises are manifest in a plethora of social ills—from the violence of racism, sexism, poverty, and homophobia, to the nihilistic dynamics of consumerism—and they bespeak "the accommodation of American religion to the political and cultural status quo."[36] West's social analysis suggests the intersection of prophetic religious critique and cultural criticism: both entail the interrogation of dominant cultural norms. This connection suggests that cultural criticism can be seen as a kind of radical spiritual practice.

As a spiritual discipline, cultural criticism provides a way for girls and women to discern and assess the meanings of popular icons and rituals that tell them what it means to be a woman and what they must do to attain salvation. This practice can enable a girl or woman to derive meaning and pleasure from popular cultural salvation myths not through patterns of consumption, conformity, or consolation, but through engaged suspicion and iconoclastic assessment of that which these myths render unsaid and unseen.

As a spiritual practice, cultural criticism provides a strategy for "discerning the spirits" that is open to persons with or without traditional religious loyalties or scholarly expertise. Because it deals primarily with the images and rituals of mass society, this practice may be a valuable tool for those who are deeply immersed in the chimeric vista of consumer-media culture. Critical consciousness, the pivotal term of cultural criticism, makes it possible to create meaning by investigating meaning, by asking, "What are the 'truths' (messages) of a particular image or story? How does it assign value? How are its meanings produced, circulated, received, and disputed by persons in diverse social situations? Who benefits in the end?"

The discipline of engaging such questions deconstructs and may destroy the conventional pleasures and enchantments of the myths of popular culture. Yet contesting the promises and stimulations of these myths may foster a more lasting kind of satisfaction: the kind that comes from working in solidarity with others to envision and create a better world. Interrogating the authority and attraction of consumer fantasies and ideals is a small but significant way of draining the corporate elites of their power to define what is sacred and true. For "First World" girls and women who must contend with the culture of eating disorders, the discipline of cultural criticism may be an everyday spiritual practice that links them to more global struggles for free-dom, such as the anticapitalist and anti-imperialist movements of liberation theology. To use this practice to define oneself in connection with such real and imagined communities may help combat the emptiness that comes from trying to fulfill the American dream of individual success. It may also instill the sense of accountability that enhances life's value.

The practice of cultural criticism also enables one to search and assess those features of popular culture that hold potential as resources for spiritual nourishment and critical vision. Certain movies, magazines, and songs may function to subvert the legacies of patriarchal religion. On the music scene, for example, a variety of popular female performers are redefining the mean-ing of salvation through song.[37] In her album *New Beginning*, folk-rock artist Tracy Chapman combines a ruthless critique of the profit ethos that orients American culture with an alternative belief:

Heaven's here on earth
In our faith in humankind
In our respect for what is earthly
In our unfaltering belief in peace and love and understanding . . .
Heaven's in our hearts . . .
The world is our temple
The world is our church
Heaven's here on earth.[38]

With a different sound but a similar vision, the Indigo Girls sing of a world where well-being does not depend on absolute certainty ("The less I seek my source in some definitive / closer I am to fine"), a world where there is no pure "individual" ("Distant nation my community / street person my responsibility"), a world in dire need of forgiveness for its crimes against humanity ("Piss and blood / in a railroad car / 100 people / gypsies, queers, and David's star") and in desperate need of hope and transformation ("What was once your pain will be your home").[39]

In different contexts, movie directors like Julia Dash, Nancy Savoca, and Jane Campion (to name a few) are challenging long-standing scenarios that depict women as decorative icons with no inner drama, divinity, or depth. The stories that these and other feminist filmmakers show and tell disrupt the visual conventions and standard narratives of womanhood, which define female subjectivity primarily in reference to physical appearance and female salvation mainly in terms of heterosexual romantic fulfillment. While no film narrative is immune to co-optation by dominant ways of thinking and seeing, practicing cultural criticism enables one to discern the visions that are pos-sible within a given text and to imagine—and when need be contest—the effects that such visions are likely to produce in a given social climate. Such discernment makes it possible to engage a diverse repertoire of spiritual images, songs, and stories, an alternative repository to which girls and women might turn for inspiration when the search for healing and wholeness seems eternally uphill.

The value of cultural criticism as a spiritual practice extends to the use of literature as another nontraditional source of postpatriarchal wisdom. As Katie Geneva Cannon has shown, black women's fiction has been a profound source of spiritual sustenance and ethical insight for the black community.[40] The transgression of boundaries between "sacred" and "profane" marks the writings of the late black feminist Audre Lorde, arguably one of the greatest cultural critics of this century. In myth, prophesy, poetry, and prose, Lorde's work gives voice to some of life's deepest questions in the face of finitude, as it summons women to speak the silences that keep them from living fully:

> In becoming forcibly and essentially aware of my mortality, and of what
> I wished and wanted for my life, however short it might be, priorities
> and omissions became strongly etched in a merciless light, and what I
> most regretted were my silences. Of what had I ever been afraid? . . . I
> was going to die, if not sooner then later, whether or not I had ever
> spoken myself. My silences had not protected me. Your silence will not
> protect you.[41]

Womanist passages such as this aim to transform the silences and sufferings of women of color into language and action that enable survival and feed the spirit. Love of this spirit is central to the very definition of "Womanist" (originally articulated by Alice Walker), a definition that, as Cheryl Townsend Gilkes points out, also contains a passionate affirmation of self-love and love for others, love of food and love of roundness in women, love of music and of dance.[42]

Other nontraditional resources for feeding girls' and women's spirit(s) are found in what is loosely referred to as the Goddess movement. Even a cursory look at the major features of this movement suggests how its resources may address some women's spiritual needs. Feminist followers of the Goddess draw on ancient traditions of Goddess worship, modifying them in ways that address their current spiritual concerns. According to feminist thealogian Carol Christ, the Goddess symbolism at the heart of this religion affirms women's spiritual powers, their bodies, their agency or will, and their bonds and heritage.[43] Such imagery also creates a different view of divinity: sacred reality is not a supreme being that exists above and beyond the tangible world; rather, divine presence resides and is manifest in the earth and its interconnected processes and bodies.

Critics of the neopagan (Goddess) movement say that its historical claims are questionable.[44] Yet the disruptive quality of its female-centered symbolism and worship in a predominantly male-centered culture suggests that the import of this movement may rest not so much in its historical content as in its imaginative power to challenge the (patriarchal) status quo. By presenting a multiplicity of images for envisioning a transcendent element of human life, including metaphors from the natural world, the Goddess movement proffers symbolic alternatives for calling attention to and fostering relationship with those aspects of life that defy rational comprehension and control. A more serious danger of Goddess religion as a countercultural spiritual resource is its valuation of the very associations (female bodies and the natural world) that have historically been used to constrict women's freedom.

If Goddess religion merits both serious consideration and criticism as a potential source of spiritual insight, so does the turn to Asian philosophies and religions that characterizes some Westerners' quests for spiritual meaning. Critics of this turn to the East are appropriately suspicious insofar as it entails the abdication of responsibility for the imperializing history and neo-colonialism of Western countries like the United States and insofar as it is based on a utopian and selective vision of the offerings of an "other" culture. Indeed, Eastern religions contain their own patriarchal legacies that both men and women ignore at their own spiritual peril.[45]

Yet for women in particular, turning to the spiritual traditions of Asia may fill in some of the gaps that the legacies of Western religion have bequeathed to (and within) them. The bodily focus of practices such as yoga, meditation, and martial arts suggest alternatives to mainstream Western forms of exercise, which often exacerbate the mind/body division they seek to mend and which seldom attend to affairs of the spirit. "Yoga," for example, means "to join," Asian feminist and community health worker Farah Shroff explains: "Joining the mind, body and spirit is a major goal of these practices. One fundamental premise upon which they operate is that the human being is a microcosm of the universe."[46] Similarly, the body awareness, techniques, and discipline that martial arts such as aikido cultivate are predicated not on rising above the conflicts and surprises of life in this world but on learning to work nonviolently with and through the difficult situations and unexpected turns that this life invariably presents. The practice of breathing at the heart of Zen meditation presents another integrative discipline. In the words of Buddhist monk, poet, and activist Thich Nhat Hanh, "Breath is the bridge which connects life to consciousness, which unites your body to your thoughts." As Nhat Hanh points out, the goal of such practice is not to isolate oneself from the unpleasant realities of the world outside but to become more effectively aware of and engaged in what is really going on in the world one seeks to change.[47]

A Different Kind of Salvation

My preliminary discussion of some possible spiritual resources for cultivating good health and healing is not meant to be or to promote a smorgasbord approach to spirituality. Rather, the variety inherent in my discussion is meant to acknowledge the complexity and diversity of spiritual hungers among girls and women who are currently starving, vomiting, and choking on the symbolic beliefs and ritualizing practices that this society normally recommends to them. Just as the histories and circumstances that shaped these hungers vary irreducibly, so must the symbolic and ritual resources engaged to more adequately nourish them. The bottom line for discerning such resources is perhaps best formulated not in terms of a fixed criterion but in terms of the question of whether and how they empower and interconnect the various struggles of girls and women and all people for a life that is meaningful and whole.

My discussion of these spiritual resources also suggests an answer to the question implicit in this book all along, namely, "What difference does it make to say that there are spiritual dimensions to girls' and women's struggles with food and their bodies?" To name these dimensions is to argue that these struggles touch on some of the most profound questions of girls' and women's lives: questions of meaning in the face of suffering and oppression, of value in the face of conflict and longing, truth in the face of plurality and uncertainty. In the end, this argument calls attention to what is currently missing not just in the discourse on eating disorders but also in the practices and perspectives, the ideals and values of this culture as a whole.

It is hard to say what is missing—perhaps because what is missing is hard to see. And it is even harder in an age when the permitted avenues and provisions for negotiating the invisible and voicing the unspoken have become as uniformly thin and firm as the lines of the female bodies that are regularly upheld for our worship. Yet to see through this thinness, to read between its narrow lines, is to encounter a hunger that could change the world. To recognize and nourish this hunger would mark the beginning of a different kind of salvation: one that did not place individual success ahead of communal ties; one that did not separate material concerns from matters of spirit; one that did not deny the limits of human knowledge and control, or the possibility of freedom and change. This revolutionary approach to redemption would create and find beauty in process and imperfection, truth in diversity and interrelations, goodness in desire and struggle. It would celebrate—not shy away from or try to shrink—female agency, passion, joy.

This redemption has already begun: where girls and women of all different sizes, colors, shapes, and cultures are opening their mouths not to gorge or vomit but to contest and transform the erasure of their longings and struggles in history; where they are sitting down to meals with each other to share their sorrow as well as their strength; where they are nurturing their bodies and spirits: writing poems of protest, singing songs of hope, marching to take back the night and arguing about books and movies, defending the dreams of children and the wisdom of the earth, baking bread and making policy, telling stories and gazing at the stars, dancing, worshiping, playing together.

May the multifaceted movements of this revolutionary redemption grow large and strong, until all girls and women can be at home in their bodies, until the world becomes a hospitable place for every body, until our myriad yearnings for something more are nourished in ways that enable us to be present to what already is, to challenge the injustices and sufferings, while honoring the pain and the uncertainty, transforming them into food for our hearts and minds, our bodies and spirits.

NOTES

Introduction

1. A number of surveys indicate that the majority of women in this country see themselves as "too fat." See, for example, Susan and Orland Wooley, "Feeling Fat in a Thin Society," *Glamour* (Feb. 1984): 198–201+; Linda Villarosa, "Dangerous Eating," *Essence* (Jan. 1994): 19–21+; Kelly Brownell, "Dieting and the Search for the Perfect Body: Where Physiology and Culture Collide," *Behavior Therapy* 22 (1991): 6; Rita Freedman, *Bodylove: Learning to Like Our Looks—and Ourselves* (New York: Harper and Row, 1988), 82. Statistics for fourth-grade girls reflect studies done in the Chicago and San Francisco areas. Among the many places these studies are cited is Joan Jacobs Brumberg's *Fasting Girls: The History of Anorexia Nervosa* (New York: Penguin, 1988), 32. Figures comparing average models with average women are cited in Katherine Gilday's documentary film *The Famine Within* (1992). On the sale of diet books, see Roberta P. Seid, *Never Too Thin: Why Women Are at War with Their Bodies* (New York: Prentice Hall, 1989), 4, 21. For figures on the diet industry, see Laura Fraser, *Losing It: America's Obsession with Weight and the Industry That Feeds On It* (New York: Dutton, 1997), 8. For statistics on bulimia and anorexia, see W. Cromie, "One in Five Female Undergraduates Has Eating Problem," *Harvard University Gazette* 88 (May 7, 1993): 3, 10; K. A. Halmi et al., "Binge Eating and Vomiting: A Survey of A College Population," *Psychological Medicine* 11 (1981): 697–706; S. Nevo, "Bulimic Symptoms: Prevalence and Ethnic Differences among College Women," *International Journal of Eating Disorders* 4 (1985): 151–68. See chapter 1 for more references regarding the prevalence and demography of eating problems.

2. Becky Thompson names some of these myths in the first chapter of her book

A Hunger So Wide and So Deep: American Women Speak Out on Eating Problems (Minneapolis: University of Minnesota Press, 1994), 1–26. For a discussion of the emergence of popular awareness of anorexia in the 1980s, see Brumberg, *Fasting Girls,* 8–10, 14–18.

3. Peter Berger uses the phrase "secularized soteriologies" to refer to nonreligious worldviews whose values compete with traditional religious perspectives in contemporary Western societies. See *The Sacred Canopy: Elements of a Sociology of Religion* (1967; reprint, New York: Doubleday, 1990), 125. I prefer to keep the term "secular" in quotes when I use it because I question the modern assumption that "secular" and "religious" myths, beliefs, and rituals can be unambiguously distinguished.

4. Throughout this book, I use the term "anorexic" to refer to people with anorexia, rather than the clinically correct term, which is "anorectic" or "anoretic." I eschew these latter terms because, as nouns, they tend to define a woman with anorexia by that disease, thereby unwittingly reinforcing an identity between her eating disorder and her self. By contrast, the more common parlance term "anorexic," though technically an adjective, is frequently used to refer to persons suffering with anorexia and may convey a greater distance between the person and the disease. The same is true for the term "bulimic," which is used both as an adjective and as a noun.

5. Becky Thompson refers to this diversion as "the politics of distraction." See *A Hunger So Wide and So Deep,* 11.

6. Seid, *Never Too Thin,* 33; Richard Gordon, *Anorexia and Bulimia: Anatomy of a Social Epidemic* (New York: Basil Blackwell, 1990), 92; Sharlene Hesse-Biber, *Am I Thin Enough Yet?: The Cult of Thinness and the Commercialization of Identity* (New York: Oxford University Press, 1996), 5; Sandra Bartky, "Foucault, Femininity, and the Modernization of Patriarchal Power," in *Femininity and Domination: Studies in the Phenomenology of Oppression* (New York: Routledge, 1990), 80; Naomi Wolf, *The Beauty Myth: How Images of Beauty Are Used against Women* (New York: Anchor, 1991), 86–130.

7. Marya Hornbacher, "Wasted," *Minneapolis–St. Paul Monthly Magazine* (Nov. 1993): 70.

8. Judith Plaskow, *Standing Again at Sinai: Judaism from a Feminist Perspective* (San Francisco: HarperCollins, 1990), 232, 237. Sallie McFague, *The Body of God: An Ecological Theology* (Minneapolis: Fortress, 1993), 208. Carol Christ, *Diving Deep and Surfacing: Women Writers on Spiritual Quest* (1980; reprint, Boston: Beacon, 1986), 8.

9. The term "thealogy," from the Greek *thea,* is meant to distinguish the work of those affiliated with the Goddess or Wiccan movements. Carol Christ, a leading feminist thealogian, defines this term as "reflections on the meaning of Goddess." See Christ, *Laughter of Aphrodite: Reflections on a Journey to the Goddess* (San Francisco: HarperCollins, 1987), ix. The term was first coined by Naomi Goldenberg in *The Changing of the Gods: Feminism and the End of Traditional Religions* (Boston: Beacon, 1979), 96–99.

10. I retain the term "feminist" to designate my work and the community and movement supporting it, even as I see the problems inherent in this nomenclature. Not only does this label lend itself to misunderstanding, given the diversity of views attached to it in society today, but perhaps more important, "feminism" has a history of being associated with the interests and concerns of women who are white and

middle-class. In my view, both the contested meanings and the spotted history of feminism call for a greater sense of accountability among those of us who have benefited from the movement to reshape its agenda in ways that speak from and to the various needs and longings of all women and all persons. My position also affirms the need for some women and feminists of color to use other terms and resources for identifying themselves and their communities.

11. Michel Foucault uses the term "subjugated knowledges" to describe the experiences and histories of those whose voices have been excluded or not taken seriously within ruling discourses and institutions. See *Power/Knowledge: Selected Interviews and Other Writings, 1927–1977* (New York: Pantheon, 1980), 81–82.

12. This approach reflects Richard Johnson's characterization of a cultural studies analysis in his essay "What Is Cultural Studies Anyway?," *Social Text* 16 (1987): 38–80.

13. This religious/theological perspective is influenced by the insights of feminist, liberation, and constructivist theologians and critically minded philosophers of religion. See chapter 1 for detailed citations of these works.

14. My awareness regarding this point has been raised by bell hooks's observations in *Teaching to Transgress: Education as the Practice of Freedom* (New York: Routledge, 1994), 89, 95–108.

Chapter One

1. Some health professionals also classify obesity as an "eating disorder." See, e.g., S. Abraham and D. Llewellyn-Jones, *Eating Disorders: The Facts* (New York: Oxford University Press, 1987); A. J. Giannini and A. E. Slaby, eds., *The Eating Disorders* (New York: Springer-Verlag, 1993). The *Diagnostic and Statistical Manual for Mental Disorders—IV* (Washington: American Psychiatric Association Press, 1994) says that obesity is a physical—not mental—problem. Some leading medical experts in the field concur. See A. S. Kaplan and P. E. Garfinkel, "Introduction," in *Medical Issues and the Eating Disorders: The Interface*, ed. Kaplan and Garfinkel (New York: Brunner/Mazel, 1993), x. In sum, the status of obesity is controversial within the field of "eating disorders."

2. The pursuit of thinness and intense fear of fat were not seen as key features of anorexia until the 1960s. This recognition distinguished anorexia from other illnesses involving malnutrition. See L. K. G. Hsu, *Eating Disorders* (New York: Guilford, 1990), 3, 12, and C. G. Fairburn and D. M. Garner, "Diagnostic Criteria for Anorexia Nervosa and Bulimia Nervosa: The Importance of Attitudes to Shape and Weight," in *Diagnostic Issues in Anorexia Nervosa and Bulimia Nervosa*, ed. D. Garner and P. Garfinkel (New York: Brunner/Mazel, 1988), 37.

3. See Abraham and Llewellyn-Jones, *Eating Disorders*, 10–11; G. F. M. Russell, "Bulimia Nervosa: An Ominous Variant of Anorexia Nervosa," *Psychological Medicine* 9 (1979): 429–48; and Russell, "The Diagnostic Formulation in Bulimia Nervosa," in Garner and Garfinkel, *Diagnostic Issues in Anorexia Nervosa and Bulimia Nervosa*, 8–9.

4. Becky Thompson, *A Hunger So Wide and So Deep: American Women Speak Out on Eating Problems* (Minneapolis: University of Minnesota Press, 1994), 94.

5. This manual is revised every several years. The most recent edition (*DSM-IV*) was published in 1994. According to C. W. Rand and J. M. Kuldau, *DSM* criteria provide the guidelines for most American studies. See "Epidemiology of Bulimia and

Symptoms in a General Population: Sex, Age, Race, and Socioeconomic Status," *International Journal of Eating Disorders* 11 (1992): 37–44.

6. See Michel Foucault, *Power/Knowledge: Selected Interviews and Other Writings, 1972–1977* (New York: Pantheon, 1980).

7. See, for example, Susan Bordo, "Whose Body Is This?: Feminism, Medicine, and the Conceptualization of Eating Disorders," in *Unbearable Weight: Feminism, Western Culture, and the Body* (Berkeley: University of California Press, 1993), 45–69.

8. While "eating disorders" in the *DSM-IV* are defined by criteria that are said to be "essential," the "diagnostic features" used to identify these illnesses have changed over time. For example, the *DSM-III* (1987) was the first edition to recognize "excessive exercise" as a form of bulimic behavior. In addition, a major debate in the 1994 *DSM-IV* revision asked whether binge eating that is not followed by "inappropriate compensatory behavior" should be designated as a separate diagnostic entity. See M. J. Devlin, "Binge Eating Disorder: The Diagnostic Debate Continues," *American Anorexia/Bulimia Association Newsletter*, Special Research Edition (Fall 1992): 8; C. G. Fairburn et al., "The Classification of Recurrent Overeating: The 'Binge Eating Disorder' Proposal," *International Journal of Eating Disorders* 13 (1993): 155–59; R. J. Spitzer et al., "Binge Eating Disorder: To Be or Not to Be in *DSM-IV*," *International Journal of Eating Disorders* 10 (1991): 627–29.

9. *DSM-IV*, 539.

10. *DSM-IV*, 545.

11. According to doctors Susan and Orland Wooley, the number one bestseller in 1981—"outselling its nearest competitor more than 2 to 1—was the *Beverly Hills Diet Book*, in which Judy Mazel advocates a form of bulimia in which binges are 'compensated' (her word) by eating massive quantities of raw fruit in order to produce diarrhea." See "The Beverly Hills Eating Disorder: The Mass Marketing of Anorexia Nervosa," *International Journal of Eating Disorders* 1 (1982): 57–69.

12. Hsu, *Eating Disorders*, 7; D. M. Garner et al., "Psychoeducational Principles in the Treatment of Bulimia and Anorexia Nervosa," *Handbook of Psychotherapy for Anorexia Nervosa and Bulimia*, ed. D. Garner and P. Garfinkel (New York: Guilford, 1985), 513, 541; D. Garner and C. G. Fairburn, "Relationship between Anorexia Nervosa and Bulimia Nervosa: Diagnostic Implications," in Garner and Garfinkel, *Diagnostic Issues in Anorexia Nervosa and Bulimia Nervosa*, 75. Not until 1980, in DSM-III, was bulimia classified as a *syndrome* with its own diagnostic criteria, rather than a *symptom* related to anorexia and/or obesity. This means that references to anorexia before this time may or may not include problems with binge-purging. See Walter Vandereycken, "Emergence of Bulimia Nervosa as a Separate Diagnostic Entity: Review of the Literature from 1960 to 1979," *International Journal of Eating Disorders* 16 (1994): 105–16. The *DSM-IV* addresses the overlap between anorexia and bulimia by classifying anorexia into two specific types (i.e., "Binge-Eating/Purging Types" and "Restricting Types"). *DSM-IV*, 545.

13. Hsu, *Eating Disorders*, 7, 27; Abraham and Llewellyn-Jones, *Eating Disorders*, 93.

14. The Eating Disorders Work Group for the *DSM-IV* (1994) consisted entirely of "experts" in the field, and most of them were male. See G. T. Wilson and B. T. Walsh, "Eating Disorders in the *DSM-IV*," *Journal of Abnormal Psychology* 100 (1991): 362–65. Matra Robertson writes: "As a category of illness, anorexia was created because it made meaningful to the medical profession—not to the starver—a set of symptoms and patterns of behavior which were unreasonable and inexplicable."

Starving in the Silences: An Exploration of Anorexia Nervosa (New York: New York University Press, 1992), ix, xiv.

15. For the criteria of "Eating Disorder Not Otherwise Specified," see *DSM-IV*, 550.

16. Linda Weltner, "Losing the Passion to Lose the Pounds," in *Eating Our Hearts Out: Personal Accounts of Women's Relationships to Food,* ed. Leslea Newman (Freedom, Calif.: Crossing Pr., 1993), 209–10. An article in *Woman's Day* features several older women whose eating disorders went undetected due to their age. One of these women was sixty-seven years old and had been starving-gorging-purging for over fifty years. See "Eating Disorders: Women at Risk" (June 3, 1997): 49–50.

17. Catrina Brown, "The Continuum: Anorexia, Bulimia, and Weight Preoccupation," in *Consuming Passions: Feminist Approaches to Weight Preoccupation and Eating Disorders*, ed. C. Brown and K. Jaspers (Toronto: Second Story, 1993), 54.

18. In addition to feminists, a number of more traditional experts in the field, particularly those who emphasize the multidetermined nature of eating problems, adopt a continuum model. See, for example, Hsu, *Eating Disorders*, 78, 144. Others who use a continuum model distinguish between "true" eating disorders and their "milder" variants. See J. Polivy and C. P. Herman, "Diagnosis and Treatment of Normal Eating," *Journal of Consulting and Clinical Psychology* 55 (1987): 635–44.

19. In his review of thirteen studies on obesity and mortality, Ancel Keys concludes that risk of early death increases only when persons are extremely obese or underweight and that weight had no significant impact on the health of the women (80 percent) between these extremes. A. Keys, "Overweight, Obesity, Coronary Heart Disease and Mortality," *Nutrition Review* 38 (1980): 297–307. Other research shows that obesity is genetically determined rather than consciously chosen. See A. J. Stunkard et al., "An Adoption Study of Human Obesity," *New England Journal of Medicine* 314 (1986): 193–98. Laura Fraser discusses the debates among "obesity researchers" in *Losing It!: False Hopes and Fat Promises in the Diet Industry* (New York: Dutton, 1997), 212–35.

20. The "set point" theory holds that body weight is regulated at a relatively set point in a manner similar to body temperature or blood pressure. The body defends its weight against external pressures to change, and deviations from the set point give rise to physical compensations (such as a lower metabolic rate) that aim to return the body to its original weight. See R. Keesey, "A Set Point Theory of Obesity," in *Handbook of Eating Disorders*, ed. K. Brownell and J. P. Foreyt (New York: Basic Books, 1986). For a summary of the two most frequently cited studies supporting the "set point" theory (Keys et al., 1950; Sims et al. 1968), see D. Garner et al., "Psychoeducational Principles in the Treatment of Bulimia and Anorexia Nervosa," 530–31.

21. See S. C. and O. W. Wooley, "Should Obesity Be Treated at All?," in *Eating and Its Disorders*, ed. A. Stunkard and E. Stellar (New York: Tavern Press, 1984), 187. In "Why Diets Fail," Donna Ciliska cites studies indicating that "there is no difference in quantities of food, speed of eating, bite size, or total caloric intake between 'large' people and the general population." In Brown and Jaspers, *Consuming Passions*, 87. See also G. Terence, "Binge Eating in Obese Patients," in Kaplan and Garfinkel, *Medical Issues and the Eating Disorders*, 40; and S. C. Wooley et al., "Theoretical, Practical, and Social Issues in Behavioral Treatments of Obesity," *Journal of Applied Behavioral Analysis* 2 (1979): 3–25.

22. Ciliska, "Why Diets Fail," 84–85. "Yo-yo dieting"—repeated cycles of

weight loss and gain—is also believed to be "a common precursor of eating disorders." R. Black et al., "Alterations in Metabolism and Energy Expenditure in Eating Disorders," in Kaplan and Garfinkel, *Medical Issues and the Eating Disorders*, 149–50, 157. See also O. Bosello et al., "Weight Cycling Syndrome: Effects on Body Weight, Body Fat Distribution, Eating Behavior, and Treatment Compliance," in *Primary and Secondary Eating Disorders: A Psychoneuroendocrine and Metabolic Approach*, ed. E. Ferrari et al. (New York: Pergamon, 1993), 397. Other articles charting the health risks linked to chronic dieting include S. A. French and R. W. Jeffrey, "Consequences of Dieting to Lose Weight: Effects on Physical and Mental Health," *Health Psychology* 13 (1994): 195–212; and J. P. Lissner and K. Brownell, "Weight Cycling, Mortality, and Cardiovascular Disease: A Review of the Epidemiological Findings," in *Obesity*, ed. P. Bjorntorp and B. Brodoff (New York: Lippincott, 1992), 653–61.

23. See M. Cuzzolaro, "Epidemiology of Eating Disorders: Some Remarks on Long-Term Trends in Incidence and on Prevalence in Western Countries," in Ferrari et al., *Primary and Secondary Eating Disorders*, 107; Hsu, *Eating Disorders*, 64; P. Leichner and A. Gertler, "Prevalence and Incidence Studies of Anorexia Nervosa," in *The Eating Disorders: Medical and Psychological Bases of Diagnoses and Treatment*, ed. B. J. Blinder et al. (New York: PMA, 1988), 147. Many experts believe that the small percentage of males who develop eating disorders are disproportionately gay and/or involved in athletics where weight is a determining issue. See Sharlene Hesse-Biber, *Am I Thin Enough Yet?: The Cult of Thinness and the Commercialization of Identity* (New York: Oxford University Press, 1996), 107. An article that appeared in *Newsweek* suggested that the gender disparity in eating disorders may partially be due to underdiagnosis. See Jean Seligman, "The Pressure to Lose: Eating Disorders and Young Men," *Newsweek* 123 (May 1994): 60–61. The greater incidence of disturbed body image and eating problems among gay men (compared to their heterosexual peers) is the subject of several essays in the collection *Looking Queer: Body Image and Identity in Lesbian, Bisexual, Gay, and Transgender Communities*, ed. Dawn Atkins (New York: The Haworth Press, 1998). Two articles that discuss dangerous eating among gay men and athletes (respectively) are Carol Ness, "Gays Find Worship of Beauty a Beast," *San Francisco Examiner* (Dec. 12, 1997): A14, and Gary Olson, "Wrestling with Fate," *St. Paul Pioneer Press* (Dec. 19, 1997): 1D. For a book-length study on eating disorders in men, see Arnold Andersen, ed., *Males with Eating Disorders* (New York: Brunner/Mazel, 1990).

24. *DSM-IV*, 543, 548. Using *DSM-III* criteria, K. A. Halmi et al. estimate that 13 percent to 20 percent of American college women suffer from bulimia. "Binge Eating and Vomiting: A Survey of a College Population," *Psychological Medicine* 11 (1981): 697–706. See also D. B. Herzog and P. M. Copeland, "Eating Disorders," *New England Journal of Medicine* 313 (1985): 295; W. Cromie, "One in Five Female Undergraduates Has Eating Problem," *Harvard University Gazette* 88 (May 7, 1993): 3.

25. M. G. Thompson and D. M. Schwartz, "Life Adjustment of Women with Anorexia Nervosa and Anorexic-like Behavior," *International Journal of Eating Disorders* 1 (1982): 47–60; see also S. Nevo, "Bulimic Symptoms: Prevalence and Ethnic Differences among College Women," *International Journal of Eating Disorders* 4 (1985): 151–68.

26. See Halmi et al., "Binge Eating and Vomiting," 483–91; R. C. Hawkins and P. F. Clement, "Development and Construct Validation of a Self-Report Measure of Binge Eating Tendencies," *Addictive Behaviors* 5 (1980): 219–26. Summarizing studies

in this country, R. L. Pyle and J. E. Mitchell write that between 57 percent and 79 percent of American women report binge eating, and between 17 percent and 21 percent do so on a weekly basis. "The Epidemiology of Bulimia," in Blinder et al., *The Eating Disorders*; 260.

27. Harris poll cited in Kelly Brownell, "Dieting and the Search for the Perfect Body: Where Physiology and Culture Collide," *Behavior Therapy* 22 (1991): 6. For exercise percentage, see S. Wooley and O. Wooley, "Feeling Fat in a Thin Society," *Glamour* (Feb. 1984): 198–201+; Thompson and Schwartz found nearly 40 percent of college women they surveyed engaging in "anorexic-like" behavior. "Life Adjustment of Women with Anorexia Nervosa and Anorexic-like Behavior," 47–60; see also Sandra Birtchnell et al., "Body Image Distortion in Non-Eating-Disordered Women," *International Journal of Eating Disorders* 6 (1987): 385–91.

28. Bridget Dolan, "Cross-Cultural Aspects of Anorexia Nervosa and Bulimia: A Review," *International Journal of Eating Disorders* 10 (1991): 67–78; Abraham and Llewellyn-Jones, *Eating Disorders*, 8. Matra Robertson cites studies that indicate an increase of anorexia among Australian women. See *Starving in the Silences*, 16.

29. See Hsu, *Eating Disorders*, 59; M. S. H. Hooper and D. Garner, "Application of the Eating Disorders Inventory to a Sample of Black, White, and Mixed Race Schoolgirls in Zimbabwe," *International Journal of Eating Disorders* 5 (1986): 161–68; C. M. Bulik, "Eating Disorders in Immigrants: Two Case Reports," *International Journal of Eating Disorders* 6 (1987): 133–41.

30. Most experts believe anorexia and bulimia to be most common among "Caucasian females from middle to upper social classes in developed countries." Hsu, *Eating Disorders*, 12. Studies showing a higher degree of disturbed eating among Caucasian females are A. H. Crisp et al., "How Common Is Anorexia Nervosa?: A Prevalence Study," *British Journal of Psychiatry* 128 (1976): 549–54; James Gray et al., "The Prevalence of Bulimia in a Black College Population," *International Journal of Eating Disorders* 6 (1987): 733–40; K. K. Abrams et al., "Disordered Eating Attitudes and Behaviours, Psychological Adjustment, and Ethnic Identity: A Comparison of Black and White Female College Students," *International Journal of Eating Disorders* 14 (1993): 49–57; Nevo, "Bulimic Symptoms," 151–68. A. Andersen and A. Hay found social class to be more a significant variable than racial identity in the demography of eating disorders. "Racial and Socioeconomic Influences in Anorexia and Bulimia," *International Journal of Eating Disorders* 4 (1985): 479–87.

31. Richard Gordon, *Anorexia and Bulimia: Anatomy of a Social Epidemic* (Cambridge: Basil Blackwell, 1990), 46; Rand and Kuldau, "Epidemiology of Bulimia and Symptoms in a General Population," 37–44; P. Robinson and A. Andersen, "Anorexia Nervosa in American Blacks," *Journal of Psychiatric Research* 19 (1985): 183–88.

32. Lionel W. Rosen et al., "Prevalence of Pathogenic Weight-Control Behaviors among Native American Women and Girls," *International Journal of Eating Disorders* 7 (1988): 807–11.

33. Although conducted in England, this study is relevant here given the relative similarities between American and British society. D. B. Mumford et al., "Sociocultural Correlates of Eating Disorders among Asian Schoolgirls in Bradford," *British Journal of Psychiatry* 158 (1991): 222–28.

34. On the increase of eating disorders among women of color, see L. Emmons, "Dieting and Purging Behavior in Black and White High School Students," *Journal of the American Diet Association* 92 (1992): 306–12; L. K. G. Hsu, "Are Eating Dis-

orders Becoming More Common in Blacks," *International Journal of Eating Disorders* 6 (1987): 113–24; T. J. Silber, "Anorexia Nervosa in Blacks and Hispanics," *International Journal of Eating Disorders* 5 (1986): 121–28; Maria Root, "Disordered Eating in Women of Color," *Sex Roles* 22 (1990): 525–36. On the age factor, see D. Blake Woodside and P. Garfinkel, "Age of Onset in Eating Disorders," *International Journal of Eating Disorders* 12 (1992): 31–36; L. K. G. Hsu and B. Zimmer, "Eating Disorders in Old Age," *International Journal of Eating Disorders* 7 (1988): 133–38; M. Gupta and N. Schork, "Aging-Related Concerns and Body-Image: Possible Future Implications for Eating Disorders," *International Journal of Eating Disorders* 14 (1993): 481–86.

35. Andersen and Hay, "Racial and Socioeconomic Influences in Anorexia and Bulimia," 479–87; I. Eisler and G. I. Szmukler, "Social Class as a Confounding Variable in the Eating Attitudes Test," *Journal of Psychiatric Research* 19 (1985): 171–76.

36. See Thompson, *A Hunger So Wide and So Deep*; Laura Brown, "Lesbians, Weight, and Eating: New Analyses and Perspectives," in *Lesbian Psychologies: Explorations and Challenges*, ed. L. Brown (Chicago: University of Illinois Press, 1987), 294–309; and Atkins, ed., *Queer Looks*.

37. J. E. Smith and J. Krejci, "Minorities Join the Majority: Eating Disturbances among Hispanic and Native American Youth," *International Journal of Eating Disorders* 10 (1991): 179–86; L. Osvold and G. Sodowsky, "Eating Disorders of White American, Racial and Ethnic Minority American, and International Women," *Journal of Multicultural Counseling and Development* 21 (1993): 143–54.

38. Thompson, *A Hunger So Wide and So Deep*, 2.

39. For a persuasive argument against the "protection" theory, see Root, "Disordered Eating in Women of Color," 527.

40. Studies that measure the significance of assimilation of white cultural ideals among minority women with eating problems include T. Furukawa, "Weight Changes and Eating Attitudes of Japanese Adolescents under Acculturative Stresses: A Prospective Study," *International Journal of Eating Disorders* 15 (1994): 71–79; Abrams et al., "Disordered Eating Attitudes and Behaviors, Psychological Adjustment, and Ethnic Identity," 49–57; Dolan, "Cross-Cultural Aspects of Anorexia Nervosa and Bulimia," 67–78; Gray et al., "The Prevalence of Bulimia in a Black College Population," 733–40; Silber, "Anorexia Nervosa in Blacks and Hispanics," 121–28. Hsu cites a study of 138 Hispanic females in the United States that found a significant correlation between disturbed eating patterns (as measured by a standard test) and level of acculturation. See *Eating Disorders*, 80.

41. For a survey of conventional approaches to eating disorders, see Kelly Bemis, "Current Approaches to the Etiology and Treatment of Anorexia Nervosa," *Psychological Bulletin* 85 (1978): 593–617.

42. See Hilde Bruch, *Eating Disorders: Obesity, Anorexia Nervosa, and the Person Within* (New York: Basic Books, 1973), 5; Bruch, "Hunger and Instinct," *Journal of Nervous and Mental Disease* 149 (1969): 91–114; and Bruch, *Conversations with Anorexics*, ed. D. Czyzewski and M. Suhr (New York: Basic Books, 1988).

43. Hilde Bruch, *The Golden Cage: The Enigma of Anorexia Nervosa* (New York: Vintage Books, 1978), 92, 98, 134–39. Based on the observation of seventy anorexic patients, this work was a watershed in the study of eating disorders.

44. Pioneering studies in this area include S. Minuchin et al., *Psychosomatic Families: Anorexia Nervosa in Context* (Cambridge: Harvard University Press, 1978), and M. S. Palazzoli et al., *Self Starvation: From the Intrapsychic to the Transpersonal*

Approach (New York: Jason Aronson, 1978). See also H. Stierlin and G. Weber, *Unlocking the Family Door: A Systematic Approach to the Understanding and Treatment of Anorexia Nervosa* (New York: Brunner/Mazel, 1989); M. Strober and L. Humphrey, "Familial Contributions to the Etiology and Course of Anorexia and Bulimia," *Journal of Consulting and Clinical Psychology* 5 (1987): 654–59.

45. Feminists offer more nuanced views of the role of the mother-daughter nexus in the development of eating problems. In *The Hungry Self: Women, Eating, and Identity* (New York: Harper and Row, 1985), Kim Chernin argues that eating problems express a woman's conflicting desires to separate from and connect with her mother.

46. R. Liebman et al., "The Role of the Family in the Treatment of Anorexia Nervosa," *Journal of the American Academy of Child Psychiatry* 13 (1974): 264–74; R. O. Schwartz et al., "Family Therapy for Bulimia," in Garner and Garfinkel, *Handbook of Psychotherapy for Anorexia Nervosa and Bulimia*, 280–310; J. Sargent and R. Liebman, "Family Therapy for Eating Disorders," in Blinder et al., *The Eating Disorders*, 447–55; D. Blake Woodside and L. Shekter-Wolfson, eds., *Family Approaches in Treatment of Eating Disorders* (Washington: American Psychological Association Press, 1991), xvi.

47. Cognitive-behavioral approaches build on the experimental animal studies of Pavlov and Thorndike. See J. Kuechler and R. Hampton, "Learning and Behavioral Approaches to the Treatment of Anorexia Nervosa and Bulimia," in Blinder et al., *The Eating Disorders*, 423; C. Fairburn, "Cognitive Behavioral Treatment for Bulimia," in Garner and Garfield, *Handbook of Psychotherapy for Anorexia Nervosa and Bulimia*, 163, 178, 188; J. C. Rosen et al., "Cognitive Behavior Therapy for Negative Body Image," *Behavior Therapy* 20 (1989): 393–404; T. Wilson and C. Fairburn, "Cognitive Treatments for Eating Disorders. Special Section: Recent Developments in Cognitive and Constructivist Psychotherapies," *Journal of Consulting and Clinical Psychology* 61 (1993): 261–69.

48. See Garner et al., "Psychoeducational Principles in the Treatment of Bulimia and Anorexia Nervosa," 513–46.

49. See, e.g., Johanna Dwyer, "Nutritional Aspects of Anorexia Nervosa and Bulimia," in *Theory and Treatment of Anorexia Nervosa and Bulimia: Biomedical, Sociocultural, and Psychological Perspectives*, ed. S. Emmett (New York: Brunner/Mazel, 1985), 28.

50. See M. de Zwaan and J. E. Mitchell, "Medical Complications of Anorexia Nervosa and Bulimia Nervosa," in Kaplan and Garfinkel, *Medical Issues and the Eating Disorders*, 60.

51. Garner et al., "Psychoeducational Principles in the Treatment of Bulimia and Anorexia Nervosa," 554–58; Abraham and Llewellyn-Jones, *Eating Disorders*, 57–65.

52. A. S. Kaplan and P. E. Garfinkel, "Introduction," in Kaplan and Garfinkel, *Medical Issues and the Eating Disorders*, ix.

53. Studies presenting different views on the role of the hypothalamus in the development of anorexia include G. I. Szmukler, "The Psychopathology of Eating Disorders," in *Handbook of the Psychophysiology of Human Eating*, ed. R. Shepard (New York: Wiley, 1989), 281–82; T. Schallert, "Animal Models of Eating Disorders: Hypothalamic Function," in Blinder et al., *The Eating Disorders*, 39–47; J. Treasure and J. Triller, "The Aetiology of Eating Disorders: Its Biological Basis," *International Review*

of Psychiatry 5 (1993): 23–31; P. Copeland, "Neuroendocrine Aspects of Eating Disorders," in Emmett, *Theory and Treatment of Anorexia Nervosa and Bulimia*, 51–68; de Zwaan and Mitchell, "Medical Complications of Anorexia Nervosa and Bulimia Nervosa," 61.

54. A. W. Brotman and D. B. Herzog, "Eating Disorders," in *The Practitioner's Guide to Psychoactive Drugs*, ed. A. J. Gelenberg et al. (New York: Plenum, 1991), 442; W. H. Kaye et al., "Serotonin Regulation in Bulimia," in *The Psychobiology of Bulimia*, edited by James Hudson and Harrison Pope (Washington: American Psychiatric Association, 1987) 159–70; K. Halmi et al., "Serotonin Responsivity and Hunger and Satiety in Eating Disorders," in Ferrari et al., *Primary and Secondary Eating Disorders*, 123–31; D. S. Goldbloom, "Serotonin in Eating Disorders: Theory and Therapy," in *The Role of Drug Treatments for Eating Disorders*, ed. P. Garfinkel and D. Garner (New York: Brunner/Mazel, 1987), 124–25; and Goldbloom et al., "The Baseline Metabolic State in Bulimia Nervosa: Abnormality and Adaptation," *International Journal of Eating Disorders* 12 (1992): 171–78.

55. Copeland, "Neuroendocrine Aspects of Eating Disorders," 52; D. Martin, "Clinical Laboratory Aspects of Eating Disorders," in Giannini and Slaby, *The Eating Disorders*, 88; Abraham and Llewellyn-Jones, *Eating Disorders*, 83. The view that overeating is a physiological response to undereating is spelled out in W. Bennet and J. Gurin's *The Dieter's Dilemma: Eating Less and Weighing More* (New York: Basic Books, 1982).

56. For a review of this hypothesis, see L. D. Hinz and D. A. Williamson, "Bulimia and Depression: A Review of the Affective Variant Hypothesis," *Psychological Bulletin* 102 (1987): 150–58; H. Pope and J. Hudson, "Biological Treatments of Eating Disorders," in Emmett, *Theory and Treatment of Anorexia Nervosa and Bulimia*, 77–78; Pope and Hudson, "Update on the Use of Fluoxetine in the Treatment of Bulimia Nervosa," *American Anorexia/Bulimia Association*, Special Research Edition (Fall 1992): 1–2; Pope and Hudson, "Affective Spectrum Disorder: Does Antidepressant Response Identify a Family of Disorders with a Common Pathophysiology?," *American Journal of Psychiatry* 147 (1990): 552–64; D. Herzog and A. Brotman, "Use of Tricyclic Antidepressants in Anorexia Nervosa and Bulimia Nervosa," in Garfinkel and Garner, *The Role of Drug Treatments for Eating Disorders*, 54. G. F. M. Russell, "The Limited Role of Drugs in the Treatment of Anorexia and Bulimia Nervosa," *The Pharmacology of Eating Disorders*, edited by Michele Carruba and John Blundell (New York: Raven, 1986) 151.

57. Bemis, "Current Approaches," 607.

58. J. E. Blundell et al., for example, argue that in addition to their use in treating eating disorders, drugs can be used as "pharmacological scalpels" to "investigate the neurochemical and physiological mechanisms involved in appetite control." See "Neurochemical Factors Involved in Normal and Abnormal Eating in Humans," in Shepard, *Handbook of the Psychophysiology of Human Eating*, 85. Proponents of the "affective variant hypothesis" are not in the majority in the field. To review discussions in this area, see M. Strober and J. L. Katz, "Depression in the Eating Disorders: A Review and Analysis of Descriptive, Family, and Biological Findings," in Garner and Garfinkel, *Diagnostic Issues in Anorexia Nervosa and Bulimia Nervosa*, 100. While some suggest that drugs like Tofranil or imipramine might be the "magic bullet" for treating eating disorders (see, e.g., Pope and Hudson, *New Hope for Binge Eaters*, 1984), others caution that "there is no established pharmacotherapy for eating disorders." Herzog and Copeland, "Eating Disorders," 300. For more critical views on

drug treatments, see M. Boskind-White and W. White, *Bulimarexia: The Binge/Purge Cycle* (New York: W. W. Norton, 1987), 138; N. Raymond, et al., "A Collaborative Approach to the Use of Medication," in *Feminist Perspectives on Eating Disorders*, ed. Patricia Fallon et al. (New York: Guilford, 1994), 231–50.

59. W. Vandereycken and H. Hoek, "Are Eating Disorders Culture-Bound Syndromes?," in *Psychobiology and Treatment of Anorexia and Bulimia Nervosa*, ed. K. A. Halmi (Washington: American Psychological Association Press, 1992), 19–36; W. Vandereycken, "The Sociocultural Roots of the Fight against Fatness: Implications for Eating Disorders and Obesity," *Eating Disorders* 1 (1993): 7–15; R. Gordon, "A Sociocultural Interpretation of the Current Epidemic of Eating Disorders," in Blinder et al., *The Eating Disorders*, 152.

60. M. Boskind-White, "Bulimarexia: A Sociocultural Perspective," in Emmett, *Theory and Treatment of Anorexia Nervosa and Bulimia*, 114. The feminist anthology *Fed Up and Hungry: Women, Oppression, and Food*, ed. Marilyn Lawrence (New York: Peter Bedrick, 1987), represents the view that there is a *range* of eating problems.

61. Chernin, *The Hungry Self*, xiii–xvi; see also Chernin's earlier book, *The Obsession: Reflections on the Tyranny of Slenderness* (New York: Harper and Row, 1981).

62. B. Silverstein et al., "Nontraditional Sex Role Aspirations, Gender Identity Conflict, and Disordered Eating among College Women," *Sex Roles* 23 (1990): 687–95; R. H. Striegel-Moore et al., "Competing on All Fronts: Achievement Orientation and Disordered Eating," *Sex Roles* 23 (1990): 697–702; B. Silverstein et al., "Bingeing, Purging and Estimates of Parental Attitudes Regarding Female Achievement," *Sex Roles* 19 (1988): 723–33; D. Perlick and B. Silverstein, "Faces of Female Discontent: Depression, Disordered Eating, and Changing Gender Roles," in Fallon et al., *Feminist Perspectives on Eating Disorders*, 77–89.

63. Susie Orbach, "Visibility/Invisibility: Social Considerations in Anorexia Nervosa—A Feminist Perspective," in Emmett, *Theory and Treatment of Anorexia Nervosa and Bulimia*, 130. See Orbach's *Hunger Strike: The Anorectic's Struggle as a Metaphor for Our Age* (New York: Avon, 1986) and *Fat Is a Feminist Issue: The Anti-Diet Guide to Permanent Weight Loss* (New York: Berkeley Medallion, 1978). For a literary reflection on the links between politically motivated fasting and the anorexic refusal to eat, see Maud Ellman, *The Hunger Artists: Starving, Writing, and Imprisonment* (Cambridge: Harvard University Press, 1993).

64. See Marlene Boskind-Lodahl's groundbreaking essay "Cinderella's Stepsisters: A Feminist Perspective on Anorexia Nervosa and Bulimia," *Signs* 2 (1976): 345–46.

65. The following authors make this comparison: C. Brown and K. Jaspers, "Introduction," in Brown and Jaspers, *Consuming Passions*, 30; M. MacSween, *Anorexic Bodies: A Feminist and Sociocultural Perspective on Anorexia Nervosa* (New York: Routledge, 1993), 3–4, 113; V. Wurman, "A Feminist Interpretation of College Student Bulimia," in *The Bulimic College Student: Evaluation, Treatment, and Prevention*, ed. L. C. Whitaker (New York: Haworth, 1989), 179; Gordon, *Anorexia and Bulimia*, 5; D. M. Schwartz et al., "Anorexia Nervosa and Bulimia: The Sociocultural Context," in Emmett, *Theory and Treatment of Anorexia Nervosa and Bulimia*, 104–5.

66. Two qualitative studies that deal with the relationship between troubled eating and incest survival are Jennifer Manlowe's *Faith Born of Seduction: Sexual Trauma, Body Image, and Religion* (New York: New York University Press, 1995) and Becky Thompson's *A Hunger So Wide and So Deep*. For discussion of the controversy surrounding the status of the sexual abuse factor in the development of eating dis-

orders, see Susan C. Wooley, "Sexual Abuse and Eating Disorders: The Concealed Debate," in Fallon et al., *Feminist Perspectives on Eating Disorders*, 171–211.

67. For example, in 1980, a New Jersey chapter of NOW (National Organization of Women) sponsored a program called "Food, Fat, and Feminism," which explored reactions to fat and fat people, food and diet. Cited in Appendix I in Dana Cassel's *The Encyclopedia of Obesity and Eating Disorders* (New York: Facts on File, 1994), 201. In 1986 in New York City, Susie Orbach organized a speak-out against eating disorders. Joan Jacobs Brumberg cites this event in *Fasting Girls: The History of Anorexia Nervosa* (New York: Penguin, 1988), 34.

68. Brumberg, *Fasting Girls*, 38. Besides Brumberg's book, the two other important historical studies of female fasting prior to the modern period in the West are Rudolph Bell's *Holy Anorexia* (Chicago: University of Chicago Press, 1985) and Caroline Walker Bynum's *Holy Feast and Holy Fast: The Religious Significance of Food for Medieval Women* (Berkeley: University of California Press, 1987). I discuss the relative merits of these works below. Other historical studies include J. Silverman, "Robert Whytt, 1714–1766, Eighteenth Century Limner of Anorexia Nervosa and Bulimia: An Essay," *International Journal of Eating Disorders* 6 (1987): 143–46; A. E. Slaby and R. Dwenger, "History of Anorexia Nervosa," in Giannini and Slaby, *The Eating Disorders*, 1–17; Dana Cassell, "Introduction: The History of Obesity and Eating Disorders," in Cassell, *The Encyclopedia of Obesity and Eating Disorders*, xi–xvii; D. Stein and W. Laakso, "Bulimia: A Historical Perspective," *International Journal of Eating Disorders* 7 (1988): 201–10; A. J. Giannini, "A History of Bulimia," in Giannini and Slaby, *The Eating Disorders*, 18; W. Vandereycken et al., "German Publications on Anorexia Nervosa in the Nineteenth Century," *International Journal of Eating Disorders* 10 (1991): 473–90.

69. In response to a religious authority who questioned the motives of her fasting, Catherine insisted that her inability to eat was an *infirmity*, not a choice. She connected her suffering caused by this infirmity to the suffering of Christ. See "Letter to a Certain Religious Person in Florence," *The Letters of Catherine of Siena*; vol. 1, trans. and ed. S. Noffke (Binghampton, New York: Medieval and Renaissance Texts and Studies, 1988), 79. On the other hand, Catherine's confessor, Raymond of Capua, interprets Catherine's fasting as proof of her supernatural holiness, confirming that "her whole life was a miracle." See Raymond of Capua, *The Life of Catherine of Siena*, trans. George Lamb (New York: P. J. Kennedy), 30, 52–57. For a discussion of the term "anorexia mirabilis," see Brumberg, *Fasting Girls*, 41.

70. Bynum, *Holy Feast and Holy Fast*, 7, 30, 95, 105–6.

71. Bell, *Holy Anorexia*, 20. Bell distinguishes between holy anorexia and anorexia nervosa (85–86). At the same time, he interprets anorexia as a "timeless" response of adolescent girls in patriarchal cultures to establish mastery over themselves and their bodies (56). Bell's theoretical perspective is primarily psychological. His criteria for identifying anorexic behavior are based on modern psychiatric measures (2–3), and his understanding of anorexia reflects a psychodynamic emphasis on adolescent development in a family environment (55).

72. Bynum, *Holy Feast and Holy Fast*, 5, 30.

73. Bynum summarizes: "First, women's food behavior—fasting and feeding—was an effective way of manipulating the environment in a world in which food was women's primary resource. Second, women's radical asceticism was less an internalizing of the church's negative views of flesh and female than a rebellion against the moderation of the high medieval church, which was moving toward a more positive

sense of the body. Third, food asceticism, food distribution, and eucharistic devotion did not, to medieval people, mean self-torture; rather, they were ways of fusing with a Christ whose suffering saves the world." Ibid., 218.

74. Bynum contends that women today "cultivate not closeness to God but physical attractiveness by food abstinence, which they call dieting." Thus, she reasons, "the self-starvation of some thirteenth-, fourteenth-, and fifteenth-century women had a resonance and a complexity that are not captured by the analogy to modern disease entities" (298–99). This comparison overlooks the variety of models used to interpret eating problems today. Bynum's view of modern anorexia is informed by psychodynamic discourse, which she treats as authoritative despite her critique of its reductionizing tendencies. See ibid., 201–6.

75. Kathleen Biddick, "Gender, Bodies, Borders: Technologies of the Visible," *Speculum* 68 (Apr. 1993): 389–418.

76. Brumberg, *Fasting Girls*, 47–48. Brumberg says that the term "fasting girls" was "used by Victorians on both sides of the Atlantic to describe cases of prolonged abstinence where there was uncertainty about the etiology of the fast and ambiguity about the intention of the faster" (62–63). Tales of fasting girls had a common plot: a fasting girl miraculously lived without food for periods ranging from weeks to decades. Popular presses publicized the stories, and both ordinary folk and elites, Catholics and Protestants alike, visited the girls (49).

77. Ibid., 49–50, 56. Brumberg tells the story of Sarah Jacobs, the daughter of Welsh farmers who began to fast in 1867 and claimed to live without eating. She starved to death ten days into a medical surveillance set up to prove that she did in fact eat on the sly. Ibid., 64–71.

78. Ibid., 60. See Brumberg's fascinating discussion of the conflicting interpretations (religious versus medical) of female fasting in late-nineteenth-century America, (77–91).

79. Almost concurrently in 1873, a famous London physician named William Gull and a notable French neurologist named Ernest Lasegue identified a new disease which they called, respectively, "anorexia nervosa" and "anorexia hysteria." The difference in modifier—*nervosa* versus *hysteria*—reflected these men's specific scientific orientations. Gull's medical interests lead him to attribute the anorexic's "lack of appetite" to nervous causes. Lasegue's preference for the term "hysteria" reflected his psychiatric interests, especially his view of such problems as part of a larger repertoire of manipulative maladies of middle-class females. Ibid., 101–25.

80. Ibid., 100.

81. Ibid., 91, 102.

82. Ibid., 140, 178, 184–87.

83. Ibid., 98. See chapter 6 of *Fasting Girls* for a fuller account of these approaches in the first half of the twentieth century.

84. Ibid., 46–47.

85. M. A. Graham, et al., "Altered Religious Practice in Patients with Eating Disorders," *International Journal of Eating Disorders* 10 (1991): 241; N. Joughin et al., "Religious Belief and Anorexia Nervosa," *International Journal of Eating Disorders* 12 (1992): 397–406; J. E. Mitchell et al., "Eating Disorders, Religious Practices, and Pastoral Counseling," *International Journal of Eating Disorders* 9 (1990): 592; D. Rampling, "Ascetic Ideals and Anorexia Nervosa," *Journal of Psychiatric Research* 19 (1985): 89–94.

86. Margaret McMullan, "My Sister's Problem with Bulimia and Me," in New-

man, *Eating Our Hearts Out*, 109; and Hendle Rumbaut, "An Image of Myself," in ibid., 124–25.

87. This is, of course, Max Weber's famous phrase, which he used to describe the rationalizing processes of the modern world that simultaneously render reality more "comprehensible" and more devoid of mystery and wonder. "Science as a Vocation," in *Max Weber: Essays in Sociology,* ed. H. H. Gerth and C. Wright Mills (New York: Oxford University Press, 1946), 155; see also M. Weber, *The Sociology of Religion,* trans. Fischoff (1922; reprint, Boston: Beacon, 1963).

88. These authors tend to echo Rudolph Bell's argument in *Holy Anorexia.* See, for example, Gail Corrington's "Anorexia, Asceticism, and Autonomy: Self-Control as Liberation and Transcendence," *Journal of Feminist Studies in Religion* 2 (Fall 1986). Two exceptions to this dehistoricizing tendency in medieval-modern comparisons are Margaret Miles, "Religion and Food: The Case of Eating Disorders," *Journal of the American Academy of Religion* 63 (Fall 1995): 549–64; and M. Reinke, " 'This Is My Body': Reflections on Abjection, Anorexia, and Medieval Women Mystics," *Journal of the American Academy of Religion* 58 (Summer 1990): 245–65. Other explorations of the ascetic aspects of anorexia nervosa include S. Sabom, "The Gnostic World of Anorexia Nervosa," *Journal of Psychology and Theology* 13 (1985): 243–54; Rampling, "Ascetic Ideals and Anorexia Nervosa," 89–94; J. H. Lacey, "Anorexia and a Bearded Female Saint," *British Medical Journal* 285 (1982): 1816–17; and B. Fallon and E. Horwath, "Asceticism: Creative Spiritual Practice or Pathological Pursuit?," *Psychiatry: Interpersonal and Biological Processes* 56 (Aug. 1992): 310–16.

89. See Cherry Boone O'Neil, *Starving for Attention* (Melbourne: Dove Communications, 1982); Cynthia Rowland, *The Monster Within: Overcoming Bulimia* (Grand Rapids: Baker Boy, 1984); Caroline Adams Miller, *My Name Is Caroline* (New York: Doubleday, 1988).

90. In *Never Too Thin: Why Women Are at War with Their Bodies* (New York: Prentice Hall, 1989), Roberta P. Seid cites a number of books and programs that enlist God in America's weight-loss campaign, including Rev. C. W. Shedd, *Pray Your Weight Away*; Frances Hunter, *God's Answer to Fat—Lose It!*; and Joan Cavanaugh, *More of Jesus, Less of Me*; as well as "The Workshop in Lenten Living," "The Prayer-Diet Club," "Overeaters Victorious," "3D [Diet, Discipline, and Discipleship]," and "The Jesus System for Weight Control." *Never Too Thin,* 107.

91. Examples of Jungian interpretations include Kim Chernin's *Reinventing Eve: Modern Woman in Search of Herself* (San Francisco: Harper and Row, 1987) and Marion Woodman's *The Owl Was a Baker's Daughter: Obesity, Anorexia Nervosa, and the Repressed Feminine* (Toronto: Inner City Books, 1980).

92. Mary L. Bringle develops this view in her article "Confessions of a Glutton," *Christian Century* 106 (Oct. 1989): 955–58, and in her book *The God of Thinness: Gluttony and Other Weighty Matters* (Nashville: Abingdon, 1992). Bringle's article examines compulsive eating with a theological lens that juxtaposes "grace" and "works." Using a Calvinist theory of human powerlessness and God's sovereignty, she contends that diets represent humans' futile efforts at self-transformation. In her book, Bringle argues that worshiping the "god of thinness" is sinful because it deflects devotion away from the "One True God" (15). Her alternative theology of food centers on "an image of God, the ground of our existence, as Feeder" (30).

93. The literature of Overeaters Anonymous (OA) includes a number of pamphlets, as well as the so-called Brown Book, entitled *Overeaters Anonymous* (Torrance, Calif.: Overeaters Anonymous, Inc., 1980), whose chapters consist of stories told by

compulsive overeaters who are recovering from their eating problems with the help of OA.

94. Patricia Hill Collins, *Black Feminist Thought: Knowledge, Consciousness, and the Politics of Empowerment* (New York: Routledge, 1991), 225–27. Elisabeth Schüssler Fiorenza draws on Hill Collin's work to construct a similar notion of "patriarchy" as a "pyramid of multiplicative oppressions." See *But She Said: Feminist Practices of Biblical Interpretation* (Boston: Beacon, 1992), 114–123; 202. In *Changing the Subject: Women's Discourses and Feminist Theology* (Minneapolis: Fortress, 1994), Mary Mc-Clintock Fulkerson suggests that the modifier "capitalist" should be attached to contemporary references to "patriarchy" to specify the mode of production through which unequal relations are currently sustained (95–98).

95. bell hooks uses this term to describe American society in *Teaching to Transgress: Education as the Practice of Freedom* (New York: Routledge, 1994), 28.

96. Becky Thompson discusses the significance of acculturation pressures in the development of eating problems among minority women in her book *A Hunger So Wide and So Deep*.

97. This understanding of meaning-production in cultural systems is put forth in Richard Johnson's influential essay "What Is Cultural Studies Anyway?," *Social Text* 16 (1987): 38–80.

98. A cultural studies analysis provides a corrective to standard theories of culture, such as the one put forth by Clifford Geertz in his classic *The Interpretation of Cultures* (New York: Basic Books, 1973), by highlighting how unequal relations of power shape the cultural production of meaning. For an excellent discussion of this cultural studies approach, see Elizabeth Traube's introduction to her book *Dreaming Identities: Class, Gender, and Generation in 1980s Hollywood Movies* (San Francisco: Westview Press, 1992), 4.

99. Foucault describes a kind of power that is central to the maintenance of social order in modern capitalist societies like the United States, where oppression by repressive violence has been "infiltrated" by more subtle forms of domination. In *Discipline and Punish*, Foucault argues that disciplinary power has infiltrated rather than replaced more centralized forms of power. *Discipline and Punish: The Birth of the Prison*, trans. A. Sheridan (New York: Vintage Books, 1979) 216. See also *The History of Sexuality*, vol. 1, trans. R. Hurley (1978; reprint, New York: Vintage Books, 1990). In Jana Sawicki's summary, Foucault sees power as a force that is exercised rather than possessed; it is productive rather than repressive, dispersed rather than centralized. *Disciplining Foucault: Feminism, Power, and the Body* (New York: Routledge, 1991), 20–21.

100. As Jana Sawicki explains, "disciplinary power" is rooted in bodily pleasures, attitudes, and practices, which are learned in relation to prevailing cultural rules and social arrangements. See *Disciplining Foucault*, 83; see also Frigga Haug, ed., *Female Sexualization: A Collective Work of Memory*, trans. Erica Carter (London: Verso, 1987).

101. I am drawing here on Susan Bordo's discussion of Foucault's distinction between the "intelligible body" (the symbolic body) and the "useful body" (the practical body). *Unbearable Weight*, 181.

102. The term "hegemony" is associated with the Italian Marxist Antonio Gramsci, who was writing during the 1920s and 1930s. See *Selections from Prison Notebooks*, ed. and trans. Q. Hoare and G. Nowell-Smith (London: Lawrence and Wishart, 1971). Since the early 1970s, "hegemony" has been used to describe "re-

lations of domination that are not visible as such." See S. During's introduction to *The Cultural Studies Reader* (New York: Routledge, 1993), 5. Pierre Bourdieu's concept of "doxa" parallels this notion of hegemony. See *Outline of a Theory of Practice*, trans. R. Nice (1972; reprint, Cambridge: Cambridge University Press, 1992), 164.

103. Bourdieu says that the "truth" of hegemonies "goes without saying because it comes without saying. . . . Every established order tends to produce (to very different degrees and with very different means) the naturalization of its own arbitrariness." *Outline for a Theory of Practice*, 164-67. Foucault also speaks of the "omnipresence of power" in *The History of Sexuality*; vol. 1, 93.

104. On the relationship between female pleasure and subjugation, see Haug, *Female Sexualization*, 79-81. See also Haug, "Victims or Culprits?: Reflections on Women's Behaviour," in *Beyond Female Masochism: Memory-Work and Politics* (London: Verso, 1992), 1-30.

105. Bruch, *The Golden Cage*, 58.

106. Margaret Miles explores this theme in her discussion of female martyrs and ascetics in *Carnal Knowing: Female Nakedness and Religious Meaning in the Christian West* (Boston: Beacon, 1989), 53-77.

107. Geertz, *The Interpretation of Cultures*, 89; Peter Berger, *The Sacred Canopy: Elements of a Sociology of Religion* (1967; reprint, New York: Doubleday, 1990), 27-28; Gordon Kaufman, *In Face of Mystery: A Constructive Theology* (Cambridge: Harvard University Press, 1993), 227-28. My emphasis on the symbolic-ritual quality of religion and religious faith does not preclude the possibility of an experiential component of religion. George Lindbeck's juxtaposition between a "cultural-linguistic" model of religion, which traces its roots to thinkers like Weber and Durkheim, and an "experiential expressive" model, which finds its origins in the ideas of Schleiermacher, may be overly dualistic. See *The Nature of Doctrine: Religion and Theology in a Postliberal Age* (Philadelphia: Westminster, 1984), 23, 33.

108. Catherine Keller, *From a Broken Web: Separation, Sexism, and Self* (Boston: Beacon, 1986), 160.

109. I am drawing on and modifying Kathleen Sands's discussion of the "rationalist" and "dualist" strategies that she argues are primary tactics for locating "truth" and positing "goodness" in classic Christian theology. See *Escape from Paradise: Evil and Tragedy in Feminist Theology* (Minneapolis: Fortress, 1994).

110. This particular reinterpretation of salvation draws on the work of Elisabeth Schüssler Fiorenza, especially *In Memory of Her: A Feminist Reconstruction of Christian Origins* (1983; reprint, New York: Crossroad; 1994), 118-30. There are numerous other works by feminist and liberation theologians that are reinterpreting Christianity in ways that draw out the liberating aspects of this tradition, inspiring Christians to use their faith to help them build a more equitable and compassionate society.

111. This point counters Emile Durkheim's claim that "sacred" and "profane" realities are essentially distinct. See *The Elementary Forms of Religious Life*, trans. J. W. Swain (New York: Collier, 1961), 52-53. For a critical discussion of the gendered subtext of Durkheim's distinction, see Victoria Lee Erickson, *Where Silence Speaks: Feminism, Social Theory, and Religion* (Minneapolis: Fortress, 1993).

112. In *The Culture of Disbelief: How American Law and Politics Trivialize Religious Devotion* (New York: Basic Books, 1994), Stephen Carter cites surveys indicating that more than 90 percent of Americans believe in God (4). Robert Bellah et al. report that "some 40 percent of Americans attend religious services at least once a week." *Habits of the Heart: Individualism and Commitment in American Life* (New York: Harper and Row, 1985), 219. According to an article in the *Christian Century*, this number

reflects Gallup poll findings over the past fifty years. See "Who Really Attends Church?" (Sept. 8–15, 1993): 848–49. Using a different methodology, C. Kirk Hadaway et al. arrive at lower percentages for church attendance (19.6 percent for Protestants and 28 percent for Catholics). See "What Polls Don't Show: A Closer Look at U.S. Church Attendance," *American Sociological Review* 58 (Dec. 1993): 741–52.

113. Peter Berger uses this term in *The Sacred Canopy*, 125. I reject both the argument of the so-called secularization thesis (Karl Lowith et al.) that the modern age is a transformed (secularized) version of an essentially religious (and specifically Christian) substance, and that of its opponents such as Hans Blumenberg, whose insistence on "modern man's [sic]" decidedly nonreligious, "self-assertive" character overlooks the inextricable relationship between religious meaning, function, and context. See H. Blumenberg, *The Legitimacy of the Modern Age*, trans. R. M. Wallace (Cambridge: MIT Press, 1983). In my view, this society is best understood as neither intrinsically secular nor inherently religious.

114. Max Weber, *The Protestant Ethic and the Spirit of Capitalism*, trans. T. Parsons (New York: Charles Scribner's Sons, 1958). Bryan Turner presents a parallel view of secularization in terms of medicalization, in *Regulating Bodies: Essays in Medical Sociology* (New York: Routledge, 1992), 18.

115. Marx's work provides an important link between religious and cultural studies. For Marx, religious processes for making meaning provided an analogy for the systems of production of modern capitalism. The similarity rests in the reifying or fetishizing processes whereby persons become alienated from the products or objects of their own imaginative creation. See Marx, "The Fetishism of Commodities," in *Critical Sociology: Selected Readings*, ed. P. Connection (Harmondsworth, England: Penguin, 1976), 75. A more recent analysis of the religious aspects of consumer capitalism is brilliantly presented by David Loy in "The Religion of the Market," *Journal of the American Academy of Religion* 65 (Summer 1997): 275–90.

116. Raymond Williams, "Advertising: The Magic System," in During, *The Cultural Studies Reader*, 335. Judith Williamson makes a similar analogy in *Decoding Advertisements: Ideology and Meaning in Advertising* (1978; reprint, New York: Marion Boyars, 1993), 138–79.

117. It is interesting to compare classic definitions of "religion" with those describing the mechanisms of commercial advertising. Consider, for example, Clifford Geertz's discussion of religious perspectives as creating a "sense of the 'really real' " (*Interpretation of Cultures*, 110–12), in the light of John Berger's analysis of different "ways of seeing" in his book *Ways of Seeing* (London: Penguin, 1972).

118. Roland Barthes refers to a "dream of wholeness" that underlies the creation and consumption of "style." See *The Fashion System*, trans. Matthew Ward and Richard Howard (New York: Hill and Wang, 1984). Stuart Ewen picks up this notion in *All Consuming Images: The Politics of Style in Contemporary Culture* (New York: Basic Books, 1988), 78–108, and Roland Marchand makes a similar point in his historical study of advertising, *Advertising the American Dream: Making Way for Modernity, 1920–1940* (Berkeley: University of California Press, 1985), especially 186, 207–27, 269–73.

Chapter Two

1. Clifford Geertz, "Ethos, World View, and the Analysis of Sacred Symbols," in *The Interpretations of Cultures* (New York: Basic Books, 1973), 126–41. See also Caroline W. Bynum's definition of religious symbols in her introduction to *Gender*

and Religion: On the Complexity of Symbols, ed. Bynum et al. (Boston: Beacon, 1986), 2. My understanding of the role of religious imagination in the creation and use of sacred images draws on the work of Gordon Kaufman, especially *The Theological Imagination: Constructing the Concept of God* (Philadelphia: Westminster, 1981) and *In Face of Mystery: A Constructive Theology* (Cambridge: Harvard University Press, 1993), and the work of Sallie McFague, especially *Models of God: Theology for an Ecological and Nuclear Age* (Philadelphia: Fortress, 1987) and *The Body of God: An Ecological Theology* (Minneapolis: Fortress, 1993).

2. Kaufman describes this process of forgetting the imaginative basis of meaning-making as "reifying"—literally, "making into a thing." *In Face of Mystery*, 330–31.

3. Though some supermodels are making their way onto the small screen, the majority of them do so not as actresses but as themselves. See the cover story of *TV Guide* (July 26, 1993): 6–15.

4. None of the magazines I consider, including *Cosmopolitan, Mademoiselle, Glamour, Seventeen, Essence, Elle, Allure, Harper's Bazaar, Vogue,* and *Mirabella*, circulates less than a million copies each month. In the March 1993 issue of *Mademoiselle*, for example, the editor claims a readership of over 5 million; in the December 1993 issue of *Glamour*, the editor claims a readership of over 9.4 million.

5. Geertz, "Religion as a Cultural System," in *The Interpretations of Cultures*, 93–95.

6. Susan Sontag, *On Photography* (New York: Doubleday, 1989), 4, 16–18, 87.

7. Mary Douglas, *Natural Symbols: Explorations in Cosmology* (1970; reprint, New York: Pantheon, 1982), xii, 115.

8. In recent years, a number of feminist film critics have shown how meanings that are not intrinsic to images are produced in viewing processes. For example, by focusing on the relationships between a film's text, its audience, its director, and the specific historical moment in which it is produced, Christine Gledhill argues that meanings are *negotiated* rather than imposed. See "Pleasurable Negotiations," in *Female Spectators: Looking at Film and Television*, ed. E. Deidre Pribram (New York: Verso, 1988), 67–68, 74, 87. In *Decoding Advertisements: Ideology and Meaning in Advertising* (1978; reprint, New York: Marion Boyars, 1993), Judith Williamson suggests a similar model of visual meaning-production.

9. See Margaret Miles, *Image as Insight: Visual Understanding in Western Christianity and Secular Culture* (Boston: Beacon, 1985). Gregor Goethals notes both the lack of compartmentalization between art and religion prior to the modern era, and the use of religious "pictures of reality" to integrate experiences on the social, individual, and cosmic levels. See *The Electronic Golden Calf: Images, Religion, and the Making of Meaning* (Cambridge: Cowley, 1990), 10, 122.

10. Joseph Frary, "The Logic of Icons," *Subernost* ser. 6 (1972): 396. Goethals suggests that such stylistic conventions aimed to convey the transcendent dimensions of religious experience. *The Electronic Golden Calf*, 17.

11. Miles, *Image as Insight*, 7–9, 128.

12. See Hal Foster's introduction to *Vision and Visuality*, ed. Foster (Seattle: Bay Press, 1988), ix.

13. Iris M. Young discusses Foucault's concept of the "gaze" in "The Scaling of Bodies and the Politics of Identity," in *Justice and the Politics of Difference* (Princeton: Princeton University Press, 1990), 125. See also Michel Foucault, *The Order of Things: An Archeology of the Human Sciences* (1970; reprint, New York: Vintage, 1973). Foucault's insights inform the works of several historians of modern science, whose studies illustrate the shift I am describing here. In *Making Sex: Body and Gender from*

the Greeks to Freud (Cambridge: Harvard University Press, 1990), Thomas Laqueur shows how medical discourses of modern Europe reinterpreted the differences between men and women in ways that responded to the sociopolitical upheavals of their times. Stephen Jay Gould examines a similar mix of science and politics in *The Mismeasure of Man* (New York: W. W. Norton, 1981), where he shows how the biological determinism of nineteenth-century science employed a normalizing gaze to reify and rank racial differences in ways that favored the socially powerful. Other works exploring the politics of modern scientific inquiry include Londa Schiebinger, *The Mind Has No Sex?: Women in the Origins of Modern Science* (Cambridge: Harvard University Press, 1989); Barbara Duden, *The Woman beneath the Skin: A Doctor's Patients in Eighteenth-Century Germany*, trans. T. Dunlap (Cambridge: Harvard University Press, 1991); Cynthia Russett, *Sexual Science: The Victorian Construction of Womanhood* (Cambridge: Harvard University Press, 1989); and Evelyn Fox Keller, *Secrets of Life/Secrets of Death: Essays on Language, Gender, and Science* (New York: Routledge, 1992).

14. Young refers to this scale throughout her essay "The Scaling of Bodies and the Politics of Identity," 122–55. Building on the work of Foucault, Young argues that this scientific way of seeing/knowing naturalized bodies by conceiving them as subject to deterministic scientific laws, while normalizing them through evaluative reference to bodies of elite men. Young's analysis also draws on the work of Sander Gilman, *Difference and Pathology: Stereotypes of Sexuality, Race, and Madness* (Ithaca: Cornell University Press, 1985), which traces the overlap in modern scientific, aesthetic, and moral discourses of otherness.

15. Building on the work of Foucault, Jonathan Crary writes that between the eighteenth and nineteenth centuries in Europe, "man [sic] emerges as a being in whom the transcendent is mapped onto the empirical." See "Modernizing Vision," in Foster, *Vision and Visuality*, 36. The scientific practice of deducing the invisible nature of the self from the body's physical appearance was most pronounced in positivist reworkings of the ancient pseudoscience called physiognomy. See P. Magli, "The Face of the Soul," in *Fragments for a History of the Human Body*, Part 2, ed. M. Feher et al. (Cambridge: Zone, MIT Press, 1989), 107. Physiognomy was widespread in the ancient world and was used as "a tool for decoding the sign of gender deviance." See M. Gleason, "The Semiotics of Gender: Physiognomy and Self-Fashioning in the Second Century C.E.," in *Before Sexuality: The Construction of the Erotic Experience in the Ancient Greek World*, ed. D. Halperin et al. (Princeton: Princeton University Press, 1990), 389–416. Despite physiognomy's long-standing presence on the margins of traditional science, the positivist procedures of late-nineteenth-century science gave it the ring of universal truth. According to Joanne Finklestein, modern physiognomists identified, reified, and ranked people's moral character on the basis of their physical appearance. *The Fashioned Self* (Philadelphia: Temple University Press, 1991), 4–7, 28, 48.

16. For a fuller exploration of these themes, see Margaret Miles's *Carnal Knowing: Female Nakedness and Religious Meaning in the Christian West* (Boston: Beacon, 1989), 18, 144. Miles also develops the significance of this absence in the struggles of contemporary anorexic girls and women in "Religion and Food: The Case of Eating Disorders," *Journal of the American Academy of Religion* 63 (Fall 1995): 549–64.

17. Sontag's discussion on photography intimates the connections between the normalizing "gaze" of modern science and that of the camera. See *On Photography*, 3.

18. Goethals argues that the symbolic universe of American media culture func-

tions as an invisible but prominent "religion." In her view, today's visual images have assumed two important roles once associated with traditional religion: the circulation of public visions of redemption and of the ultimate order of things. See *The Electronic Golden Calf*, 57–58, 81, 156–60.

19. Wolf writes: "Magazines transmit the beauty myth as the gospel of a new religion. Reading them, women participate in re-creating a belief system as powerful as that of any of the churches whose hold on them has so rapidly loosened." *The Beauty Myth: How Images of Beauty Are Used against Women* (New York: Doubleday, 1991), 86. Wolf was not the first to see the quasi-religious quality of media images of women. In her analysis of popular women's magazines, Marjorie Ferguson argues that these texts collectively constitute a "cult of femininity." This cult "is manifested both as a social group to which all those born female can belong, and as a set of practices and beliefs: rites and rituals, sacrifices and ceremonies, whose periodic performance reaffirms a common femininity and shared group membership." *Forever Feminine: Women's Magazines and the Cult of Femininity* (London: Heinemann, 1983), 184. By 1960, one magazine writer for *Vogue* had already perceived the centrality of slenderness in this "cult," observing that "weight control is emerging as the new morality; fat, one of the deadlier sins. . . . The bathroom scales are a shrine to which believers turn daily. Converts are marked by the usual unctuous zeal. Doctors become father confessors to whom grievous sins are whispered. . . . Perhaps we are witnessing the first stirrings of a gigantic Puritan revival, designed to lead the nation along a stony path of self-denial." Quoted by Laura Fraser in *Losing It!: False Hopes and Fat Profits in the Diet Industry* (New York: Dutton, 1997), 57. For a more recent analysis of the "cult of slenderness" among American women, see Sharlene Hesse-Biber, *Am I Thin Enough Yet?: The Cult of Thinness and the Commercialization of Identity* (New York: Oxford University Press, 1996).

20. Despite the oversights in her work, Wolf's contribution to feminism has been invaluable. A number of feminists have deplored media images of female beauty, but Wolf's book popularized this critique, introducing millions to the insight that women's apparently frivolous concerns with their bodies have deep political meanings.

21. Wolf, *The Beauty Myth*, 9–11. This assertion is both bold and somewhat nuanced. The problem with media images of women is not (according to Wolf) simply that they exist "but that they proliferate at the expense of other female heroines, role models, villains, eccentrics, buffoons, visionaries, sex goddesses, and pranksters" (2). Perhaps to illustrate her point that popular women's magazines are not in and of themselves bad for women, Wolf has appeared in a number of them since the publication of *The Beauty Myth*. See, for example, "Loving Men," *Glamour* (Dec. 1993): 196–97.

22. Wolf, *The Beauty Myth*, 66–67.

23. For a critique of Friedan's assumptions from a multicultural feminist perspective, see bell hooks, *Feminist Theory: From Margin to Center* (Boston: South End, 1984), 2–3. hooks offers her own critique of Wolf in *Outlaw Culture: Resisting Representations* (New York: Routledge, 1994), 91–100.

24. Wolf, *The Beauty Myth*, 9.

25. For Wolf, "religion" is the basic paradigm for the beauty myth's oppressive power. See especially 86–89, 92. Wolf's derogatory comments are confusing in light of her later assertion that "the beauty culture attests to a spiritual hunger for female ritual and rites of passage" (279). Perhaps this assertion anticipates an emerging

interest in "spirituality" that Wolf discusses in her recent essay "Starting on My Spiritual Path," *Tikkun* 13 (Jan./Feb. 1998): 18–20.

26. Wolf, *The Beauty Myth*, 93–94.

27. For an example of the antireligious sentiments in feminist discourse, see Debbie Cameron's "Can You Feel the Force (and Should You Give In to It)?," *Trouble and Strife* 31 (Summer 1995): 4–10.

28. Wolf, *The Beauty Myth*, 86. In "Under Western Eyes: Feminist Scholarship and Colonial Discourses," Chandra Talpade Mohanty notes how appeals to secularity inform "First World" feminism's snapshots of "Third World women" as "other": "Universal images of 'the third world woman' (the veiled woman, chaste virgin, etc.), images constructed from adding the 'third world difference' to 'sexual difference,' are predicated upon (and hence obviously bring into sharper focus) assumptions about Western women as secular, liberated, and having control over their own lives." See *Third World Women and the Politics of Feminism*, ed. C. Talpade Mohanty et al. (Bloomington: Indiana University Press, 1991), 74.

29. This approach is spelled out in Richard Johnson's "What Is Cultural Studies Anyway?," *Social Text* 16 (198–7): 38–80. For another introduction to a cultural studies approach, see Elizabeth Traube, introduction to *Dreaming Identities: Class, Gender, and Generation in 1980s Hollywood Movies* (San Francisco: Westview, 1992).

30. Sante D'Orazio, quoted in *Allure* (May 1993): 29.

31. Iris Young makes this point in "The Scaling of Bodies and the Politics of Identity," 135–36. See also Sandra Bartky, *Femininity and Domination: Studies in the Phenomenology of Oppression* (New York: Routledge, 1990), especially 65–80; and Susan Bordo, *Unbearable Weight: Feminism, Western Culture, and the Body* (Berkeley: University of California Press, 1993).

32. Mainstream women's magazines continue to circulate the kind of "gender advertisements" that Erving Goffman described almost twenty-five years ago: images that construct and advertise a hierarchical gender order by positioning women's bodies subordinately in relation to men, out of balance in relation to themselves, or submissively in relation to the viewer. *Gender Advertisements* (New York: Harper and Row, 1976), 45. While Goffman's analysis of these images highlighted how gender is a constructed "display" rather than a natural identity, it did not assess the ways in which such construction depends on specific ideologies of race, class, sexuality, and age.

33. Patricia Hill Collins, *Black Feminist Thought: Knowledge, Consciousness, and the Politics of Empowerment* (New York: Routledge, 1991), 67–78. Hill Collins traces these images to the dominant ideologies that evolved out of the slave era. For another reflection on the damaging effects of such stereotypes, see Cheryl Townsend Gilkes, "The 'Loves' and 'Troubles' of African-American Women's Bodies: The Womanist Challenge to Cultural Humiliation and Community Ambivalence," in *A Troubling in My Soul: Womanist Perspectives on Evil and Suffering*, ed. Emilie Townes (Maryknoll, N.Y.: Orbis, 1993), 232–59.

34. Vron Ware, *Beyond the Pale: White Women, Racism, and History* (New York: Verso, 1992), 4, 11–18.

35. Kwok Pui-lan writes: "The white missionary women who travelled long distances to save their 'heathen' sisters were portrayed almost as saints in missionary literature and their 'hagiographic' biographies. . . . The original purpose of their missionary career was to save feminine souls. Judging from their own standards, however, missionary women found that their sisters could not possibly be 'saved' without

adopting some of their customs and values" (21–24). See "The Image of the 'White Lady': Gender and Race in Christian Mission," in *Concilium: The Special Nature of Women?*, ed. A. Carr and E. Schüssler Fiorenza (Philadelphia: Trinity, 1991), 19–27.

36. See Ware, *Beyond the Pale*, 14. For a graphic example of contemporary advertising's use of the juxtaposition between the "white lady" and her "heathen" sisters, see the photo on page 225.

37. Ibid., 229.

38. A Latin American study found that over 50 percent of the ads in women's magazines in Mexico, Colombia, Chile, and Venezuela featured the products of multinational corporations. The ideal woman presented in these ads was "young, white, and thin." J. Gay, "Sweet Darlings in the Media: How Foreign Corporations Sell Western Images of Women to the Third World," in *Being Beautiful: Deciding for Yourself* (Washington: Center for the Study of Responsive Law, 1986).

39. "Ans," quoted in Wendy Chapkis, *Beauty Secrets: Women and the Politics of Appearance* (Boston: South End, 1986), 60.

40. Kim Shayo Buchanan, "Creating Beauty in Blackness," in *Consuming Passions: Feminist Approaches to Weight Preoccupation and Eating Disorders*, ed. C. Brown and K. Jaspers (Toronto: Second Story Press, 1993), 37.

41. Andrea Tebay, age sixteen, quoted in Louise Lague et al., "How Thin Is Too Thin?," *People* (Sept. 20, 1993): 74. See also Gerri Hirshey, "How Fashion Broke Free: A Special Report on a Half-Century of Fashions of the Times," *New York Times Magazine* (Oct. 24, 1993): 114–15.

42. Louis Banner, *American Beauty* (Chicago: University of Chicago Press, 1983), 261.

43. *Young Miss* (Oct. 1993): 52–60. Model searches are especially common in magazines that target younger women. In the same month as the *Young Miss* feature on becoming a model, the cover of *Seventeen* magazine featured "The Making of a Cover Model."

44. Christine Fellingham, "The Secret Lives of Models," *Glamour* (Dec. 1994): 202–7.

45. bell hooks, *Black Looks: Race and Representation* (Boston: South End, 1992), 72.

46. Ibid., 63–67, 71–72.

47. Diana Fuss, "Fashion and the Homospectatorial Look," *Critical Inquiry* 18 (Summer 1992): 713. While Fuss raises interesting issues regarding the "gaze" that magazine images of women construct and circulate, I think a reading of these texts as "subversive" is too textualized; it depends on a level of consciousness not available to most girls and women in a culture where heterosexuality is *materially* and *institutionally* compulsory.

48. "Women in Love," *Mademoiselle* (Mar. 1993): 180–83, 208.

49. See Adrienne Rich, "Compulsory Heterosexuality and Lesbian Existence," *Signs* 5 (Summer 1980): 631–60.

50. hooks, *Black Looks*, 21. Susan Bordo makes a similar point when she warns that "consumer capitalism depends on the continual production of novelty, of fresh images to stimulate desire," and it "frequently drops into marginalized neighborhoods in order to find them." *Unbearable Weight*, 25. David Tetzlaff cautions that while new representations may make some people feel more empowered, "feeling empowered and being empowered are not the same thing." See "Material Girl:—patriarchy—postmodernism—power—money—Madonna," in *The Madonna Connection: Represen-*

tational Politics, Subcultural Identities, and Cultural Theory, ed. Cathy Schwichtenberg (Boulder, Colo.: Westview, 1993), 262. In "Feminist Politics and Postmodern Seductions: Madonna and the Struggle for Political Articulation," Roseann Mandziuk warns that it is politically dangerous to mistake individual play for social intervention. In Schwichtenberg, *The Madonna Connection,* 183.

51. This is evident in their continued predominance. *Essence* magazine reports that female models of color are underrepresented in magazine advertising. Though African Americans comprise about 11.3 percent of the readership of all consumer magazines and 12.5 percent of the U.S. population, only 3.4 percent of ads in these texts depicted African Americans in 1991. See Deborah Gregory and Patricia Jacobs, "The Ugly Side: The Modeling Business," *Essence* (Sept. 9, 1993): 89–90, 126.

52. Carol Mithers, "Strength in Diversity," *Mirabella* (Mar. 1993): 154+.

53. Sally Wadyka, *Mademoiselle* (Mar. 1993): 195+.

54. In the words of author and former anorexic-bulimic Marya Hornbacher, thinness has become a key ingredient in "the yuppification of the body and soul." *Wasted: A Memoir of Anorexia and Bulimia* (New York: HarperFlamingo, 1998), 46. For an analysis of the relationship between social distinction, class taste, and body codes, see Pierre Bourdieu, *Distinction: A Social Critique of the Judgment of Taste,* trans. R. Nice (Cambridge: Harvard University Press, 1984).

55. Roberta P. Seid, "Too 'Close to the Bone': The Historical Context for Women's Obsession with Slenderness," in *Feminist Perspectives on Eating Disorders,* ed. Patricia Fallon et al. (New York: Guilford, 1994), 4. See also Roberta P. Seid, *Never Too Thin: Why Women Are at War with Their Bodies* (New York: Prentice Hall, 1989), 15. Figures comparing model women with average women are stated in the documentary film *The Famine Within,* written and directed by Katherine Gilday, 1992, and in Hesse-Biber, *Am I Thin Enough Yet?,* 96. Research suggests that young women recognize this shrinking trend. The college women that Robin Lakoff and Raquel Scherr surveyed in 1984 identified slenderness as the distinguishing feature of the ideal female body. All of the women said they wanted to lose between five and twenty-five pounds, regardless of their current body size. See Lakoff and Scherr, *Face Value: The Politics of Beauty* (Boston: Routledge and Kegan Paul, 1984), 141–42, 168–69.

56. One magazine characterizes "waifs" as "more subdued" and "ethereal." Their look "emphasizes innocence to the point of preconscious sexuality." K. Russel Rich, "This Year's Models," *Allure* (May 1993): 172. Figures for Moss's height and weight reported by Cathy Horyn in "The Thin Girl," *Allure* (May 1994): 165.

57. Andrea Tebay, quoted in "How Thin Is Too Thin?," 74.

58. Seid, *Never Too Thin,* 85, 15, 82, 148.

59. See Ann Braude, *Radical Spirits: Spiritualism and Women's Rights in Nineteenth-Century America* (Boston: Beacon, 1989), 82; Nancy Cott, *The Grounding of Modern Feminism* (New Haven: Yale University Press, 1987); and Russett, *Sexual Science.*

60. Banner traces these ideals of femininity in *American Beauty.*

61. Fabien Baron, creative director at *Harper's Bazaar,* quoted in *Harper's Bazaar* (July 1993): 78.

62. See Walter Benjamin, "The Work of Art in the Age of Mechanical Reproduction," in *Illuminations,* ed. Hannah Arendt, trans. H. Zohn (New York: Schocken, 1969), 217–51.

63. Sallie Tisdale, "A Weight That Women Carry: The Compulsion to Diet in

a Starved Culture," in *Minding the Body: Women Writers on Body and Soul*, ed. Patricia Foster (New York: Doubleday, 1994), 16.

64. The slippage of "reality" is portrayed in Jean Beaudrillard's "The Precession of Simulacra," in *Art after Modernism: Rethinking Representation*, ed. Brian Wallis (New York: New Museum of Contemporary Art, 1984), 253–81.

65. Bordo, *Unbearable Weight*, 201–2.

66. Bordo, " 'Material Girl': The Effacements of Postmodern Culture," in Schwichtenberg, *The Madonna Connection*, 265–66.

67. Victoria Geibel, *Harper's Bazaar* (Mar. 1993): 167. For a feminist reading of such contradictions, see Brown and Jaspers's introduction to *Consuming Passions*, 20, 28.

68. Bordo makes a similar point in *Unbearable Weight*, 206–7.

69. Chris Marcil and Sam Johnson, "Lives of the Supermodels: Niki Taylor," *Elle* (Nov. 1993): 66.

70. Seid, *Never Too Thin*, 161–62, 27–28; Sandra Birtchnell et al., "Body Image Distortion in Non-Eating Disordered Women," *International Journal of Eating Disorders* 6 (1987): 385–91.

71. Pam Houston, "Out of Habit, I Start Apologizing," in Patricia Foster, *Minding the Body*, 148.

72. Hornbacher, *Wasted*, 92, 231–32.

73. See Susan and Orland Wooley, "Feeling Fat in a Thin Society," *Glamour* (Feb. 1984): 198–201+. Studies show that women tend to rate their own bodies as less attractive after viewing media images of model women. See T. F. Cash et al., "Mirror, Mirror on the Wall . . . ?: Contrast Effects and Self-Evaluation of Physical Attractiveness," *Personality and Social Psychology Bulletin* 9 (1983): 351–58. On a CBS News edition of *48 Hours*, Dan Rather reported that 68 percent of women surveyed said that they felt worse about their own appearance after looking at magazine images of female models (Mar. 2, 1994). See also Nancy Wartik, "Can Media Images Trigger Eating Disorders?," *American Health* 14 (Apr. 1995): 26–27.

74. Kim Lorton and Elena Levkin, "Re-figuring Ourselves: Two Voices on Eating Disorders," in *Eating Our Hearts Out: Personal Accounts of Women's Relationship to Food*, ed. Leslea Newman (Freedom, Calif.: Crossing Press, 1993), 218–19.

75. Houston, "Out of Habit, I Start Apologizing," 150.

76. Lorton and Levkin, "Re-figuring Ourselves," 220.

77. Tisdale, "A Weight That Women Carry," 20. That the fear of fat runs wide and deep among Americans in general, and American females in particular, is indicated by surveys on the subject. A 1990 *Newsweek* poll reported that 11 percent of surveyed couples would opt to abort a fetus that was known to be predisposed to obesity. In 1997, 15 percent of female respondents in a *Psychology Today* survey said they would be willing to die five years younger if they could achieve their "ideal" weight. These surveys are cited in Terry Poulton's book *No Fat Chicks: How Big Business Profits by Making Women Hate Their Bodies—And How to Fight Back* (Secaucas, N.J.: Carol Publishing, 1997), 63–64. In 1994, more than half of the 1,000 women polled by *Esquire* magazine said they would rather be run over by a truck than gain 150 pounds. See Laura Fraser in "The Body Beautiful," *Diablo* (Jan. 1998): 58+.

78. Richard Klein, *Eat Fat* (New York: Vintage, 1996), 36. Klein calls for a transvaluation and reversal of the value of fat—from ugly, sickly, and a sign of lethargy, to beautiful, healthy, and a sign of strength (25).

79. Hillel Schwartz, *Never Satisfied: A Cultural History of Diets, Fantasies, and Fat*, (New York: Free Press, 1986), 18–19.

80. See Judith Gaines, " 'Beefcake' Advertising Offers New Sex Objects," *Boston Globe* (Sept. 5, 1993): 1, 11. In this article, the term "beefcake" is used by an advertising executive to describe the marketing trend of using semi-nude males with large, tightly defined, muscular bodies. For an analysis of popular idealization of the male physique, see William Doty, "Baring the Flesh: Aspects of Contemporary Male Iconography," in *Men's Bodies, Men's Gods*, ed. B. Krondorfer (New York: New York University Press, 1996), 267–308.

81. John Berger, *Ways of Seeing* (London: Penguin, 1972), 47. For an interesting reflection on men's use of images of women's bodies as a language for defining, controlling, and exploiting male sexuality, see O. W. Wooley, ". . . And Man Created 'Woman': Representations of Women's Bodies in Western Culture," in Fallon et al., *Feminist Perspectives on Eating Disorders*, 19–44.

82. The racial and economic subtexts of the disdain of fat and its coding as a sign of social deviancy represent a historical shift in modern America. Whereas in the nineteenth century, the thin body was a sickly body, signifying poverty and social vulnerability, by the end of World War I, the plump body came to signify ethnic, racial, and/or economic "difference"—as defined in reference to a norm of white, northern European privilege. See Schwartz, *Never Satisfied*, 143. Today, some fat-liberationists claim that "fattism" is the last form of oppression in an era when other prejudices have been condemned. See, for example, Shelly Bovey, *The Forbidden Body: Why Being Fat Is Not a Sin* (London: HarperCollins, 1994). I suggest that the cultural disdain for big-bodied women also provides a socially approved idiom for expressing dislike of other "deviant" bodies.

83. "Fat Liberation Manifesto," quoted by Judy Freespirit and Aldebaran, "Writings from the Fat Underground," in *Shadow on a Tightrope: Writings by Women on Fat Oppression*, ed. L. Schoenfielder and B. Wieser (San Francisco: Aunt Lute, 1983), 55.

84. Beth MacInnis, "Fat Oppression," in Brown and Jaspers, *Consuming Passions*, 77. According to *The Black Women's Health Book: Speaking for Ourselves*, ed. Evelyn C. White (Seattle: Seal Press, 1990), nearly 35 percent of African American women between the ages of twenty and forty-four weigh 20 percent more than the "ideal" weight for their height and age (28). Such numbers concur with Albert Stunkard's classic "Midtown Manhattan Study," which found women's weights to be lower if their husbands' incomes were higher. Cited in Seid, *Never Too Thin*, 16.

85. *Time* magazine reports that obesity is more common among black, Native American, and Mexican American females compared to their white counterparts but offers no social analysis of these figures. See P. Elmer-Dewitt, "Fat Times," *Time* (Jan. 16, 1995): 63. The war on fat has a prolific arm in the mainstream news media. Other cover stories include "Are You Too Fat?," *U.S. News and World Report* (Jan. 6, 1996): 52+; "How the Stars Fight Fat," *People* (Jan. 22, 1996): 72+; "Fat-Free Fat?," *Time* (Jan. 8, 1996): 52+. Michael Fumento's book *The Fat of the Land: The Obesity Epidemic and How Overweight Americans Can Help Themselves* (New York: Viking, 1997) adds to this depoliticizing discourse. By contrast, see Angela Davis, "Sick and Tired of Being Sick and Tired: The Politics of Black Women's Health," in White, *The Black Women's Health Book* (19–20), for an analysis of the sociopolitical anatomy of obesity. For the political underpinnings of obesity and eating problems among

American Indian women, see H. Mitzi Doane, "Historical Approach to Diet and Community Support Systems for Chronic Disease," in *Mashkiki: Old Medicine Nourishing the New*, ed. E. Haller and L. Aitkin (Lanham, Md.: University Press of America, 1992), 108–9.

86. Linda. Villarosa, "Dangerous Eating," *Essence* (Jan. 1994): 18–21+.

87. Retha Powers, "Fat Is a Black Woman's Issue," *Essence* (Oct. 1989): 78.

88. "Katie," quoted in Maya Browne, "Dying to Be Thin," *Essence* (June 1993): 126.

89. Christy Haubegger, "I'm Not Fat, I'm Latina," *Essence* (Dec. 1994): 48.

90. Lois Fine, "Happy Loser," in Newman, *Eating Our Hearts Out*, 136.

91. Marianne Banks, "A Fat Dyke Tells All," in ibid., 215–216. Many of the women Becky Thompson interviewed for her multicultural study saw slenderness as a sign of heterosexual success. See *A Hunger So Wide and So Deep: American Women Speak Out on Eating Problems* (Minneapolis: University of Minnesota Press, 1994), 39.

92. Rosemary Bray, "Heavy Burden," *Essence* (Jan. 1992): 54, 90.

93. Horyn, "The Thin Girl," 165. More recently, controversy has focused on the actress Calista Flockart, star of *Ally McBeal*, whose weight loss has fueled speculation that she has an eating disorder. See Karen Schneider, "Arguing Her Case," *People* (Nov. 9, 1998): 92–101.

94. Lague et al., "How Thin Is Too Thin?," 74.

95. Horyn, "The Thin Girl," 165.

96. Tina Gaudoin, "Body of Evidence," *Harper's Bazaar* (July 1993): 77.

97. Amber Valetta, quoted in Lague et al., "How Thin Is Too Thin?," 79. In this article, Kate Moss is quoted as saying that she never weighs herself, never exercises, and tries to eat more "so I won't be so waiflike" (74). Women's magazines add to the controversy. One survey found that only 35 percent of supermodels diet (Fellingham, "The Secret Life of Models," 202), but another survey reports that this number is closer to 60 percent. See George Wayne, "Statistical Models," *Allure* (June 1993): 170.

98. For these models, the article reports, "success meant constant gnawing hunger." Kim Alexis admits that " 'there's a lot of pressure when your job depends on your weight.' " Carol Alt advises that " 'anybody who thinks that society pressures women to live up to our image . . . should think of what we have to go through to maintain that image.' " Beverly Johnson, the first black model to appear on the cover of *Vogue*, recalls her modeling days: " 'I ate nothing, I mean *nothing*.' " Eventually she developed bulimia. See Elizabeth Sporkin, "Famous Models, Dangerous Diets," *People* (Jan. 1, 1993).

99. Rose Shepart, "The Hunger: Terrible Pangs and a Craving for Control: Confessions of an Anorexic," *Mirabella* (Apr. 1993): 120–24.

100. Hornbacher, *Wasted*, 44.

101. L. Fraser mentions this study in "The Body Beautiful," 61.

102. Hornbacher, *Wasted*, 64, 69, 123–24.

103. Lorton and Levkin, "Re-figuring Ourselves," 219.

104. Ibid.

105. Pamela Gross, "A Separation of Self," in Newman, *Eating Our Hearts Out*, 63.

106. Laurie Rizzo, "Toward Fullness," in ibid., 186.

107. Thompson, *A Hunger So Wide and So Deep*, 11.

108. Ida Siegal, quoted in "Crosstalk," reported by D. Chen, *Young Miss* (Oct. 1993): 60.

109. This episode (*20/20* [Jan. 6, 1983], Tom Hoving reporting) is described in Stephen Fried's *Thing of Beauty: The Tragedy of Supermodel Gia* (New York: Pocket Books, 1993), 1.

Chapter Three

1. Paula Cooey makes a similar point in *The Religious Imagination and the Body: A Feminist Analysis* (New York: Oxford University Press, 1994), where she explores the "ambiguous status of the body as both location and artifact of human imagination." Cooey argues that "religious traditions provide a pedagogical context for the sociocultural transfiguration of human pain and pleasure in ways that continually recreate and destroy human subjectivity, the world within which it emerges, and the transcendent realities with which the subject seeks relation" (7, 9). While this exploration produces a number of interesting insights, its insights are short-circuited by Cooey's narrow definition of "religious imagination" as "governed and expressed through religious imagery" (4–5). This focus on the contents (rather than the functions and processes) of religious meaning-making creates an unnecessarily rigid distinction between "secular" and "religious" images that blunts the critical edge of her argument.

2. The view that creating and giving practical meaning and orientation in the world is central to the function of religious rites and ideals is elaborated in Gordon Kaufman's *In Face of Mystery: A Constructive Theology* (Cambridge: Harvard University Press, 1993). Kaufman writes, "A major function of what we have come to regard as religious practices and ideas has been to provide a comprehensive framework of orientation which enables humans to gain some insight into and understanding of themselves, their most profound problems, and the sort of fulfillment or salvation that might be available to them" (70).

3. Clifford Geertz, "Religion as a Cultural System," in *The Interpretation of Cultures* (New York: Basic Books, 1973), 98, 89.

4. Mary Douglas, *Purity and Danger: An Analysis of the Concepts of Pollution and Taboo* (1966; reprint, New York: Routledge, 1991), 2–3, 68–72.

5. Catherine Bell, *Ritual Theory, Ritual Practice* (New York: Oxford University Press, 1992), 8, 67, 74. Bell's theory highlights how rituals *make* meanings, rather than *have* or *reflect* meanings. Ritual practices do not dramatize the symbols they reference; rather, they generate their meanings for practical (not logical) purposes.

6. Ibid., 48–49, 83–85, 90. Bell is drawing on the insights of Antonio Gramsci, Pierre Bourdieu, and Michel Foucault. From Gramsci, she uses the concept of "hegemony" to highlight "the dominance and subordination that exist within people's practical and un-self-conscious awareness of the world" and their sense of "identity" and "reality" therein (82–83). Bell's notion of the "ritualized body" is close to Bourdieu's concept of the "socially informed body," the body that has incorporated the moral, aesthetic, and scientific codes of its society into its everyday habits of being (80). From Foucault, Bell picks up the idea that the body is basic to all sociopolitical relations of power (202).

7. Sallie Tisdale, "A Weight That Women Carry: The Compulsion to Diet in a Starved Culture," in *Minding the Body: Women Writers on Body and Soul*, ed. Patricia Foster (New York: Doubleday, 1994), 17.

8. Atema Eclai was a master's student at Harvard Divinity School in 1996. I am grateful to her for this and many other illuminating conversations.

9. Roberta P. Seid lists a number of popular diets in *Never Too Thin: Why Women Are at War with Their Bodies* (New York: Prentice Hall, 1989), 5, 102.

10. The word "diet" stems from the Greek word *diaita*, meaning "way of life." Bryan S. Turner's *The Body and Society: Explorations in Social Theory* (New York: Basil Blackwell, 1984) discusses the dual meanings of the term, namely, as "a regulation of the individual or a regulation of the body politics" (165).

11. See Seid, *Never Too Thin*, 54; and Susan Sprecher and Elaine Hatfield, *Mirror, Mirror . . . : The Importance of Looks in Everyday Life* (Albany: State University of New York Press, 1986), 9.

12. A number of historians concur that fatness had primarily positive connotations throughout the nineteenth century. See Seid, *Never Too Thin*, 76; Harvey Levenstein, *Revolution at the Table: The Transformation of the American Diet* (New York: Oxford University Press, 1988), 13.

13. By situating the beginnings of modern dieting in the writings and practices of early modern men rather than the practices of medieval holy women, I am following the work of cultural historians such as Seid and Levenstein, and especially that of Hillel Schwartz's *Never Satisfied: A Cultural History of Diets, Fantasies, and Fat* (New York: Free Press, 1986).

14. Ibid., 16–17.

15. Ibid. According to Schwartz, Cornaro was outspoken about his views regarding the perils of gluttony. " 'O wretched, miserable Italy!' " he wrote. " 'Dost not thou plainly see, that Gluttony deprives thee of more Souls yearly, than either a War, or the Plague itself could have done?' " However, the moral tone of such warnings focused not on the size of one's body but on the state of one's soul. Ibid., 9–10.

16. This emphasis on monitoring one's own physical and spiritual conduct was encoded in a series of new social norms for "outward bodily propriety" and restraint in the early modern period. Such norms "privatized" and "civilized" certain bodily functions. They engendered new hopes for prolonging the life of the body, as well as a new sense of shame. See Norbert Elias, *The Civilizing Process, vol. 1: The History of Manners*, trans. E. Jephcott (1939; reprint, New York: Pantheon, 1978), xiii, 53–54. While new codes of behavior did not originate in priestly circles, Elias notes that the Church played a central role in their dispersion (140, 101).

17. Carolyn Merchant, *The Death of Nature: Women, Ecology, and the Scientific Revolution* (1980; reprint, San Francisco: HarperCollins, 1990). Merchant sums up some of the major shifts the mechanistic model implied: "The primacy of organic process gave way to the stability of mathematical laws and identities. Force was external to matter rather than immanent within it. Matter was corpuscular, passive, and inert; change was simply the rearrangement of particles as motion was transmitted from one part to another in a causal nexus" (102–3, 194, 234). As this worldview functioned to legitimate the manipulation of nature, it was also extremely compatible with the new directions of commercial capitalism. Merchant's reading of the scientific revolution as gendered informs her whole account.

18. Turner, *The Body and Society*, 36–37. See also Turner's more recent book, *Regulating Bodies: Essays in Medical Sociology* (New York: Routledge, 1992).

19. The dietary regimes of George Cheyne (1671–1743) illustrate this trend. A popular physician and Fellow of the Royal Society in London, Cheyne's plan centered on moderating one's food intake and engaging in light exercise. Although this program was devised for a group of London elites, some of its principles reached a wider audience through the interests of Methodist founder John Wesley. See Turner, *Body and Society*, 77–78, and *Regulating Bodies*, 190. Turner draws an interesting parallel between Foucault's account of the body's imprisonment through the modern forms of disciplinary power and Max Weber's conception of the rationalization of human experience with the rise of modern capitalism. Both thinkers suggest the decisive role that religious practices (ironically) played in the rise of modern industrial capitalism; both understood that "religious models of thought and practice provide one historical location for the growth and spread of rational surveillance of human populations." *Body and Society*, 163–64, and *Regulating Bodies*, 4, 11, 180–81.

20. Stephen Nissenbaum, *Sex, Diet, and Debility in Jacksonian America: Sylvester Graham and Health Reform* (Chicago: Dorsey, 1980), ix, 142; Schwartz, *Never Satisfied*, 25–28.

21. See James C. Whorton, *Crusaders for Fitness: The History of American Health Reformers* (Princeton: Princeton University Press, 1982), 6. The lack of conflict between religious and scientific programs for healthy/holy living is evident in the nineteenth-century American Physiological Society, whose members attended lectures and put forth resolutions regarding health reform, one of which read: "Resolved, That the highest moral and religious interests of man require a strict conformity in the dietetic and the voluntary habits to all the physiological laws of his nature." Quoted in Whorton, *Crusaders for Fitness*, 59–60. Seid explains that "Enlightenment notions about natural science had slowly spread the heady idea that human beings could control their health. . . . These beliefs merged with religious aspirations. Perfecting the body became part of the wave of religious Perfectionism of the period, which argued that if people bettered themselves morally and physically, they would either hasten the Second Coming or could ensure they were not one of the damned." *Never Too Thin*, 69.

22. Prior to Banting's text, health reformers were concerned not with creating a thinner population but with the way eating influenced one's physical and moral condition. Though Banting was British, his book had wide and popular influence in this country: it went through five printings in just one year and was republished for nearly fifty years thereafter. Seid, *Never Too Thin*, 64, 69.

23. According to Levenstein, these turn-of-the-century ideas, which he refers to as the "New Nutrition," planted the seeds for present-day attitudes toward nutrition and diet, especially the beliefs that "taste is not a true guide to what should be eaten, that one should not simply eat what one enjoys; that the important components of food cannot be seen or tasted, but are discernible only in scientific laboratories; and that experimental science has produced rules of nutrition which will prevent illness and encourage longevity." *Revolution at the Table*, 46, 210.

24. Throughout this century, scientifically sanctioned eating practices and bodily standards have been deployed to Americanize certain ethnic groups, rewarding "different" individuals for absorbing mainstream cultural norms. Schwartz writes: "Fatness was careless, selfish, wasteful, treacherous and un-American. During the

prewar era, for the first time, fatness had been specifically associated with immigrant groups. Americanization began to imply an actual physical change toward uniform American (Yankee) features." *Never Satisfied,* 142–43. For more on the "Americanization" of minority and working-class cultures through the monitoring of body size, see Seid, *Never Too Thin,* 91, 226; Schwartz, *Never Satisfied,* 248–49; and Levenstein, *Revolution at the Table,* 104.

25. According to Levenstein, members of immigrant groups and the working class, many of whom were not secure about their own food supplies, were slow or unwilling to adopt the new scientific guidelines designed to "improve" (and Americanize) their eating patterns. Eventually, these guidelines were introduced to mainstream America. See *Revolution at the Table,* 43, 104, 176–77, 210–11.

26. Schwartz notes that even the Great Depression years did not abate the cultural shift toward a narrower body ideal. *Never Satisfied,* 75, 80–81, 192–93.

27. Alongside new medical theories about the detriments of obesity, psychoanalytic models not only blamed obesity on overeating but also assumed that people who overate did so because of unsatisfied emotional needs. Seid, *Never Too Thin,* 126; Schwartz, *Never Satisfied,* 192–94, 153–55.

28. Seid, *Never Too Thin,* 18–19.

29. Ibid., 105–6, 108.

30. The best source for current statistics and data regarding the economics of the diet industry is Laura Fraser's *Losing It: America's Obsession with Weight and the Industry That Feeds On It* (New York: Dutton, 1997). The above figures draw on references from pages 8, 82, 120, 141 of this book. Other sources for figures on diet food and soft drink sales include Schwartz, *Never Satisfied,* 245, 255, and Levenstein, *Revolution at the Table,* 205. According to the President's Council on Physical Fitness and Sports, Americans spent $31 billion on diet and fitness in 1984. See A. Thresher, "Girth of a Nation (Diet Entrepreneurs)," *Nation's Business* 74 (Dec. 1986): 50–51. In "War of the Diets," Joanne Silberner cites figures indicating that about 53 million adult Americans, mostly women, were expected to go on diets in 1992, spending $36 billion in the process. See *U.S. News and World Report* 112 (Feb. 3, 1992): 55–60. On commercial weight-loss centers, see A. Miller, "Diets Incorporated," *Newsweek* 114 (Sept. 11, 1989): 56+. On the failure of commercial weight-loss programs to keep weight off, see "Losing Weight: What Works, What Doesn't," *Consumer Reports* 58 (June 1993): 347–57. On the revenues for programs like Weight Watchers, see B. O'Reilly, "Diet Centers Are Really in Fat City," *Fortune* 119 (June 5, 1989): 137+. On scandals and debates that have hurt this industry, see M. Schroeder, "The Diet Business Is Getting a Lot Skinnier," *Business Week* (June 24, 1991): 132–34. On pharmaceutical dieting, see Schwartz, *Never Satisfied,* 245, and Seid, *Never Too Thin,* 106, 138–39. The $77 billion figure, which does not include money spent on "aesthetic" surgery, is cited in Lynette Lamb, "Your Body: Friend, Foe, or Total Stranger," *Utne Reader* (May/June 1992): 53.

31. Seid, *Never Too Thin,* 164–66. The fitness industry today is a $42.9 billion business, including health clubs, exercise videos, home exercise equipment, clothing, and accessories. Sharlene Hesse-Biber cites this figure in *Am I Thin Enough Yet?: The Cult of Thinness and the Commercialization of Identity* (New York: Oxford University Press, 1996), 47.

32. See Warren Belasco's *Appetite for Change: How the Counterculture Took On the Food Industry* (Ithaca: Cornell University Press, 1989) for an account of the 1960s

and 1970s countercultural critique of mainstream eating and dieting practices, the social challenge underlying this critique, and its eventual absorption by mainstream culture and capitalist markets.

33. For example, in a survey conducted by *Essence* on issues related to troubled eating and body-hatred, 74.5 percent of respondents said that they exercise to burn calories. See Linda Villarosa, "Dangerous Eating," *Essence* (Jan. 1994): 19.

34. These stats for advertising exposure are cited in Jean Kilbourne's "Still Killing Us Softly: Advertising and the Obsession with Thinness," in *Feminist Perspectives on Eating Disorders*, ed. Patricia Fallon et al. (New York: Guilford, 1994), 395.

35. Marjorie Rosen et al., "Diet Wars: Who's Winning, Who's Sinning," *People* (Jan. 13, 1992): 72–82; K. Jackovich and A. Lynn, "Diet Winners and Sinner of the Year," *People* (Jan. 10, 1994): 36–53.

36. This study was conducted by Purdue University and is cited by Julia Lieblich in "Christian Dieting: Get Righteous, Get Thin," *San Francisco Examiner* (Apr. 19, 1998): A18. Body and Soul Aerobics quote found on that program's Web site. For additional information on Christian dieting and fitness programs, see John Allen Jr., "Christian Diets Point to Getting 'Slim for Him,' " *National Catholic Reporter* 34 (Dec. 12, 1997): 39–40.

37. R. Marie Griffith, *God's Daughters: Evangelical Women and the Power of Submission* (Berkeley: University of California Press, 1997), 143. See especially 139–50.

38. Ibid., 143–45, 149–50.

39. Shamblin quote from Lieblich, "Christian Dieting," A18. An advertisement for the Weigh Down Workshop that appeared in a newsletter for the women of the Evangelical Free Church in Walnut Creek, California, asks its readers: "Did you know that the Bible has some things to say about food and eating habits, and by following some simple principles of hunger and fullness you can finally lose that extra weight you've lost and found several times before? The class costs $103 for a 12-week session and includes video lectures, group sessions, and your own workbook with 12 audio tapes." From *Women in Touch* 1 (Feb.–Apr. 1997): 7.

40. Allen, "Christian Diets Point to Getting 'Slim for Him,' " 39–40.

41. Fraser, *Losing It!*, 121.

42. This saying is quoted by Lois Fine in her essay "Happy Loser," in *Eating Our Hearts Out: Personal Accounts of Women's Relationship to Food*, ed. Leslea Newman (Freedom, Calif.: Crossing Press, 1993), 136.

43. Quoted in Fraser, *Losing It!*, 67.

44. Ray Kybartas, *Fitness Is Religion: Keep the Faith* (New York: Simon and Schuster, 1997), 19.

45. These examples are cited in Fraser, *Losing It!*, 74.

46. Alison Thresher charts this trend in "Girth of a Nation (Diet Entrepreneurs)," 50–51. Sybil Ferguson shared her weight-loss strategies with her friends for free until she realized the potential profits generated by her own experience. She opened her first Diet Center in 1969 and by 1986 had over 2,000 franchises. Weight Watchers's founder, Jean Nidetch, has a similar story. In an article on the quasi-religious qualities of diet programs, Natalie Allon reports on visits to more than ninety group diet meetings. Allon highlights the religious rhetoric of the women who discussed their efforts to lose weight: "These dieters labeled overweight as a sinful deviation, buttressed by the religious argot of saint, sinner, angel, devil, guilt, confession and absolution. Some stated that they had innocently caught this sin. . . .

Others claimed that they had actively acquired their sinful state." N. Allon, "Fat Is a Dirty Word: Fat as a Sociological and Social Problem," in *Recent Advances in Obesity Research: 1*, ed. A. N. Howard (London: Newman Publishing, 1975), 244–47.

47. Powter quoted in Rebecca Sherman, "Stop the Lies," *Boston Phoenix* (Jan. 14, 1994): 3, 8. For a detailed discussion of Powter's tactics, see Fraser, *Losing It!*, 50–51, 74–79.

48. Sherman, "Stop the Lies," 3, 8. See also James Servin, "Lean and Mean," *Allure* (Oct. 1993): 114; Elizabeth Kaye, "Powter Keg," *Lears* 6 (1994): 56, 91.

49. Melanie Menagh, "Starting Late: How to Get Fit When Your Life Gets in the Way," *Lears* 6 (1994): 63.

50. For more examples of the use of religious discourse in advertisements for weight-loss products, see Kilbourne, "Still Killing Us Softly," especially 409–11.

51. Deborah Gregory, "Heavy Judgment," *Essence* (Aug. 1994): 110.

52. Tisdale, "A Weight That Women Carry," 18–19.

53. Pamela Gross, "A Separation of Self," in Newman, *Eating Our Hearts Out*, 65; Patricia J. Washburn, "Losing It," in ibid., 56.

54. Retha Powers, "Fat Is a Black Woman's Issue," *Essence* (Oct. 1989): 78.

55. See Deborah Tolman and Elizabeth Debold, "Conflicts of Body and Image: Female Adolescents, Desire, and the No-Body Body," in Fallon et al., *Feminist Perspectives on Eating Disorders*, 307.

56. "Janine," quoted in Jennifer Manlowe, "Seduced by Faith: Sexual Traumas and Their Embodied Effects," *Critical Matrix* 8, no. 2 (1994): 85–99.

57. Joan Dickenson, "Some Thoughts on Fat," in *Shadow on a Tightrope: Writings by Women on Fat Oppression*, ed. L. Schoenfielder and B. Wieser (San Francisco: Aunt Lute, 1983), 39.

58. "Conversation with Nancy," in ibid., 181.

59. Gladys M. Murphy, "Some Days I Even Eat Breakfast," In Newman, *Eating Our Hearts Out*, 145.

60. Becky Thompson also notes the inadequacy of terms like "body image" for describing women's eating problems. She suggests the term "body-consciousness" as a corrective to conventional discourse. See *A Hunger So Wide and So Deep*, 16–20. I prefer the term "body sense," which has the advantage of calling attention to the multiple levels on which meanings are made, insofar as the term "sense" encompasses thought, feeling, and physical sensation.

61. The concept of the "ritualized body" is Catherine Bell's (see above), though she draws heavily on the work of Pierre Bourdieu, especially his notion of the "socially informed body," which he explains in his *Outline of a Theory of Practice*, trans. R. Nice (1977; reprint, Cambridge: Cambridge University Press, 1992). Bourdieu's concept of the "socially informed body" focuses attention on the body's social training through its senses, including not just "the five traditional senses, which never escape the structuring action of social determinisms—but also the sense of necessity and the sense of duty, the sense of direction and the sense of reality, the sense of balance and the sense of beauty, common sense and the sense of the sacred, tactical sense and the sense of responsibility, business sense and the sense of propriety, the sense of humor and the sense of absurdity, moral sense and the sense of practicality, and so on" (94, 124). Bourdieu's idea of the "socially informed body" is close to Foucault's notion of modern society's "political technology of the body." Foucault writes, "There may be a 'knowledge' of the body that is not exactly the science of its functioning, and a mystery of its forces that is more than the ability to conquer them:

this knowledge and this mastery constitute what might be called the political technology of the body." *Discipline and Punish: The Birth of the Prison*, trans. A. Sheridan (1978; reprint, New York: Vintage Books, 1990), 26.

62. In *Bodylove: Learning to Like Our Looks—and Ourselves* (New York: Harper and Row, 1988), Rita Freedman suggests that "if you listen with respect instead of mistrust—to pain, pleasure, hunger, fatigue—your body will tell you how to nurture it" (4). Such advice overlooks the degree to which women's bodies—their hungers, pains, and pleasures—are always already shaped by their social environments.

63. Sima Rabinowitz, "The Unanswered Echo," in Newman, *Eating Our Hearts Out,* 78, 81.

64. Marya Hornbacher, "Wasted," *Minneapolis–St. Paul Monthly Magazine* (Nov. 1993): 69.

65. "Janis," quoted in Elizabeth Karleberg, "I Have an Eating Disorder," *Teen* (Dec. 1992): 98.

66. "Megan," quoted in ibid., 97.

67. Doris Grumbach, "Coming to the End Zone," in Foster, *Minding the Body*, 77.

68. Marjory Nelson, "Fat and Old: Old and Fat," in Schoenfielder and Wieser, *Shadow on a Tightrope,* 229–30.

69. Marianne Banks, "A Fat Dyke Tells All," in Newman, *Eating Our Hearts Out,* 215.

70. Lee Lynch, "Lesbian Stew," in ibid., 212.

71. Christy Haubegger, "I'm Not Fat, I'm Latina," *Essence* (Dec. 1994): 48.

72. Julia Boyd, "Ethnic and Cultural Diversity in Feminist Therapy: Keys to Power," in *The Black Women's Health Book: Speaking for Ourselves,* ed. Evelyn C. White (Seattle: Seal Press, 1990), 231.

73. Georgiana Arnold, "Coming Home: One Black Woman's Journey to Health and Fitness," in ibid., 270.

74. See J. E. Smith and J. Krejci, "Minorities Join the Majority: Eating Disturbances among Hispanic and Native American Youth," *International. Journal of Eating Disorders* 10 (1991): 179–86; Lionel Rosen et al., "Prevalence of Pathogenic Weight-Control Behaviors among Native American Women and Girls," *International. Journal of Eating Disorders* 7 (1988): 807–11; Maria Root, "Disordered Eating in Women of Color," *Sex Roles* 22 (1990): 525–36.

75. Thompson, *A Hunger So Wide and So Deep*, 44, 36, and "Food, Bodies, and Growing Up Female: Childhood Lessons about Culture, Race, and Class," in Fallon et al., *Feminist Perspectives on Eating Disorders,* 372.

76. Rabinowitz, "The Unanswered Echo," 80.

77. "Interview with Deb," in Schoenfielder and Wieser, *Shadow on a Tightrope,* 86.

78. "Kathy," quoted in Wendy Chapkis, *Beauty Secrets: Women and the Politics of Appearance* (Boston: South End, 1986), 159.

79. Barbara Katz, "Weighing the Cost," in Newman, *Eating Our Hearts Out,* 189.

80. Deonne L. Kahler, "No Simple Feast," in ibid., 228.

81. Deane Curtin, "Food/Body/Person," in *Cooking, Eating, Thinking: Transformative Philosophies of Food*, ed. D. Curtin and L. Heldke (Bloomington: Indiana University Press, 1992), 3–22.

82. Susan Bordo, *Unbearable Weight: Feminism, Western Culture, and the Body* (Berkeley: University of California Press, 1993), 27.

83. See Frigga Haug, *Beyond Female Masochism: Memory-Work and Politics* (London: Verso, 1992), 9, 26. See also Haug, ed., *Female Sexualization: A Collective Work of Memory*, trans. Erica Carter (London: Verso, 1987).

84. See Margaret Morrison's " 'In Only Four Weeks,' " reprinted in *Being Beautiful: Deciding for Yourself* (Washington: Center for the Study of Responsive Law, 1986).

85. Deborah Pike, "Redefining the Body," *Vogue* (Jan. 1994): 105, 166.

86. Martha Barnette, "Perfect Endings," *Allure* (Nov. 93): 160–63.

87. Bordo makes this point about the transvaluation of muscles in *Unbearable Weight*, 193–95.

88. See Victoria Johnson's "Body Sculpting," *Essence* (Apr. 1994): 65–69. The advertising trend toward targeting minority women is cited by Fraser in *Losing It!*, 143–44.

89. Schwartz, *Never Satisfied*, 254. According to Schwartz, caricatures of male dieters are similar in all respects except for age, which was assumed to be between thirty-five and fifty-four. In a chapter entitled "Work(ing) Out," Susan Willis suggests that a similar demographic makeup (white and middle- or upper-class) characterizes those women who "work out" on a regular basis. See *A Primer for Daily Life* (New York: Routledge, 1991), 65.

90. Rosemary Bray makes these points in "Heavy Burden," *Essence* (Jan. 1992): 54.

91. On the economic demographics of "healthy eating," see Belasco, *Appetite for Change*, 194, 201, 228.

Chapter Four

1. Reported by Eric Pace, "Obituaries," *New York Times* (July 28, 1994). See also Merrell Noden, "Dying to Win," *Sports Illustrated* 81 (Aug. 1994): 52–60+.

2. Joan Jacobs Brumberg notes that Carpenter's death in 1983 fueled both popular and professional interest in anorexia nervosa. *Fasting Girls: The History of Anorexia Nervosa* (New York: Penguin, 1988), 15.

3. Kimberly Sender, "My Hero, Myself," in *Eating Our Hearts Out: Personal Accounts of Women's Relationship to Food*, ed. Leslea Newman (Freedom, Calif.: Crossing Press, 1993), 30.

4. Karen Twenhofel, "Do You Diet?," in ibid., 201–2.

5. Maya Browne, "Dying to Be Thin," *Essence* (June 1993): 87.

6. Cherry Boone O'Neil, *Starving for Attention* (New York: Continuum, 1982), 38.

7. Hilde Bruch, *Conversations with Anorexics,* ed. Danita Czyzewski and Melanie A. Suhr (New York: Basic Books, 1988), 4. See also Bruch, *The Golden Cage: The Enigma of Anorexia Nervosa* (New York: Vintage Books, 1978).

8. "Ida," in Bruch, *Conversations with Anorexics*, 26, 72, 132.

9. Elena Levkin and Kim Lorton, "Re-figuring Ourselves: Two Voices on Eating Disorders," in Newman, *Eating Our Hearts Out*, 217.

10. Lynn Woodland, "Filling the Void: Healing Food Addiction," *The Phoenix* (Minneapolis) 14, no. 12 (Dec. 1994): 1; anonymous woman quoted in Linda Villarosa, "Dangerous Eating," *Essence* (Jan. 1994): 20.

11. Twenhofel, "Do You Diet?," 199.

12. Ibid., "Helen," in Bruch, *Conversations with Anorexics*, 92.

13. Marya Hornbacher, "Wasted," *Minneapolis–St. Paul Monthly Magazine* (Nov. 1993): 170.

14. Twenhofel, "Do You Diet?," 201.

15. Caroline Adams Miller, *My Name Is Caroline* (New York: Doubleday, 1988), 17–18.

16. Anni Acker, "Scenes from a Life with Food," in Newman, *Eating Our Hearts Out*, 177.

17. Marya Hornbacher, *Wasted: A Memoir of Anorexia and Bulimia* (New York: HarperFlamingo, 1998), 108, 154, 133.

18. See chapter 1. I do not refer to "binge eating" or "compulsive eating" separately in this chapter because I see this problem as a form of bulimic behavior and thus on the same continuum as anorexia.

19. Barbara Katz, "Weighing the Cost," in Newman, *Eating Our Hearts Out*, 191–93.

20. It is important to remember that not all women who eat compulsively are fat—just as not all women who are fat eat compulsively. Though they are often related, eating compulsively and being "overweight" are not automatically linked in a causal chain. See my discussion of these issues in chapter 1.

21. Sima Rabinowitz, "The Unanswered Echo," in Newman, *Eating Our Hearts Out*, 79.

22. Tillich's view of the relationship between "religion" and "culture" is summed up in his claim that "religion is the substance of culture, culture is the form of religion." For Tillich, the crises of meaning that many modern persons experience is the result of living in a culture where religion has been relegated to a narrow and insular domain. *Theology of Culture* (New York: Oxford University Press, 1959), 8, 42, 46. In his article "Reconsidering the Status of Popular Culture in Tillich's Theology of Culture," Kelton Cobb points out that Tillich's notion of "culture" tacitly referred to the culture of the elite. See *Journal of the American Academy of Religion* 63 (Spring 1995): 53–84.

23. Hornbacher, *Wasted*, 231.

24. "Kim," an anorexic woman interviewed by Sharlene Hesse-Biber in *Am I Thin Enough Yet?: The Cult of Thinness and the Commercialization of Identity* (New York: Oxford University Press, 1996), 83.

25. Lorton and Levkin, "Re-figuring Ourselves," 221.

26. Hornbacher, "Wasted," 70.

27. Anonymous woman quoted in Villarosa, "Dangerous Eating," 20.

28. "Ida," in Bruch, *Conversations with Anorexics*, 131–36, 175.

29. Hornbacher, *Wasted*, 86, 125–26.

30. Patricia Foster, "Reading the Body: An Introduction," in *Minding the Body: Women Writers on Body and Soul*, ed. Foster (New York: Doubleday, 1994), 4–5.

31. Retha Powers, "Fat Is a Black Woman's Issue," *Essence* (Oct. 1989): 78.

32. "Paula," in Bruch, *Conversations with Anorexics*, 48–49.

33. Ibid., 4–6, 8.

34. "Megan," in ibid., 149.

35. Hornbacher, "Wasted," 70.

36. "Ida," in Bruch, *Conversations with Anorexics*, 132, 204

37. "Annette," in ibid., 20–21.

38. Deonne Lynn Kahler, "No Simple Feast," in Newman, *Eating Our Hearts Out*, 229–30.

39. Hornbacher, "Wasted," 70, 68.

40. "Helen," in Bruch, *Conversations with Anorexics*, 83.

41. Woodland, "Filling the Void," 1.

42. "Ida," in Bruch, *Conversations with Anorexics*, 175.

43. Jennifer Manlowe, *Faith Born of Seduction: Sexual Trauma, Body Image, and Religion* (New York: New York University Press, 1995), 60. Of course, historically, those who defined and monitored such virtues often managed to exempt themselves from their codes. Moreover, as historian Elizabeth Clark has noted, martyrdom was one of the few avenues open to early Christian women for moving beyond their "sex" and enabling them to claim a limited form of spiritual power. According to Clark, the early church fathers agreed that "in martyrdom, no difference of sex obtained. . . . Martyrdom not only provided an opportunity—if one may call it that—for the elevation of females; it also furnished heroic subject matter about women for writers of both prose and poetry." *Women in the Early Church* (Collegeville, Minn.: Liturgical Press, 1983) 22. See also Margaret Miles's discussion on female martyrs and ascetics and the religious trope of "becoming male" in chapter 2 of *Carnal Knowing: Female Nakedness and Religious Meaning in the Christian West* (Boston: Beacon, 1989), 53–77.

44. Nancy Jay, *Throughout Your Generations Forever: Sacrifice, Religion, and Paternity* (Chicago: University of Chicago Press, 1992), xxiii. Jay's account focuses on the opposition between sacrifice and childbirth, or between sacrifice and childbearing women (mothers and potential mothers), that is present in diverse sacrificial traditions. This study illustrates how fear/rejection of female flesh is central to the reproduction of patriarchal religious authority.

45. Sender, "My Hero, Myself," 29–30.

46. Anonymous, *Re-Imagining*, ed. Pamela Carter Jones (Minneapolis), issue 1 (Nov. 1994): 9.

47. Starhawk contrasts the notion of "power-over" with the alternative view of "power-from-within" in *Dreaming the Dark: Magic, Sex, and Politics* (Boston: Beacon, 1982), 1–14. Sallie McFague discusses the "monarchical" model of power that has shaped much traditional Christian theology in "Imagining a Theology of Nature: The World as God's Body," in *Liberation Theology: An Introductory Reader*, ed., Curt Cadorette, et al. (Maryknoll, N.Y.: Orbis, 1992), 269–89.

48. Twenhofel, "Do You Diet?," 202; and "Megan," in Bruch, *Conversations with Anorexics*, 149.

49. Abra Fortune Chernik, "The Body Politic," in *Listen Up: Voices from the Next Feminist Generation*, ed. Barbara Findlen (Seattle: Seal Press, 1995), 78.

50. Browne, "Dying to Be Thin," 87.

51. Bruch, *Conversations with Anorexics*, 8, 21, 59, 183.

52. Adams Miller, *My Name Is Caroline*, 96.

53. "Esther," in Bruch, *Conversations with Anorexics*, 98.

54. "Lucy," in ibid., 83.

55. On the "oversubmissiveness" of anorexics, see Bruch, *The Golden Cage*, 47. On the "overcompliance" of bulimics, see Marlene Boskind-Lodahl's classic essay "Cinderella's Stepsisters: A Feminist Perspective on Anorexia Nervosa and Bulimia," *Signs* 2 (1976): 342–46, and M. Boskind-White and W. White, *Bulimarexia: The Binge/Purge Cycle* (New York: W. W. Norton, 1987), 68. On the cultural specificity

of this gender trait, see Becky Thompson, "Food, Bodies, and Growing Up Female: Childhood Lessons about Culture, Race, and Class," in *Feminist Perspectives on Eating Disorders*, ed. Patricia Fallon et al. (New York: Guilford, 1994), 358, 372.

56. "Fawn," in Bruch, *Conversations with Anorexics,* 104, 109.

57. Rabinowitz, "The Unanswered Echo," 78–79.

58. Lois Fine, "Happy Loser," in Newman, *Eating Our Hearts Out*, 135.

59. Hornbacher, "Wasted," 170.

60. "Annette," in Bruch, *Conversations with Anorexics*, 120–21, 125.

61. "Lucy," in ibid., 81.

62. "Annette," in ibid., 120–21, 125.

63. Hornbacher, *Wasted*, 118, 229.

64. "Fawn," in Bruch, *Conversations with Anorexics*, 141–42.

65. Hornbacher, *Wasted*, 108.

66. "Ida," in Bruch, *Conversations with Anorexics,* 205, 207.

67. "Helen," 92, and "Lucy," in ibid., 81.

68. "Ida," in ibid., 132.

69. See Margaret Miles, "Religion and Food: The Case of Eating Disorders," *Journal of the American Academy of Religion* 63 (Fall 1995): 549–64.

70. "Ida," in Bruch, *Conversations with Anorexics,* 132.

71. See Margaret Miles, *Fullness of Life: Historical Foundations for a New Asceticism* (Philadelphia: Westminster, 1981). This work challenges the widespread assumption that Christian authors assumed or posited a total separation between mind and body. Through a close and contextualized reading of primary Christian texts, Miles reconstructs a Christian history of the human body that underscores classical authors' assumptions that the human "body" and "soul," while distinct, were inseparable.

72. Rabinowitz, "The Unanswered Echo," 80.

73. "Elsa," quoted in Thompson, *A Hunger So Wide and So Deep*, 73.

74. Kathryn Zerbe, "Whose Body Is It Anyway?: Understanding and Treating Psychosomatic Aspects of Eating Disorders," *Bulletin of the Menninger Clinic* 57 (Spring 1993): 161.

75. In *Body and Soul: The Black Women's Guide to Physical Health and Emotional Well-Being*, Linda Villarosa cites studies suggesting that African American females between the ages of nine and twelve are more often the victims of sexual abuse than their white female counterparts (New York: HarperPerennial, 1994), 7.

76. According to Thompson, between one-third and two-thirds of those who suffer from eating problems have experienced sexual abuse. *A Hunger So Wide and So Deep*, 20, 47. See also Manlowe, *Faith Born of Seduction*, and Susan C. Wooley, "Sexual Abuse and Eating Disorders: The Concealed Debate," in Fallon et al., *Feminist Perspectives on Eating Disorders*, 171–211.

77. "Ida," in Bruch, *Conversations with Anorexics*, 204.

78. Ariadne Northstar, "Eating," in Newman, *Eating Our Hearts Out*, 75.

79. "Nora," in Bruch, *Conversations with Anorexics*, 152.

80. Northstar, "Eating," 77.

81. "Fawn," in Bruch, *Conversations with Anorexics*, 140.

82. Browne, "Dying to Be Thin," 86.

83. Lou Ann Thomas, "Fill 'er Up," in Newman, *Eating Our Hearts Out*, 181.

84. Fine, "Happy Loser," 135.

85. Katz, "Weighing the Cost," 191; Heisel, "Food for Life," 237–38; Northstar, "Eating," 75.

86. Northstar, "Eating," 75–76.

87. "Ida," in Bruch, *Conversations with Anorexics*, 203.

88. "Lucy," in ibid., 80–81.

89. Heisel, "Food for Life," 237.

90. Laurie Rizzo, "Toward Fullness," in Newman, *Eating Our Hearts Out*, 188.

91. Thomas, "Fill 'er Up," 180.

92. "Mira," in Bruch, *Conversations with Anorexics*, 42.

93. Ellie Mamber, "Orgy for One," in Newman, *Eating Our Hearts Out*, 37.

94. Ruth Hinkel, "Confessions of a Food Junkie," in ibid., 235.

95. Linda Weltner, "Tempted by the Demons of an Eating Disorder," in ibid., 10.

96. Lorton and Levkin, "Re-figuring Ourselves," 220.

97. Northstar, "Eating," 75–76.

98. "Nora," in Bruch, *Conversations with Anorexics*, 151.

99. Rabinowitz, "The Unanswered Echo" 79.

100. Sender, "My Hero, Myself," 29.

101. Kahler, "No Simple Feast," 227–30.

102. Northstar, "Eating," 74–75.

103. Quoted from page 4 of the insert to the Indigo Girls' double-disk release *1200 Curfews* (1995), produced by Indigo Girls and Russell Carter, recorded on Epic. Ray is describing her song "Pushing the Needle Too Far."

104. Quoted from Bruch, *The Golden Cage*, 74–75.

105. "Helen," in Bruch, *Conversations with Anorexics*, 147.

106. This suggests that anorexic and bulimic women are neither passive victims nor political heroines. While it is crucial to recognize the search for freedom that permeates their struggles, it is important to see the limits of the "resistance" these struggles creates. Susie Orbach fails to sufficiently recognize these limits in her comparison of anorexic women with female suffragists in "Visibility/Invisibility: Social Considerations in Anorexia Nervosa—A Feminist Perspective," in *Theory and Treatment of Anorexia Nervosa and Bulimia: Biomedical, Sociocultural, and Psychological Perspectives*, ed. S. Emmett (New York: Brunner/Mazel, 1985), 130. Maud Ellman also probes the relationship between the anorexic struggle and the hunger strikes of political activists and prisoners. Her phenomenological analysis of the "dream of miraculous transfiguration" that underlies both forms of self-starvation is intriguing, but such intrigue has the effect of depoliticizing the issues she means to illuminate. Ellman is more fascinated by than critical of these "arts of disincarnation" and "deconstruction of the flesh." See *The Hunger Artists: Starving, Writing, and Imprisonment* (Cambridge: Harvard University Press, 1993), 4.

107. Northstar, "Eating," 75–77.

108. "Lucy," in Bruch, *Conversations with Anorexics*, 81.

109. Northstar, "Eating," 76.

110. "Ida," in Bruch, *Conversations with Anorexics*, 204.

111. "Annette," in ibid., 128–29, 157.

112. Hornbacher, *Wasted*, 266.

Chapter Five

1. Joan Iten Sutherland, "Body of Radiant Knots: Healing as Remembering," *Being Bodies: Buddhist Women on the Paradox of Embodiment* (Boston: Shambhala, 1997), 3.

2. Nina Silver, "The Midnight Prowl," in *Eating Our Hearts Out: Personal Accounts of Women's Relationship to Food*, ed. Leslea Newman (Freedom, Calif.: Crossing Press, 1993), 41.

3. In liberation theology, the term "conscientization" describes this shift in consciousness. Paulo Freire first used this term in *Pedagogy of the Oppressed* (New York: Seabury Press, 1973). Elisabeth Schüssler Fiorenza discusses its importance for feminist liberation theology in *But She Said: Feminist Practices of Biblical Interpretation* (Boston: Beacon, 1992), 53.

4. Abra Fortune Chernik, "The Body Politic," in *Listen Up: Voices from the Next Feminist Generation*, ed. Barbara Findlen (Seattle: Seal Press, 1995), 82.

5. See, for example, Mary Daly, *Beyond God the Father: Toward a Philosophy of Women's Liberation* (1973; reprint, Boston: Beacon, 1985), and Carol Christ, *Diving Deep and Surfacing: Women Writers on Spiritual Quest* (1980; reprint, Boston: Beacon, 1986).

6. Newman, introduction to *Eating Our Hearts Out*, 3.

7. Jennifer Semple Siegel, "Are You Thin Yet?," in ibid., 206. For an interesting essay on the need for anorexic and bulimic women to let go of the dream of slenderness in their search for health and healing, see Andria Siegler, "Grieving the Lost Dream of Thinness," in *Consuming Passions: Feminist Approaches to Weight Preoccupation and Eating Disorders*, ed. Catrina Brown and Karin Jaspers (Toronto: Second Story 1993), 151–60.

8. Georgiana Arnold, "Coming Home: One Black Woman's Journey to Health and Fitness," in *The Black Women's Health Book: Speaking for Ourselves*, ed. Evelyn C. White (Seattle: Seal Press, 1990), 269–79.

9. Patricia J. Washburn, "Losing It," in Newman, *Eating Our Hearts Out*, 57.

10. My thinking on this point is influenced by a conversation between Gail Rubin and Judith Butler, entitled "Sexual Traffic," published in *Difference* 6 (1994): 63–98. In this discussion, Rubin suggests that "the acquisition of our sexual and gender programming is much like the learning of our native cultural system or language. It is much harder to learn new languages, or to be as facile in them as in our first language" (70).

11. My emphasis on the importance of countercultural communities is influenced by Sharon Welch's book *Communities of Resistance and Solidarity: A Feminist Theology of Liberation* (Maryknoll, N.Y.: Orbis, 1985). The concept of "imagined communities" is from Chandra Talpade Mohanty's introductory essay to the collection *Third World Women and the Politics of Feminism*, ed. C. Talpade Mohanty et al. (Bloomington: Indiana University. Press, 1991), entitled "Cartographies of Struggle: Third World Women and the Politics of Feminism." For Mohanty, the notion of "imagined community" defines political struggles for liberation on the basis of political—rather than biological or cultural—affinity: "It is not color or sex which constructs the ground for these struggles. Rather, it is the way we think about race, class, and gender—the political links we choose to make along and between struggles. Thus, potentially women of all colors (including white women) can align themselves with and participate in these imagined communities" (4).

12. Byllye Y. Avery makes this point in her essay "Breathing Life into Ourselves: The Evolution of the National Black Women's Health Project," in White, *The Black Women's Health Book*, 7.

13. This is Nelle Morton's famous idea, elaborated in her book *The Journey Is Home* (Boston: Beacon, 1985). See especially 17–19, 54–55. For an early religious feminist essay on the value of consciousness-raising, see Judith Plaskow, "The Com-

ing of Lilith: Toward a Feminist Theology," in *Womanspirit Rising: A Feminist Reader in Religion*, ed. C. Christ and J. Plaskow (San Francisco: HarperCollins, 1979), 198–209. Building on the format of consciousness-raising groups, Frigga Haug proposes "memory work" as a collective strategy for raising consciousness and "denaturalizing" the female body. "Memory work" involves women coming together to "rewrit[e] the narratives through which their bodies have historically become what they are." Such narratives become the basis for building alternative perspectives within which the processes of female socialization and sexualization can be interrogated and transformed. See Hang, ed., *Female Sexualization: A Collective Work of Memory*, trans. E. Carter (London: Verso, 1987), 14.

14. For a critique of consciousness-raising tactics and theory, see Iris M. Young, "The Ideal of Community and the Politics of Difference," in *Feminism/Postmodernism*, ed. L. Nicholson (New York: Routledge, 1990), 300–323. Young argues that the ideal of community "privileges unity over difference, immediacy over mediation, sympathy over recognition of the limits of one's understanding of others from their point of view" (300). For a critique of the quest for theoretical purity (at the cost of pragmatic concerns for efficacy and accessibility), see Susan Bordo, "Feminism, Postmodernism, and Gender Scepticism," in ibid., *Feminism/Postmodernism*, 133–56. For an example of the effectiveness of consciousness-raising groups in the 1990s, see bell hooks, *Sisters of the Yam: Black Women and Self-Recovery* (Boston: South End, 1993).

15. In addition to various pamphlets and a newsletter called "Lifeline," the main text for Overeaters Anonymous is the "Brown Book," called *Overeaters Anonymous* (Torrence, Calif.: Overeaters Anonymous, Inc., 1980).

16. This is the title of the last chapter of Judith Plaskow's book, *Standing Again at Sinai: Judaism from a Feminist Perspective* (San Francisco: HarperCollins, 1990), 211–38.

17. Alison Bass, " 'Anorexic Marketing' Faces Boycott," *Boston Globe* (Apr. 25, 1994): 1, 16. Another example of this "talking back" strategy is About Face, a San Francisco group that combats anorexic advertising through education, humor, and advertising. See Kathy Bruin, "Diary of an Urban Guerrilla," *Bitch* 3 no. 2 (1998): 19–21.

18. See bell hooks, *Talking Back* (Boston: South End, 1989).

19. Ariadne Northstar, "Eating," in Newman, *Eating Our Hearts Out*, 76–77.

20. Laura Rizzo, "Toward Fullness," in ibid., 187.

21. Schüssler Fiorenza, *But She Said*, 158.

22. See hooks, *Sisters of the Yam*; Audre Lorde, *Sister Outsider: Essays and Speeches* (Freedom, Calif.: Crossing Press, 1984); Cornel West, *Keeping Faith: Philosophy and Race in America* (New York: Routledge, 1993).

23. Marya Hornbacher, *Wasted: A Memoir of Anorexia and Bulimia* (New York: HarperFlamingo, 1998), 286.

24. Ibid., 111.

25. "Ruthie," quoted in Becky Thompson, *A Hunger So Wide and So Deep: American Women Speak Out on Eating Problems* (Minneapolis: University of Minnesota Press, 1994), 124.

26 Marya Hornbacher, "Wasted," *Minneapolis–St. Paul Monthly Magazine* (Nov. 1993): 173–74.

27. Elisabeth Schüssler Fiorenza, *In Memory of Her: A Feminist Reconstruction of Christian Origins* (1983; reprint, New York: Crossroad, 1994), 121, 118–30.

28. Schüssler Fiorenza, *But She Said*, see especially 11–14.

29. Plaskow, *Standing Again at Sinai*,1, 122, 135.

30. Jacquelyn Grant, "The Sin of Servanthood: And the Deliverance of Discipleship," in *A Troubling in My Soul: Womanist Perspectives on Evil and Suffering*, ed. Emilie Townes (Maryknoll, N.Y.: Orbis, 1993), 199–218.

31. Delores Williams, *Sisters in the Wilderness: The Challenge of Womanist God-Talk* (Maryknoll, N.Y.: Orbis, 1993).

32. Chung Hyung Kyung, *The Struggle to Be the Sun Again: Introducing Asian Women's Theology* (Maryknoll, N.Y.: Orbis, 1990).

33. Ada Maria Isasi-Diaz, *En la Lucha, In the Struggle: A Hispanic Women's Liberation Theology* (Minneapolis: Fortress, 1993).

34. Rosemary Radford Ruether, *Sexism and God-Talk: Toward a Feminist Theology* (Boston: Beacon, 1983), 18–23.

35. See Carol Christ's "A Spirituality for Women," in *Laughter of Aphrodite: Reflections on a Journey to the Goddess* (San Francisco: HarperCollins, 1987), 57–71, and Plaskow, *Standing Again at Sinai*, 5–6.

36. Cornel West, *Prophetic Fragments: Illuminations of the Crisis in American Religion and Culture* (Trenton, N.J.: Africa World Press, 1988), ix. See also bell hooks and Cornel West, *Breaking Bread: Insurgent Black Intellectual Life* (Boston: South End, 1991).

37. In the summers of 1997 and 1998, for example, the "Lilith Fair" festival, featuring a rotating lineup of sixty-one popular female singer-songwriters, toured the United States. While the diversity of its talents and sounds defy simple categorization, these women's music is connected by common themes of female empowerment and social critique of a world that stands in its way. See C. John Farley, "The First Ladies of Song," *Time* 150 (July 21, 1997): 60–67.

38. Tracy Chapman's *New Beginning* (1995) is produced by Don Gehman and Tracy Chapman on Elektra Entertainment Group, a division of Warner Communications, Inc.

39. See—or, rather, listen to—"Closer to Fine," on *Indigo Girls* (Virgin Songs, Inc., 1988); "Watershed," on *Indians, Nomads, Saints* (Virgin Songs, Inc., 1990); "This Train Revised," on *Swamp Ophelia* (Virgin Songs, Inc., 1994); and "Everything in Its Own Time," on *Shaming of the Sun* (Virgin Songs, Inc., 1997).

40. Katie Geneva Canon, *Black Womanist Ethics* (Atlanta: Scholars Press, 1988); "Moral Wisdom in the Black Women's Literary Tradition," in *Weaving the Visions: New Patterns in Feminist Spirituality*, ed. J. Plaskow and C. Christ (San Francisco: Harper and Row, 1989), 281–92; and *Katie's Canon: Womanism and the Soul of Black Community* (New York: Continuum, 1995).

41. Audre Lorde, "The Transformation of Silence into Language and Action," in *Sister Outsider*, 41.

42. The term "womanist" comes from Alice Walker, whose definition is presented ("Definition of Womanist") in *Making Face, Making Soul: Hacienndo Caras: Creative and Critical Perspectives by Feminists of Color*, ed. Gloria Anzaldua (San Francisco: Aunt Lute, 1990), 370. Delores Williams elaborates the significance of this term for black women's theology: "Many women in church and society have appropriated it as a way of affirming themselves as black while simultaneously owning their connection with feminism and with the Afro-American community, male and female. The concept of womanist allows women to claim their roots in black history, religion, and culture." D. Williams, "Womanist Theology," in Plaskow and Christ, *Weaving the Visions*, 179. See also Cheryl Townsend Gilkes, "The 'Loves' and 'Troubles' of

African-American Women's Bodies: The Womanist Challenge to Cultural Humiliation and Community Ambivalence," in Townes, *A Troubling in My Soul*, 232–49.

43. Carol Christ, "Why Women Need the Goddess," in *Laughter of Aphrodite*, 120.

44. For example, see Rosemary R. Ruether, *Gaia and God: An Ecofeminist Theology of Earth Healing* (New York: HarperCollins, 1992), especially 149–55; and Marsha Hewitt, *Critical Theory of Religion: A Feminist Analysis* (Minneapolis: Fortress, 1995), 184–206.

45. Rita Nakashima Brock and Susan Brooks Thistlethwaite sketch a broad but careful overview of some of the misogynist and anti-body messages of various Eastern philosophies and religions in their study of the religious underpinnings of prostitution in Asia and America. See *Casting Stones: Prostitution and Liberation in Asia and the United States* (Minneapolis: Fortress, 1996), especially 23–66.

46. Farah Shroff, "¡Deliciosa!: The Body, Passion, and Pleasure," in Brown and Jaspers, *Consuming Passions*, 115.

47. Thich Nhat Hanh, *The Miracle of Mindfulness: A Manual on Meditation*, trans. Mobi Ho (Boston: Beacon, 1975), 15; see also Nhat Hahn, *Being Peace*, ed. Arnold Kotler (Berkeley: Parallax, 1987).

SELECT BIBLIOGRAPHY

Abraham, S., and D. Llewellyn-Jones. 1987. *Eating Disorders: The Facts*. 2d ed. New York: Oxford University Press.

Abrams, K. K., et al. 1993. "Disordered Eating Attitudes and Behaviours, Psychological Adjustment, and Ethnic Identity: A Comparison of Black and White Female College Students." *International Journal of Eating Disorders* 14: 49–57.

Allen, John L. 1997. "Christian Diets Point to Getting 'Slim for Him.'" *National Catholic Reporter* 34 (December 7): 27–28.

American Psychiatric Association. 1994. *Diagnostic and Statistical Manual for Mental Disorders IV*. Washington: American Psychiatric Association Press.

Andersen, A., and A. Hay. 1985. "Racial and Socioeconomic Influences in Anorexia and Bulimia." *International Journal of Eating Disorders* 4: 479–87.

Anzaldua, Gloria, ed. 1990. *Making Face, Making Soul: Hacienndo Caras: Creative and Critical Perspectives by Feminists of Color*. San Francisco: Aunt Lute.

Arnold, Georgiana. 1991. "Coming Home: One Black Woman's Journey to Health and Fitness." Pp. 269–79 in White 1991.

Atkins, Dawn, ed. 1998. *Queer Looks: Body Image and Identity in Lesbian, Bisexual, Gay and Transgender Communities*. Binghamton, N.Y.: The Haworth Press.

Banner, Louis. 1983. *American Beauty*. Chicago: University of Chicago Press.

Bartky, Sandra. 1990. *Femininity and Domination: Studies in the Phenomenology of Oppression*. New York: Routledge.

Beaudrillard, Jean. 1984. "The Precession of Simulacra." Pp. 253–81 in *Art after Modernism: Rethinking Representation*, ed. Brian Wallis. New York: New Museum of Contemporary Art.

Beauvior, Simone de. 1952. *The Second Sex*. New York: Vintage.

Belasco, Warren. 1993. *Appetite for Change: How the Counterculture Took on the Food Industry*. Ithaca: Cornell University Press.

Bell, Catherine. 1992. *Ritual Theory, Ritual Practice*. New York: Oxford University Press.

Bell, Rudolph. 1985. *Holy Anorexia*. Chicago: University of Chicago Press.

Bellah, Robert, et al. 1985. *Habits of the Heart: Individualism and Commitment in American Life*. New York: Harper and Row.

Bemis, Kelly. 1978. "Current Approaches to the Etiology and Treatment of Anorexia Nervosa." *Psychological Bulletin* 85: 593–617.

Benhabib, Seyla. 1992. *Situating the Self: Gender, Community, and Postmodernism in Contemporary Ethics*. New York: Routledge.

Benhabib, S., and Drucilla Cornell, eds. 1987. *Feminism as Critique*. Minneapolis: University of Minnesota Press.

Benjamin, Walter. 1969. "The Work of Art in the Age of Mechanical Reproduction." Pp. 217–51 in *Illuminations*, ed. Hannah Arendt. New York: Schocken.

Berger, John. 1972. *Ways of Seeing*. London: Penguin.

Berger, Peter. 1990 [1967]. *The Sacred Canopy: Elements of a Sociology of Religion*. New York: Doubleday.

Birtchnell, Sandra, et al. 1987. "Body Image Distortion in Non-Eating Disordered Women." *International Journal of Eating Disorders* 6: 385–91.

Bjorntorp, P., and B. Brodoff, eds. 1992. *Obesity*. New York: Lippincott.

Blinder, Barton J., et al., eds. 1988. *The Eating Disorders: Medical and Psychological Bases of Diagnoses and Treatment*. New York: PMA Publishers.

Bordo, Susan. 1993. *Unbearable Weight: Feminism, Western Culture, and the Body*. Berkeley: University of California Press.

Boskind-Lodahl, Marlene. 1976. "Cinderella's Stepsisters: A Feminist Perspective on Anorexia Nervosa and Bulimia." *Signs* 2: 342–56.

Boskind-White, M., and W. White. 1987. *Bulimarexia: The Binge/Purge Cycle*. New York: W. W. Norton.

Bourdieu, Pierre. 1992 [1972]. *Outline of a Theory of Practice*. Cambridge: Cambridge University Press.

——. 1984. *Distinction: A Social Critique of the Judgment of Taste*. Cambridge: Harvard University Press.

Bray, Rosemary L. 1992. "Heavy Burden." *Essence*. January: 53–54+.

Bringle, Mary Louise. 1992. *The God of Thinness: Gluttony and Other Weighty Matters*. Nashville: Abingdon.

Brock, Rita Nakashima, and Susan Brooks Thistlethwaite. 1996. *Casting Stones: Prostitution and Liberation in Asia and the United States*. Minneapolis: Fortress.

Brown, Catrina. 1993. "The Continuum: Anorexia, Bulimia, and Weight Preoccupation." Pp. 53–68 in Brown and Jaspers 1993.

Brown, Catrina, and Karin Jaspers, eds. 1993. *Consuming Passions: Feminist Approaches to Weight Preoccupation and Eating Disorders*. Toronto: Second Story Press.

Brown, Laura. 1987. "Lesbians, Weight, and Eating: New Analyses and Perspectives." Pp. 294–309 in *Lesbian Psychologies: Exploration and Challenges*, ed. L. Brown. Chicago: University of Illinois Press.

Browne, Maya. 1993. "Dying to Be Thin." *Essence*. June: 86–87+.

Brownell, Kelly. 1991. "Dieting and the Search for the Perfect Body: Where Physiology and Culture Collide." *Behavior Therapy* 22: 1–12.

Bruch, Hilde. 1973. *Eating Disorders: Obesity, Anorexia Nervosa, and the Person Within*. New York: Basic Books.

———. 1978. *The Golden Cage: The Enigma of Anorexia Nervosa*. New York: Vintage.

———. 1988. *Conversations with Anorexics*. Edited by D. Czyzewski and M. Suhr. New York: Basic Books.

Brumberg, Joan Jacobs. 1988. *Fasting Girls: The History of Anorexia Nervosa*. New York: Penguin.

Butler, Judith. 1990. *Gender Trouble: Feminism and the Subversion of Identity*. New York: Routledge.

Butler, Judith, and Joan Scott, eds. 1992. *Feminists Theorize the Political*. New York: Routledge.

Bynum, Caroline Walker. 1987. *Holy Feast and Holy Fast: The Religious Significance of Food for Medieval Women*. Berkeley: University of California Press.

Cannon, Katie Geneva. 1988. *Black Womanist Ethics*. Atlanta: Scholars Press.

———. 1995. *Womanism and the Soul of the Black Community*. New York: Continuum.

Carruba, Michele, and J. Blundell, eds. 1986. *The Pharmacology of Eating Disorders: Theoretical and Clinical Developments*. New York: Raven.

Cassel, Dana. 1994. *The Encyclopedia of Obesity and Eating Disorders*. New York: Facts on File.

Chapkis, Wendy. 1986. *Beauty Secrets: Women and the Politics of Appearance*. Boston: South End.

Chernik, Abra Fortune. 1995. "The Body Politic." Pp. 75–84 in Findlen 1995.

Chernin, Kim. 1981. *The Obsession: Reflections on the Tyranny of Slenderness*. New York: Harper and Row.

———. 1985. *The Hungry Self: Women, Eating, and Identity*. New York: Harper and Row.

Christ, Carol. 1986. *Diving Deep and Surfacing: Women Writers on Spiritual Quest*. Boston: Beacon.

———. 1987. *Laughter of Aphrodite: Reflection on a Journey to the Goddess*. San Francisco: Harper and Row.

Christ, Carol, and Judith Plaskow, eds. 1979. *Womanspirit Rising: A Feminist Reader in Religion*. San Francisco: Harper and Row.

Chung, Hyung Kyung. 1990. *Struggle to Be the Sun Again: Introducing Asian Women's Theology*. Maryknoll, N.Y.: Orbis.

Ciliska, Donna. 1993. "Why Diets Fail." Pp. 80–90 in Brown and Jaspers 1993.

Clark, Elizabeth. 1983. *Women in the Early Church*. Collegeville, Minn.: Liturgical Press.

Cooey, Paula. 1994. *The Religious Imagination and the Body: A Feminist Analysis*. New York: Oxford University Press.

Crisp, A. H. 1980. *Anorexia Nervosa: Let Me Be Me*. London: Plenum.

Curtin, Deane, and Lisa Heldke, eds. 1992. *Cooking, Eating, Thinking: Transformative Philosophies of Food*. Bloomington: Indiana University Press.

Daly, Mary. 1973. *Beyond God the Father: Toward a Philosophy of Women's Liberation*. Boston: Beacon.

Diamond, Irene, and Lee Quinby, eds. 1988. *Feminism and Foucault: Reflections on Resistance*. Boston: Northeastern University Press.

Dolan, Bridget. 1991. "Cross-Cultural Aspects of Anorexia Nervosa and Bulimia: A Review." *International Journal of Eating Disorders* 10: 67–78.

Donovan, Josephine. 1985. *Feminist Theory: The Intellectual Traditions of American Feminism*. New York: Ungar.

Douglas, Mary. 1991 [1966]. *Purity and Danger: An Analysis of the Concepts of Pollution and Taboo*. New York: Routledge.

————. 1982 [1970]. *Natural Symbols: Explorations in Cosmology*. New York: Pantheon.

Duden, Barbara. 1991. *The Woman beneath the Skin: A Doctor's Patients in Eighteenth-Century Germany*. Cambridge: Harvard University Press.

During, Simon, ed. 1993. *The Cultural Studies Reader*. New York: Routledge.

Durkheim, Emile. 1961. *The Elementary Forms of Religious Life*. New York: Collier.

Eisler, I., and G. I. Szmukler. 1985. "Social Class as a Confounding Variable in the Eating Attitudes Test." *Journal of Psychiatric Research* 19: 171–76.

Elias, Norbert. 1978 [1939]. *The Civilizing Process*; vol. 1: *The History of Manners*. New York: Pantheon.

Ellman, Maud. 1993. *The Hunger Artists: Starving, Writing, and Imprisonment*. Cambridge: Harvard University Press.

Emmett, Rev. Steven Wiley, ed. 1985. *Theory and Treatment of Anorexia Nervosa and Bulimia: Biomedical, Sociocultural, and Psychological Perspectives*. New York: Brunner/Mazel.

Emmons, L. 1992. "Dieting and Purging Behavior in Black and White High School Students." *Journal of the American Diet Association* 92: 306–12.

Erickson, Victoria Lee. 1993. *Where Silence Speaks: Feminism, Social Theory, and Religion*. Minneapolis: Fortress.

Ewen, Stuart. 1988. *All Consuming Images: The Politics of Style in Contemporary Culture*. New York: Basic Books.

Fallon, Patricia, Melanie Katzman, and Susan Wooley, eds. 1994. *Feminist Perspectives on Eating Disorders*. New York: Guilford.

Fausto-Sterling, Anne. 1985. *Myths of Gender: Biological Theories about Women and Men*. New York: Basic Books.

Ferguson, Marjorie. 1983. *Forever Feminine: Women's Magazines and the Cult of Femininity*. London: Heinemann Educational Books.

Ferrari, E., et al., eds. 1993. *Primary and Secondary Eating Disorders: A Psychoneuroendocrine and Metabolic Approach*. New York: Pergamon.

Findlen, Barbara, ed. 1995. *Listen Up: Voices from the Next Feminist Generation*. Seattle: Seal Press.

Finkelstein, Joanne. 1991. *The Fashioned Self*. Philadelphia: Temple. University Press.

Foster, Hal, ed. 1988. *Vision and Visuality*. Seattle: Bay Press.

Foster, Patricia, ed. 1994. *Minding the Body: Women Writers on Body and Soul*. New York: Doubleday.

Foucault, Michel. 1973. *The Order of Things: An Archeology of the Human Sciences*. New York: Vintage.

————. 1990 [1978]. *History of Sexuality*; vol. 1. New York: Vintage.

————. 1979. *Discipline and Punish: The Birth of the Prison*. New York: Vintage.

————. 1980. *Power/Knowledge: Selected Interviews and Other Writings, 1972–1977*. New York: Pantheon.

Fox, Richard Wightman, and T. J. Jackson Lears, eds. 1983. *The Culture of Consumption: Critical Essays in American History, 1880–1980*. New York: Pantheon.

Fraser, Laura. 1997. *Losing It!: False Hopes and Fat Profits in the Diet Industry*. New York: Plume.

————. 1998. "The Body Beautiful." *Diablo*. January: 58+.

Friedman, Lenore, and Susan Moon, eds. 1997. *Being Bodies: Buddhist Women on the Paradox of Embodiment*. Boston: Shambhala Press.

Fulkerson, Mary McClintock. 1994. *Changing the Subject: Women's Discourses and Feminist Theology*. Minneapolis: Fortress.

Furukawa, Toshiaki. 1994. "Weight Changes and Eating Attitudes of Japanese Adolescents under Acculturative Stresses: A Prospective Study." *International Journal of Eating Disorders* 15: 71–79.

Garfinkel, P., and D. Garner. 1987. *The Role of Drug Treatments for Eating Disorders*. New York: Brunner/Mazel.

Garner, David, et al. 1985. "Psychoeducational Principles in the Treatment of Bulimia Nervosa." Pp. 513–72 in *Handbook of Psychotherapy for Anorexia Nervosa and Bulimia*, edited by D. Garner and P. Garfinkel. New York: Guilford.

Garner, D. M., and P. E. Garfinkel, eds. 1988. *Diagnostic Issues in Anorexia Nervosa and Bulimia Nervosa*. New York: Brunner/Mazel.

Geertz, Clifford. 1973. *The Interpretation of Cultures*. New York: Basic Books.

Giannini, A. J., and A. E. Slaby, eds. 1993. *The Eating Disorders*. New York: Springer-Verlag.

Gledhill, Christine. 1988. "Pleasurable Negotiations." Pp. 64–87 in *Female Spectators: Looking at Film and Television,*. ed. E. Diedre Pribram. New York: Verso.

Goethals, Gregor. 1990. *The Electronic Golden Calf: Images, Religion, and the Making of Meaning*. Cambridge: Cowley.

Goffman, Erving. 1976. *Gender Advertisements*. New York: Harper and Row.

Gordon, Richard. 1990. *Anorexia and Bulimia: Anatomy of a Social Epidemic*. New York: Basil Blackwell.

Gould, Stephen Jay. 1981. *The Mismeasure of Man*. New York: W. W. Norton.

Gramsci, Antonio. 1971. *Selections from the Prison Notebooks*. London: Lawrence and Wishart.

Gray, James J., et al. 1987. "The Prevalence of Bulimia in a Black College Population." *International Journal of Eating Disorders* 6: 733–40.

Griffith, R. Marie. 1997. *God's Daughters: Evangelical Women and the Power of Submission*. Berkeley: University of California Press.

Hahn, Thich Nhat. 1975. *The Miracle of Mindfulness: A Manual on Meditation*. Boston: Beacon.

Hall, Stuart. 1993. "Encoding, Decoding." Pp. 90–103 in During 1993.

Halmi, K. A., ed. 1992. *Psychobiology and Treatment of Anorexia and Bulimia Nervosa*. Washington: American Psychiatric Association Press.

Halmi, K. A., et al. 1981. "Binge Eating and Vomiting: A Survey of a College Population." *Psychological Medicine* 11: 483–91.

Haug, Frigga, ed. 1987. *Female Sexualization: A Collective Work of Memory*. London: Verso.

————. 1992. *Beyond Female Masochism: Memory-Work and Politics*. London: Verso.

Herzog, David, et al. 1992. "The Current Status of Treatment for Anorexia Nervosa and Bulimia Nervosa." *International Journal of Eating Disorders* 12: 215–20.

Hesse-Biber, Sharlene. 1996. *Am I Thin Enough Yet?: The Cult of Thinness and the Commercialization of Identity*. New York: Oxford University Press.

Hill Collins, Patricia. 1991. *Black Feminist Thought: Knowledge, Consciousness, and the Politics of Empowerment*. New York: Routledge.

hooks, bell. 1984. *Feminist Theory: From Margin to Center*. Boston: South End.

———. 1989. *Talking Back*. Boston: South End.

———. 1990. *Yearning: Race, Gender, and Cultural Politics*. Boston: South End.

———. 1992. *Black Looks: Race and Representation*. Boston: South End.

———. 1993. *Sisters of the Yam: Black Women and Self-Recovery*. Boston: South End.

———. 1994a. *Outlaw Culture: Resisting Representations*. New York: Routledge.

———. 1994b. *Teaching to Transgress: Education as the Practice of Freedom*. New York: Routledge.

hooks, bell, and Cornel West. 1991. *Breaking Bread: Insurgent Black Intellectual Life*. Boston: South End.

Hornbacher, Marya. 1993. "Wasted." *Minneapolis–St. Paul Monthly Magazine*. November: 66–71+.

———. 1998. *Wasted: A Memoir of Anorexia and Bulimia*. New York: Harper-Flamingo.

Houston, Pam. 1994. "Out of Habit, I Start Apologizing." Pp. 147–58 in Foster 1994.

Hsu, L. K. G. 1987. "Are Eating Disorders Becoming More Prevalent in Blacks?" *International Journal of Eating Disorders* 6: 113–24.

———. 1990. *Eating Disorders*. New York: Guilford.

Hubbard, Ruth. 1990. *The Politics of Women's Biology*. New Brunswick, N.J.: Rutgers University Press.

Hudson, J., and H. Pope, eds. 1987. *The Psychobiology of Bulimia*. Washington: American Psychiatric Association Press.

Isasi-Diaz, Ada Maria. 1993. *En la Lucha, In the Struggle: A Hispanic Women's Liberation Theology*. Minneapolis: Fortress.

Isasi-Diaz, Ada Maria, and Yolanda Tarango. 1988. *Hispanic Women: Prophetic Voice in the Church*. San Francisco: Harper and Row.

Jaggar, Alison, and Susan Bordo, eds. 1989. *Gender/Body/Knowledge: Feminist Reconstructions of Being and Knowing*. New Brunswick, N.J.: Rutgers University Press.

Jay, Nancy. 1992. *Throughout Your Generations Forever: Sacrifice, Religion, and Paternity*. Chicago: University of Chicago Press.

Johnson, Richard. 1987. "What Is Cultural Studies Anyway?" *Social Text* 16: 38–80.

Kaplan, A. S., and P. E. Garfinkel, eds. 1993. *Medical Issues and the Eating Disorders: The Interface*. New York: Brunner/Mazel.

Kaufman, Gordon D. 1979. [1975]. *Essay on Theological Method*. Atlanta: Scholars Press.

———. 1981. *The Theological Imagination: Constructing the Concept of God*. Philadelphia: Westminster.

———. 1993. *In Face of Mystery: A Constructive Theology*. Cambridge: Harvard University Press.

Keesey, R. E. 1986. "A Set Point Theory of Obesity." In *Handbook of Eating Disorders*, edited by K. Brownell and J. P. Foreyt. New York: Basic Books.

Keller, Catherine. 1986. *From a Broken Web: Separation, Sexism, and Self*. Boston: Beacon.

Keller, Evelyn Fox. 1992. *Secrets of Life/Secrets of Death: Essays on Language, Gender, and Science*. New York: Routledge.

Klein, Richard. 1996. *Eat Fat*. New York: Vintage.

Kwok Pui-lan. 1991. "The Image of the 'White Lady': Gender and Race in Christian Mission." Pp. 19–27 in *Concilium: The Special Nature of Women?*, edited by A. Carr and E. Schüssler Fiorenza. Philadelphia: Trinity.

Lakoff, R., and Raquel Scherr. 1984. *Face Value: The Politics of Beauty*. Boston: Routledge and Kegan Paul.

Laqueur, Thomas. 1990. *Making Sex: Body and Gender from the Greeks to Freud*. Cambridge: Harvard University Press.

Lawrence, Marilyn, ed. 1987. *Fed Up and Hungry: Women, Oppression, and Food*. New York: Peter Bedrick Books.

Levenstein, Harvey. 1988. *Revolution at the Table: The Transformation of the American Diet*. New York: Oxford University Press.

Lieblich, Julia. 1998. "Christian Dieting: Getting Righteous, Getting Thin." *San Francisco Examiner*, April 19, 1998: A18.

Lloyd, Genevieve. 1984. *The Man of Reason: "Male" and "Female" in Western Philosophy*. Minneapolis: University of Minnesota Press.

Lorde, Audre. 1984. *Sister Outsider: Essays and Speeches by Audre Lorde*. Freedom, Calif.: Crossing Press.

MacInnis, Beth. 1993. "Fat Oppression." Pp. 69–79 in Brown and Jaspers 1993.

MacSween, Morag. 1993. *Anorexic Bodies: A Feminist and Sociocultural Perspective on Anorexia Nervosa*. New York: Routledge.

Manlowe, Jennifer. 1995. *Faith Born of Seduction: Sexual Trauma, Body Image, and Religion*. New York: New York University Press.

Marchand, Roland. 1985. *Advertising the American Dream: Making Way for Modernity, 1920–1940*. Berkeley: University of California Press.

McFague, Sallie. 1987. *Models of God: Theology for an Ecological, Nuclear Age*. Philadelphia: Fortress.

————. 1993. *The Body of God: An Ecological Theology*. Minneapolis: Fortress.

Merchant, Caroline. 1990 [1980]. *The Death of Nature: Women, Ecology, and the Scientific Revolution*. San Francisco: HarperCollins.

Miles, Margaret. 1981. *Fullness of Life: Historical Foundations for a New Asceticism*. Philadelphia: Westminster.

————. 1985. *Image as Insight: Visual Understanding in Western Christianity and Secular Culture*. Boston: Beacon.

————. 1989. *Carnal Knowing: Female Nakedness and Religious Meaning in the Christian West*. Boston: Beacon.

————. 1995. "Religion and Food: The Case of Eating Disorders." *Journal of the American Academy of Religion* 63: 549–64.

Miller, Caroline Adams. 1988. *My Name Is Caroline*. New York: Doubleday.

Mohanty, Chandra Talpade, et al., eds. 1991. *Third World Women and the Politics of Feminism*. Bloomington: Indiana University Press.

Nevo, Shoshana. 1985. "Bulimic Symptoms: Prevalence and Ethnic Differences among College Women." *International Journal of Eating Disorders* 4: 151–68.

Newman, Leslea, ed. 1993. *Eating Our Hearts Out: Personal Accounts of Women's Relationships to Food*. Freedom, Calif.: Crossing Press.

Nicholson, Linda, ed. 1990. *Feminism/Postmodernism*. New York: Routledge.

Nissenbaum, Stephen. 1980. *Sex, Diet, and Debility in Jacksonian America: Sylvester Graham and Health Reform*. Chicago: Dorsey.

O'Niel, Cherry Boone. 1982. *Starving for Attention*. Melbourne: Dove Communications.

Orbach, Susie. 1978. *Fat Is a Feminist Issue: The Anti-Diet Guide to Permanent Weight Loss*. New York: Berkeley Medallion Books.

————. 1986. *The Hunger Strike: The Anorectic's Struggle as a Metaphor for Our Age*. New York: Avon.

Osvold, L. L., and G. R. Sodowsky. 1993. "Eating Disorders of White American, Racial and Ethnic Minority American, and International Women." *Journal of Multicultural Counseling and Development* 21: 143–54.

Palazzoli, M. S., et al. 1978. *Self-Starvation: From the Intrapsychic to the Transpersonal Approach*. New York: Jason Aronson.

Plaskow, Judith. 1990. *Standing Again at Sinai: Judaism from a Feminist Perspective*. San Francisco: HarperCollins.

Plaskow, Judith, and Carol Christ, eds. 1989. *Weaving the Visions: New Patterns in Feminist Spirituality*. San Francisco: Harper and Row.

Poulton, Terry. 1997. *No Fat Chicks: How Big Business Profits by Making Women Hate Their Bodies—and How to Fight Back*. Secaucas, N.J.: Carol Publishing Group.

Powers, Retha. 1989. "Fat is a Black Woman's Issue." *Essence*. October: 75–78+.

Rand, C. S. W., and J. M. Kuldau. 1992. "Epidemiology of Bulimia and Symptoms in a General Population: Sex, Age, Race, and Socioeconomic Status." *International Journal of Eating Disorders* 11: 37–44.

Robertson, Matra. 1992. *Starving in the Silences: An Exploration of Anorexia Nervosa*. New York: New York University Press.

Robinson, P., and A. Andersen. 1985. "Anorexia Nervosa in American Blacks." *Journal of Psychiatric Research* 19: 183–88.

Root, Maria. 1990. "Disordered Eating in Women of Color." *Sex Roles* 22: 525–36.

Rosen, L. W., et al. 1988. "Prevalence of Pathogenic Weight-Control Behaviours among Native American Women and Girls." *International Journal of Eating Disorders* 7: 807–11.

Rubin, Gail, and J. Butler. 1994. "Sexual Traffic." *Differences* 6: 63–98.

Ruether, Rosemary R. 1983. *Sexism and God-Talk: Toward a Feminist Theology*. Boston: Beacon.

Russell, Letty, et al., eds. 1988. *Inheriting Our Mother's Gardens: Feminist Theology in Third World Perspective*. Philadelphia: Westminster.

Russett, Cynthia. 1989. *Sexual Science: The Victorian Construction of Womanhood*. Cambridge: Harvard University Press.

Sands, Kathleen. 1994. *Escape from Paradise: Evil and Tragedy in Feminist Theology*. Minneapolis: Fortress.

Sawicki, Jana. 1991. *Disciplining Foucault: Feminism, Power, and the Body*. New York: Routledge.

Schoenfielder, L., and B. Wieser, eds. 1983. *Shadow on a Tightrope: Writings by Women on Fat Oppression*. San Francisco: Spinsters/Aunt Lute.

Schüssler Fiorenza, Elisabeth. 1984. *Bread Not Stone: The Challenge of Feminist Biblical Interpretation*. Boston: Beacon.

————. 1994 [1984]. *In Memory of Her: A Feminist Reconstruction of Christian Origins*. New York: Crossroad.

————. 1992. *But She Said: Feminist Practices of Biblical Interpretation*. Boston: Beacon.

Schwartz, Hillel. 1986. *Never Satisfied: A Cultural History of Diets, Fantasies, and Fat*. New York: Free Press.

Schwichtenberg, Cathy, ed. 1993. *The Madonna Connection: Representational Politics, Subcultural Identities, and Cultural Theory*. Boulder, Colo.: Westview.

Seid, Roberta Pollack. 1989. *Never Too Thin: Why Women Are at War with Their Bodies*. New York: Prentice Hall.

Silber, T. 1986. "Anorexia Nervosa in Blacks and Hispanics." *International Journal of Eating Disorders* 5: 121–28.

Smith, J. E., and J. Krejci. 1991. "Minorities Join the Majority: Eating Disturbances among Hispanic and Native American Youth." *International Journal of Eating Disorders* 10: 179–86.

Sontag, Susan. 1989. *On Photography*. New York: Doubleday.

Spelman, Elizabeth. 1988. *Inessential Woman: Problems in Contemporary Feminist Thought*. Boston: Beacon.

Stierlin, H., and G. Weber. 1989. *Unlocking the Family Door: A Systematic Approach to the Understanding and Treatment of Anorexia Nervosa*. New York: Brunner/Mazel.

Stunkard, A. J., and E. Stellar, eds. 1984. *Eating and Its Disorders*. New York: Tavern.

Thompson, Becky. 1994. *A Hunger So Wide and So Deep: American Women Speak Out on Eating Problems*. Minneapolis: University of Minnesota Press.

Thompson, M. G., and D. M. Schwartz. 1982. "Life Adjustment of Women with Anorexia Nervosa and Anorexic-like Behavior." *International Journal of Eating Disorders* 1: 47–60.

Tillich, Paul. 1959. *Theology of Culture*. New York: Oxford University Press.

Tisdale, Sallie. 1994. "A Weight That Women Carry: The Compulsion to Diet in a Starved Culture." Pp. 15–32 in Foster 1994. Also published in *Harper's* (March 1993): 49–55.

Townes, Emilie, ed. 1993. *A Troubling in My Soul: Womanist Perspectives on Evil and Suffering*. Maryknoll, N.Y.: Orbis.

Townsend Gilkes, Cheryl. 1993. "The 'Loves' and 'Troubles' of African-American Women's Bodies: The Womanist Challenge to Cultural Humiliation." Pp. 232–59 in Townes 1993.

Traube, Elizabeth. 1992. *Dreaming Identities: Class, Gender, and Generation in 1980s Hollywood Movies*. San Francisco: Westview.

Turner, Bryan S. 1984. *The Body and Society: Explorations in Social Theory*. New York: Basil Blackwell.

———. 1992. *Regulating Bodies: Essays in Medical Sociology*. New York: Routledge.

Vandereycken, Walter. 1994. "Emergence of Bulimia Nervosa as a Separate Diagnostic Entity: A Review of the Literature from 1960 to 1979." *International Journal of Eating Disorders* 16: 105–16.

Villarosa, Linda. 1994. "Dangerous Eating." *Essence* January: 19–21+.

———, ed. 1994. *Body and Soul: The Black Women's Guide to Physical Health and Emotional Well-Being*. New York: HarperPerennial.

Walsh, B. T., ed. 1988. *Eating Behavior and Eating Disorders*. Washington: American Psychiatric Association Press.

Ware, Vron. 1992. *Beyond the Pale: White Women, Racism, and History*. New York: Verso.

Weber, Max. 1964 [1922]. *The Sociology of Religion*. Boston: Beacon.

———. 1958. *The Protestant Ethic and the Spirit of Capitalism*. New York: Charles Scribner's Sons.

Welch, Sharon. 1987. *Feminist Liberation Theology: Communities of Solidarity and Resistance*. Maryknoll, N.Y.: Orbis.

————. 1990. *A Feminist Ethic of Risk*. Minneapolis: Fortress.

West, Cornel. 1988. *Prophetic Fragments: Illuminations of the Crisis of American Religion and Culture*. Trenton, N.Y.: Africa World Press.

————. 1993. *Keeping Faith: Philosophy and Race in America*. New York: Routledge.

Whitaker, L. C., ed. 1989. *The Bulimic College Student: Evaluation, Treatment, and Prevention*. New York: Haworth.

White, Evelyn, ed. 1991. *The Black Women's Health Book: Speaking for Ourselves*. Seattle: Seal Press.

Whorton, James C. 1982. *Crusaders for Fitness: The History of American Health Reformers*. Princeton: Princeton University Press.

Williams, Delores. 1993. *Sisters in the Wilderness: The Challenge of Womanist God-Talk*. Maryknoll: Orbis.

Williams, Raymond. 1993. "Advertising: The Magic System." Pp. 320–38 in During 1993.

Williamson, Judith. 1978. *Decoding Advertisements: Ideology and Meaning in Advertising*. New York: Marion Boyars.

Wolf, Naomi. 1991. *The Beauty Myth: How Images of Beauty Are Used against Women*. New York: Anchor.

Woodside, D. Blake, and L. Shekter-Wolfson, eds. 1991. *Family Approaches in Treatment of Eating Disorders*. Washington: American Psychiatric Association Press.

Wooley, Susan. 1994. "Sexual Abuse and Eating Disorders: The Concealed Debate." Pp. 171–211 in Fallon 1994.

Wooley, Susan C., and O. W. Wooley. 1984. "Feeling Fat in a Thin Society." *Glamour* February: 198–201+.

Young, Iris M. 1990. *Justice and the Politics of Difference*. Princeton: Princeton University Press.

————. 1990. *Throwing Like a Girl and Other Essays in Feminist Philosophy and Social Theory*. Bloomington: Indiana University Press.

INDEX

absolute dependence, 118–19
acculturative pressures, 21, 87–89. *See
    also* women of color
  for black women, 46, 57–58, 92
  diet as a tool for Americanizing, 72,
    177 n.24
  for Latina women, 88, 92, 156 n.40
adolescent girls
  and dieting, 4, 86, 89
  and family pressures, 63
  as feeling too fat, 53–54, 86,
    171 n.55
  morality of eating of, 82
  as typical age of onset, 22
  and women's magazines, 46–47, 50,
    64–65
advertising
  average American's exposure to, 75
  gender advertisements in, 169 n.32
  images of men in, 56, 173 n.80
  market profiles of a typical dieter in,
    92, 182 n.89
  protest of anorexic advertising, 134–
    35, 188 n.17

resemblance to religious ways of
    seeing, 37–38, 165 nn.117–18
  as targeting minority women, 92
  as a tool of neocolonialism, 46,
    170 n.38
  use of religious conventions in, 75,
    78–79, 93–94
affective variant hypothesis, 24
age as a variable in eating problems,
    18, 21–22, 86–87, 153 n.16
aikido, 125, 145
Americanizing ethnic eating habits, 72,
    177 n.24
anorexia, 5, 80–91, 96–124
  the admiration of anorexics, 98, 101
  and asceticism, 114–15
  the beauty of, 113
  as defined by *DSM* criteria, 17
  and the denial of hunger, 100
  and the desire for control, 108–12
  and the fear of ordinariness, 104–5,
    107
  history of, 29–30
  and the loss of control, 99–102